Henrik
Ibsen
Four Plays

Henrik Ibsen
Four Plays

Translated by EVA LE GALLIENNE

Illustrated by Tony Eubanks

THE FRANKLIN LIBRARY
Franklin Center, Pennsylvania

Contents

A Doll's House

A Play in Three Acts

Characters

TORVALD HELMER,
an attorney

NORA,
his wife

DR. RANK

MRS. KRISTINE LINDE

NILS KROGSTAD,
an attorney

HELMER'S THREE SMALL CHILDREN

ANNE-MARIE,
the nurse at the Helmers'

HELENE,
the maid at the Helmers'

A PORTER

The action takes place in the HELMER *residence.*

Act One

SCENE: *A comfortable room furnished with taste, but not expensively. In the back wall a door on the right leads to the hall; another door on the left leads to* HELMER'S *study. Between the two doors a piano. In the left wall, center, a door; farther downstage a window. Near the window a round table with an armchair and a small sofa. In the right wall upstage a door, and further downstage a porcelain stove around which are grouped a couple of armchairs and a rocking chair. Between the stove and the door stands a small table. Engravings on the walls. A whatnot with china objects and various bric-a-brac. A small bookcase with books in fancy bindings. The floor is carpeted; a fire is burning in the stove. A winter day.*

NORA: Be sure and hide the Christmas tree carefully, Helene, the children mustn't see it till this evening, when it's all decorated. *(To the* PORTER, *taking out her purse)* How much?

PORTER: Fifty, ma'am.

NORA: Here you are. No—keep the change.

(The PORTER *thanks her and goes.* NORA *closes the door. She laughs gaily to herself as she takes off her outdoor things. She takes a bag of macaroons out of her pocket and eats a couple, then goes cautiously to the door of her husband's study and listens)* Yes—he's home. *(She goes over to the table right, humming to herself again.)*

HELMER *(From his study)*: Is that my little lark twittering out there?

NORA *(Busily undoing the packages)*: Yes, it is.

HELMER: Is that my little squirrel bustling about?

NORA: Yes.

HELMER: When did my squirrel get home?

NORA: Just this minute. *(She puts the bag of macaroons back in her pocket and wipes her mouth)* Oh, Torvald, do come in here! You must see what I have bought.

HELMER: Now, don't disturb me! *(A moment afterward he opens the door and looks in—pen in hand)* Did you say "bought"? That—all *that?* Has my little spendthrift been flinging money about again?

NORA: But, Torvald, surely this year we ought to let ourselves go a bit! After all, it's the first Christmas we haven't had to be careful.

HELMER: Yes, but that doesn't mean we can afford to *squander* money.

NORA: Oh, Torvald, we can squander a bit, can't we? Just a little tiny bit? You're going to get a big salary and you'll be making lots and lots of money.

HELMER: After the first of the year, yes. But remember there'll be three whole months before my salary falls due.

NORA: We can always borrow in the meantime.

HELMER: Nora! *(Goes to her and pulls her ear playfully)* There goes my little featherbrain! Let's suppose I borrowed a thousand crowns today, you'd probably squander it all during Christmas week; and then let's suppose that on New Year's Eve a tile blew off the roof and knocked my brains out—

NORA *(Puts her hand over his mouth)*: Don't say such frightful things!

HELMER: But let's suppose it happened—then what?

NORA: If anything as terrible as *that* happened, I shouldn't care whether I owed money or not.

HELMER: But what about the people I'd borrowed from?

NORA: Who cares about them? After all they're just strangers.

HELMER: Oh, Nora, Nora! What a little woman you are! But seriously, Nora, you know my feelings about such things. I'll have no borrowing—I'll have no debts! There can be no freedom—no, nor beauty either—in a home based upon loans and credit. We've held out bravely up to now, and we shall continue to do so for the short time that remains.

NORA *(Goes toward the stove)*: Just as you like, Torvald.

HELMER *(Following her)*: Come, come; the little lark mustn't droop her wings. Don't tell me my little squirrel is sulking! *(He opens his purse)* Nora! Guess what I have here!

NORA *(Turns quickly)*: Money!

HELMER: There you are! *(He hands her some notes)* Don't you suppose I know that money is needed at Christmas time.

NORA *(Counts the notes)*: Ten, twenty, thirty, forty. Oh, thank you, thank you, Torvald—this'll last me a long time!

HELMER: Better see that it does!

NORA: Oh, it will—I know. But do come here. I want to show you everything I've bought, and all so cheap too! Here are some new clothes for Ivar, and a little sword—and this horse and trumpet are for Bob, and here's a doll for Emmy—and a doll's bed. They're not worth much, but she's sure to tear them to pieces in a minute anyway. This is some dress material and handkerchiefs for the maids. Old Anne-Marie really should have had something better.

HELMER: And what's in that other parcel?

NORA *(With a shriek)*: No, Torvald! You can't see that until this evening!

HELMER: I can't, eh? But what about you—you little squanderer? Have you thought of anything for yourself?

NORA: Oh, there's nothing I want, Torvald.

HELMER: Of course there is!—now tell me something sensible you'd really like to have.

NORA: But there's nothing—really! Except of course—

HELMER: Well?

NORA *(She fingers the buttons on his coat; without looking at him)*: Well—If you really want to give me something—you might—you might—

HELMER: Well, well, out with it!

NORA *(Rapidly)*: You might give me some money, Torvald—just anything you feel you could spare; and then one of these days I'll buy myself something with it.

HELMER: But Nora—

NORA: Oh, please do, dear Torvald—I beg you to! I'll wrap it up in beautiful gold paper and hang it on the Christmas tree. Wouldn't that be fun?

HELMER: What's the name of the bird that eats up money?

NORA: The spendthrift bird—I know! But do let's do as I say, Torvald!—it will give me a chance to choose something I really need. Don't you think that's a sensible idea? Don't you?

HELMER *(Smiling)*: Sensible enough—providing you really *do* buy something for yourself with it. But I expect you'll fritter it away on a lot of unnecessary household expenses, and before I know it you'll be coming to me for more.

NORA: But, Torvald—

HELMER: You can't deny it, Nora dear. *(Puts his arm round her waist)* The spendthrift is a sweet little bird—but it costs a man an awful lot of money to support one!

NORA: How can you say such nasty things—I save all I can!

HELMER: Yes, I dare say—but that doesn't amount to much!

NORA *(Hums softly and smiles happily)*: You don't know, Torvald, what expenses we larks and squirrels have!

HELMER: You're a strange little creature; exactly like your father. You'll go to any lengths to get a sum of money—but as soon as you have it, it just slips through your fingers. You don't know yourself what's become of it. Well, I suppose one must just take you as you are. It's in your blood. Oh, yes! such things are hereditary, Nora.

NORA: I only wish I had inherited a lot of Father's qualities.

10

HELMER: And I wouldn't wish you any different than you are, my own sweet little lark. But Nora, it's just occurred to me—isn't there something a little—what shall I call it—a little guilty about you this morning?

NORA: About me?

HELMER: Yes. Look me straight in the eye.

NORA *(Looking at him)*: Well?

HELMER *(Wags a threatening finger at her)*: Has my little sweet tooth been breaking rules today?

NORA: No! What makes you think that?

HELMER: Are you sure the sweet tooth didn't drop in at the confectioner's?

NORA: No, I assure you, Torvald—

HELMER: She didn't nibble a little candy?

NORA: No, really not.

HELMER: Not even a macaroon or two?

NORA: No, Torvald, I assure you—really—

HELMER: There, there! Of course I'm only joking.

NORA *(Going to the table right)*: It would never occur to me to go against your wishes.

HELMER: Of course I know that—and anyhow—you've given me your word—*(Goes to her)* Well, my darling, I won't pry into your little Christmas secrets. They'll be unveiled tonight under the Christmas tree.

NORA: Did you remember to ask Dr. Rank?

HELMER: No, it really isn't necessary. He'll take it for granted he's to dine with us. However, I'll ask him when he stops by this morning. I've ordered some specially good wine. I am so looking forward to this evening, Nora dear!

NORA: So am I—And the children will have such fun!

HELMER: Ah! How nice it is to feel secure; to look forward to a good position with an ample income. It's a wonderful prospect—isn't it, Nora?

NORA: It's simply marvelous!

HELMER: Do you remember last Christmas? For three whole weeks—you locked yourself up every evening until past midnight—making paper flowers for the Christmas tree—and a lot of other wonderful things you wanted to surprise us with. I was never so bored in my life!

NORA: I wasn't a bit bored.

HELMER *(Smiling)*: But it all came to rather a sad end, didn't it, Nora?

NORA: Oh, do you have to tease me about that again! How could I help the cat coming in and tearing it all to pieces.

HELMER: Of course you couldn't help it, you poor darling! You meant to give us a good time—that's the main thing. But it's nice to know those lean times are over.

NORA: It's wonderful!

HELMER: Now I don't have to sit here alone, boring myself to death; and you don't have to strain your dear little eyes, and prick your sweet little fingers—

NORA *(Claps her hands)*: No, I don't—do I, Torvald! Oh! How lovely it all is. *(Takes his arm)* I want to tell you how I thought we'd arrange things after Christmas. *(The doorbell rings)* Oh, there's the bell. *(Tidies up the room a bit)* It must be a visitor—how tiresome!

HELMER: I don't care to see any visitors, Nora—remember that.

HELENE *(In the doorway)*: There's a lady to see you, ma'am.

NORA: Well, show her in.

HELENE *(To HELMER)*: And the Doctor's here too, sir.

HELMER: Did he go straight to my study?

HELENE: Yes, he did, sir.

(HELMER goes into his study. HELENE ushers in MRS. LINDE, who is dressed in traveling clothes, and closes the door behind her.)

MRS. LINDE *(In a subdued and hesitant tone)*: How do you do, Nora?

NORA *(Doubtfully)*: How do you do?

MRS. LINDE: You don't recognize me, do you?

NORA: No, I don't think—and yet—I seem to—*(With a sudden outburst)* Kristine! Is it really you?

MRS. LINDE: Yes, it's really I!

NORA: Kristine! And to think of my not knowing you! But how could I when—*(More softly)* You've changed so, Kristine!

MRS. LINDE: Yes, I suppose I have. After all—it's nine or ten years—

NORA: Is it *that* long since we met? Yes, so it is. Oh, these last eight years have been such happy ones! Fancy your being in town! And imagine taking that long trip in midwinter! How brave you are!

MRS. LINDE: I arrived by the morning boat.

NORA: You've come for the Christmas holidays, I suppose—what fun! Oh, what a good time we'll have! Do take off your things. You're not cold, are you? *(Helping her)* There; now we'll sit here by the stove. No, you take the armchair; I'll sit here in the rocker. *(Seizes her hands)* Now you look more like yourself again. It was just at first—you're a bit paler, Kristine—and perhaps a little thinner.

MRS. LINDE: And much, much older, Nora.

NORA: Well, perhaps a *little* older—a tiny, tiny bit—not much, though. *(She suddenly checks herself; seriously)* Oh, but Kristine! What a thoughtless wretch I am, chattering away like that—Dear, darling Kristine, do forgive me!

MRS. LINDE: What for, Nora dear?

NORA *(Softly)*: You lost your husband, didn't you, Kristine! You're a widow.

MRS. LINDE: Yes; my husband died three years ago.

NORA: Yes, I remember; I saw it in the paper. Oh, I *did* mean to write to you, Kristine! But I kept on putting it off, and all sorts of things kept coming in the way.

MRS. LINDE: I understand, dear Nora.

NORA: No, it was beastly of me, Kristine! Oh, you poor darling! What you must have gone through!—And he died without leaving you anything, didn't he?

MRS. LINDE: Yes.

NORA: And you have no children?

MRS. LINDE: No.

NORA: Nothing then?

MRS. LINDE: Nothing—Not even grief, not even regret.

NORA (*Looking at her incredulously*): But how is that possible, Kristine?

MRS. LINDE (*Smiling sadly and stroking her hair*): It sometimes happens, Nora.

NORA: Imagine being so utterly alone! It must be dreadful for you, Kristine! I have three of the loveliest children! I can't show them to you just now, they're out with their nurse. But I want you to tell me all about yourself—

MRS. LINDE: No, no; I'd rather hear about you, Nora—

NORA: No, I want you to begin. I'm not going to be selfish today. I'm going to think only of you. Oh! but one thing I *must* tell you. You haven't heard about the wonderful thing that's just happened to us, have you?

MRS. LINDE: No. What is it?

NORA: My husband's been elected president of the Joint Stock Bank!

MRS. LINDE: Oh, Nora—How splendid!

NORA: Yes; isn't it? You see, a lawyer's position is so uncertain, especially if he refuses to handle any cases that are in the least bit—shady; Torvald is very particular about such things—and I agree with him, of course! You can imagine how glad we are. He's to start at the bank right after the New Year; he'll make a big salary and all sorts of percentages. We'll be able to live quite differently from then on—we'll have everything we want. Oh, Kristine! I'm so happy and excited! Won't it be wonderful to have lots and lots of money, and nothing to worry about!

MRS. LINDE: It certainly would be wonderful to have enough for one's needs.

NORA: Oh, not just for one's *needs*, Kristine! But heaps and heaps of money!

MRS. LINDE *(With a smile)*: Nora, Nora, I see you haven't grown up yet! I remember at school you were a frightful spendthrift.

NORA *(Quietly; smiling)*: Yes; that's what Torvald always says. *(Holding up her forefinger)* But I haven't had much chance to be a spendthrift. We have had to work hard—both of us.

MRS. LINDE: You too?

NORA: Oh, yes! I did all sorts of little jobs: needlework, embroidery, crochet—that sort of thing. *(Casually)* And other things as well. I suppose you know that Torvald left the government service right after we were married. There wasn't much chance of promotion in his department, and of course he had to earn more money when he had me to support. But that first year he overworked himself terribly. He had to undertake all sorts of odd jobs, worked from morning till night. He couldn't stand it; his health gave way and he became deathly ill. The doctors said he absolutely *must* spend some time in the South.

MRS. LINDE: Yes, I heard you spent a whole year in Italy.

NORA: Yes, we did. It wasn't easy to arrange, I can tell you. It was just after Ivar's birth. But of course we had to go. It was a wonderful trip, and it saved Torvald's life. But it cost a fearful lot of money, Kristine.

MRS. LINDE: Yes, it must have.

NORA: Twelve hundred dollars! Four thousand eight hundred crowns! That's an awful lot of money, you know.

MRS. LINDE: You were lucky to have it.

NORA: Well, you see, we got it from Father.

MRS. LINDE: Oh, I see. Wasn't it just about that time that your father died?

NORA: Yes, it was, Kristine. Just think! I wasn't able to go to him—I couldn't be there to nurse him! I was expecting Ivar at the time, and then I had my poor sick Torvald to look after. Dear, darling Papa! I never saw him again, Kristine. It's the hardest thing I have had to go through since my marriage.

MRS. LINDE: I know you were awfully fond of him. And after that you went to Italy?

NORA: Yes; then we had the money, you see; and the doctors said we must lose no time; so we started a month later.

MRS. LINDE: And your husband came back completely cured?

NORA: Strong as an ox!

MRS. LINDE: But—what about the doctor then?

NORA: How do you mean?

MRS. LINDE: Didn't the maid say something about a doctor, just as I arrived?

NORA: Oh, yes; Dr. Rank. He's our best friend—it's not a professional call; he stops in to see us every day. No, Torvald hasn't had a moment's illness since; and the children are strong and well, and so am I. *(Jumps up and claps her hands)* Oh, Kristine, Kristine! How lovely it is to be alive and happy! But how disgraceful of me! Here I am talking about nothing but myself! *(Seats herself upon a footstool close to* KRISTINE *and lays her arms on her lap)* Please don't be cross with me—Is it really true, Kristine, that you didn't love your husband? Why did you marry him then?

16

MRS. LINDE: Well, you see—Mother was still alive; she was bedridden; completely helpless; and I had my two younger brothers to take care of. I didn't think it would be right to refuse him.

NORA: No, I suppose not. I suppose he had money then?

MRS. LINDE: Yes, I believe he was quite well off. But his business was precarious, Nora. When he died it all went to pieces, and there was nothing left.

NORA: And then—?

MRS. LINDE: Then I had to struggle along as best I could. I had a small shop for a while, and then I started a little school. These last three years have been one long battle—but it is over now, Nora. My dear mother is at rest—She doesn't need me any more. And my brothers are old enough to work, and can look after themselves.

NORA: You must have such a free feeling!

MRS. LINDE: No—only one of complete emptiness. I haven't a soul to live for! *(Stands up restlessly)* I suppose that's why I felt I had to get away. I should think here it would be easier to find something to do—something to occupy one's thoughts. I might be lucky enough to get a steady job here—some office work, perhaps—

NORA: But that's so terribly tiring, Kristine; and you look so tired already. What you need is a rest. Couldn't you go to some nice watering-place?

MRS. LINDE *(Going to the window)*: I have no father to give me the money, Nora.

NORA *(Rising)*: Oh, please don't be cross with me!

MRS. LINDE *(Goes to her)*: My dear Nora, you mustn't be cross with me! In my sort of position it's hard not to become bitter. One has no one to work for, and yet one can't give up the struggle. One must go on living, and it makes one selfish. I'm ashamed to admit it—but, just now, when you told me the good news about your husband's new position—I was glad—not so much for your sake as for mine.

NORA: How do you mean? Oh, of course—I see! You think Torvald might perhaps help you.

MRS. LINDE: That's what I thought, yes.

NORA: And so he shall, Kristine. Just you leave it to me. I'll get him in a really good mood—and then bring it up quite casually. Oh, it would be such fun to help you!

MRS. LINDE: How good of you, Nora dear, to bother on my account! It's especially good of you—after all, you've never had to go through any hardship.

NORA: I? Not go through any—?

MRS. LINDE *(Smiling)*: Well—good heavens—a little needlework, and so forth—You're just a child, Nora.

NORA *(Tosses her head and paces the room)*: You needn't be so patronizing!

MRS. LINDE: No?

NORA: You're just like all the rest. You all think I'm incapable of being serious—

MRS. LINDE: Oh, come now—

NORA: You seem to think I've had no troubles—that I've been through nothing in my life!

MRS. LINDE: But you've just told me all your troubles, Nora dear.

NORA: I've only told you trifles! *(Softly)* I haven't mentioned the important thing.

MRS. LINDE: Important thing? What do you mean?

NORA: I know you look down on me, Kristine; but you really shouldn't. You take pride in having worked so hard and so long for your mother.

MRS. LINDE: I don't look down on anyone, Nora; I can't help feeling proud and happy too, to have been able to make Mother's last days a little easier—

NORA: And you're proud of what you did for your brothers, too.

MRS. LINDE: I think I have a right to be.

NORA: Yes, so do I. But I want you to know, Kristine—that I, too, have something to be proud of.

MRS. LINDE: I don't doubt that. But what are you referring to?

NORA: Hush! We must talk quietly. It would be dreadful if Torvald overheard us! He must never know about it! No one must know about it, except you.

MRS. LINDE: And what is it, Nora?

NORA: Come over here. *(Draws her down beside her on sofa)* Yes, I have something to be proud and happy about too. I saved Torvald's life, you see.

MRS. LINDE: Saved his life? But how?

NORA: I told you about our trip to Italy. Torvald would never have recovered if it hadn't been for that.

MRS. LINDE: Yes, I know—and your father gave you the necessary money.

NORA *(Smiling)*: That's what everyone thinks—Torvald too; but—

MRS. LINDE: Well—?

NORA: Papa never gave us a penny. I raised the money myself.

MRS. LINDE: All that money! You?

NORA: Twelve hundred dollars. Four thousand eight hundred crowns. What do you think of that?

MRS. LINDE: But, Nora, how on earth did you do it? Did you win it in the lottery?

NORA *(Contemptuously)*: The lottery! Of course not! Any fool could have done that!

MRS. LINDE: Where did you get it then?

NORA *(Hums and smiles mysteriously)*: H'm; tra-la-la-la.

MRS. LINDE: You certainly couldn't have borrowed it.

NORA: Why not?

MRS. LINDE: A wife can't borrow without her husband's consent.

NORA *(Tossing her head)*: Oh, I don't know! If a wife has a good head on her shoulders—and has a little sense of business—

MRS. LINDE: I don't in the least understand, Nora—

NORA: Well, you needn't. I never said I borrowed the money. I may have got it some other way. *(Throws herself back on the sofa)* Perhaps I got it from some admirer. After all when one is as attractive as I am—!

MRS. LINDE: What a mad little creature you are!

NORA: I'm sure you're dying of curiosity, Kristine—

MRS. LINDE: Nora, are you sure you haven't been a little rash?

NORA *(Sitting upright again)*: Is it rash to save one's husband's life?

MRS. LINDE: But mightn't it be rash to do such a thing behind his back?

NORA: But I couldn't tell him—don't you understand that! He wasn't even supposed to know how ill he was. The doctors didn't tell him—they came to me privately, told me his life was in danger and that he could only be saved by living in the South for a while. At first I tried persuasion; I cried, I begged, I cajoled—I said how much I longed to take a trip abroad like other young wives; I reminded him of my condition and told him he ought to humor me—and finally, I came right out and suggested that we borrow the money. But then, Kristine, he was almost angry; he said I was being frivolous and that it was his duty as my husband not to indulge my whims and fancies—I think that's what he called them. Then I made up my mind he must be saved in spite of himself—and I thought of a way.

MRS. LINDE: But didn't he ever find out from your father that the money was not from him?

NORA: No; never. You see, Papa died just about that time. I was going to tell him all about it and beg him not to give me away. But he was so very ill—and then, it was no longer necessary—unfortunately.

MRS. LINDE: And you have never confided all this to your husband?

NORA: Good heavens, no! That's out of the question! He's much too strict in matters of that sort. And besides— Torvald could never bear to think of owing anything to me! It would hurt his self-respect—wound his pride. It would ruin everything between us. Our whole marriage would be wrecked by it!

MRS. LINDE: Don't you think you'll ever tell him?

NORA *(Thoughtfully; half-smiling)*: Perhaps some day—a long time from now when I'm no longer so pretty and attractive. No! Don't laugh! Some day when Torvald is no longer as much in love with me as he is now; when it no longer amuses him to see me dance and dress up and act for him—then it might be useful to have something in reserve. *(Breaking off)* Oh, what nonsense! That time will never come! Well—what do you think of my great secret, Kristine? Haven't I something to be proud of too? It's caused me endless worry, though. It hasn't been easy to fulfill my obligations. You know, in business there are things called installments, and quarterly interest—and they're dreadfully hard to meet on time. I've had to save a little here and there, wherever I could. I couldn't save much out of the housekeeping, for of course Torvald had to live well. And I couldn't let the children go about badly dressed; any money I got for them, I spent on them, the darlings!

MRS. LINDE: Poor Nora! I suppose it had to come out of your own allowance.

NORA: Yes, of course. But after all, the whole thing was my doing. Whenever Torvald gave me money to buy some new clothes, or other things I needed, I never spent more than half of it; I always picked out the simplest, cheapest dresses. It's a blessing that almost anything looks well on me—so Torvald never knew the difference. But it's been hard sometimes, Kristine. It's so nice to have pretty clothes—isn't it?

MRS. LINDE: I suppose it is.

NORA: And I made money in other ways too. Last winter I was lucky enough to get a lot of copying to do. I shut myself up in my room every evening and wrote far into the night. Sometimes I was absolutely exhausted—but it was fun all the same—working like that and earning money. It made me feel almost like a man!

MRS. LINDE: How much have you managed to pay off?

NORA: Well, I really don't know exactly. It's hard to keep track of things like that. All I know is—I've paid every penny I could scrape together. There were times when I didn't know which way to turn! *(Smiles)* Then I used to sit here and pretend that some rich old gentleman had fallen madly in love with me—

MRS. LINDE: What are you talking about? *What* old gentleman?

NORA: I'm just joking! And then he was to die and when they opened his will, there in large letters were to be the words: "I leave all my fortune to that charming Nora Helmer to be handed over to her immediately."

MRS. LINDE: But who *is* this old gentleman?

NORA: Good heavens, can't you understand? There never *was* any such old gentleman; I just used to make him up, when I was at the end of my rope and didn't know where to turn for money. But it doesn't matter now—the tiresome old fellow can stay where he is as far as I am concerned. I no longer need him nor his money; for now my troubles are over. *(Springing up)* Oh, isn't it wonderful to think of, Kristine. No more troubles! No more worry! I'll be able to play and romp about with the children; I'll

be able to make a charming lovely home for Torvald—
have everything just as he likes it. And soon spring will
be here, with its great blue sky. Perhaps we might take a
little trip—I might see the ocean again. Oh, it's so marvelous to be alive and to be happy!
(The hall doorbell rings.)

MRS. LINDE *(Rising)*: There's the bell. Perhaps I had better go.

NORA: No, no; do stay! It's probably just someone for Torvald.

HELENE *(In the doorway)*: Excuse me, ma'am; there's a gentleman asking for Mr. Helmer—but the doctor's in there—
and I didn't know if I should disturb him—

NORA: Who is it?

KROGSTAD *(In the doorway)*: It is I, Mrs. Helmer.
(MRS. LINDE starts and turns away to the window.)

NORA *(Goes a step toward him, anxiously; in a low voice)*: You?
What is it? Why do you want to see my husband?

KROGSTAD: It's to do with bank business—more or less. I have
a small position in the Joint Stock Bank, and I hear your
husband is to be the new president.

NORA: Then it's just—?

KROGSTAD: Just routine business, Mrs. Helmer; nothing else.

NORA: Then, please be good enough to go into his study.
*(KROGSTAD goes. She bows indifferently while she closes the door
into the hall. Then she goes to the stove and tends the fire.)*

MRS. LINDE: Who was that man, Nora?

NORA: A Mr. Krogstad—he's a lawyer.

MRS. LINDE: I was right then.

NORA: Do you know him?

MRS. LINDE: I used to know him—many years ago. He worked
in a law office in our town.

NORA: Yes, so he did.

MRS. LINDE: How he has changed!

NORA: He was unhappily married, they say.

MRS. LINDE: Is he a widower now?

NORA: Yes—with lots of children. There! That's better! *(She closes the door of the stove and moves the rocking chair a little to one side.)*

MRS. LINDE: I'm told he's mixed up in some rather questionable business.

NORA: He may be; I really don't know. But don't let's talk about business—it's so tiresome.

(DR. RANK comes out of HELMER'S room.)

RANK *(Still in the doorway)*: No, no, I won't disturb you. I'll go in and see your wife for a moment. *(Sees MRS. LINDE)* Oh, I beg your pardon. I seem to be in the way here, too.

NORA: Of course not! *(Introduces them)* Dr. Rank—Mrs. Linde.

RANK: Well, well, I've often heard that name mentioned in this house; didn't I pass you on the stairs when I came in?

MRS. LINDE: Yes; I'm afraid I climb them very slowly. They wear me out!

RANK: A little on the delicate side—eh?

MRS. LINDE: No; just a bit overtired.

RANK: I see. So I suppose you've come to town for a good rest—on a round of dissipation!

MRS. LINDE: I have come to look for work.

RANK: Is that the best remedy for tiredness?

MRS. LINDE: One has to live, Doctor.

RANK: Yes, I'm told that's necessary.

NORA: Oh, come now, Dr. Rank! You're not above wanting to live yourself!

RANK: That's true enough. No matter how wretched I may be, I still want to hang on as long as possible. All my patients have that feeling too. Even the *morally* sick seem to share it. There's a wreck of a man in there with Helmer now—

MRS. LINDE *(Softly)*: Ah!

NORA: Whom do you mean?

RANK: A fellow named Krogstad, he's a lawyer—you wouldn't know anything about him. He's thoroughly depraved—rotten to the core—Yet even he declared, as though it were a matter of paramount importance, that he must live.

NORA: Really? What did he want with Torvald?

RANK: I've no idea; I gathered it was some bank business.

NORA: I didn't know that Krog—that this man Krogstad had anything to do with the bank?

RANK: He seems to have some sort of position there. *(To MRS. LINDE)* I don't know if this is true in your part of the country—but there are men who make it a practice of prying about in other people's business, searching for individuals of doubtful character—and having discovered their secret, place them in positions of trust, where they can keep an eye on them, and make use of them at will. Honest men—men of strong moral fiber—they leave out in the cold.

MRS. LINDE: Perhaps the weaklings need more help.

RANK *(Shrugs his shoulders)*: That point of view is fast turning society into a clinic.

(NORA, deep in her own thoughts, breaks into half-stifled laughter and claps her hands.)

RANK: Why should that make you laugh? I wonder if you've any idea what "society" is?

NORA: Why should I care about your tiresome old "society"? I was laughing at something quite different—something frightfully amusing. Tell me, Dr. Rank—will all the employees at the bank be dependent on Torvald now?

25

RANK: Is *that* what strikes you as so amusing?

NORA *(Smiles and hums)*: Never you mind! Never you mind! *(Walks about the room)* What fun to think that we—that Torvald—has such power over so many people. *(Takes the bag from her pocket)* Dr. Rank, how about a macaroon?

RANK: Well, well!—macaroons, eh? I thought they were forbidden here.

NORA: These are some Kristine brought—

MRS. LINDE: What! I—

NORA: Now, you needn't be so frightened. How could you possibly know that Torvald had forbidden them? He's afraid they'll spoil my teeth. Oh, well—just for once! Don't you agree, Dr. Rank? There you are! *(Puts a macaroon into his mouth)* You must have one too, Kristine. And I'll have just one—just a tiny one, or at most two. *(Walks about again)* Oh, dear, I *am* so happy! There's just one thing in all the world that would give me the greatest pleasure.

RANK: What's that?

NORA: It's something I long to say in front of Torvald.

RANK: What's to prevent you?

NORA: Oh, I don't dare; it isn't nice.

MRS. LINDE: Not nice?

RANK: It might be unwise then. But you can certainly say it to us. What is it you so long to say in front of Torvald?

NORA: I'd so love to say "Damn!—damn!—damn it all!"

RANK: Have you gone crazy?

MRS. LINDE: Good gracious, Nora!

RANK: Go ahead and say it—here he comes!

NORA *(Hides the macaroons)*: Hush—sh—sh.

(HELMER comes out of his room; he carries his hat and overcoat.)

NORA *(Going to him)*: Well, Torvald dear, did you get rid of him?

HELMER: He has just gone.

NORA: Let me introduce you. This is Kristine, who has just arrived in town . . .

HELMER: Kristine? I'm sorry—but I really don't . . .

NORA: Mrs. Linde, Torvald dear—Kristine Linde.

HELMER: Oh, yes! I suppose you're one of my wife's school friends?

MRS. LINDE: Yes. We knew each other as children.

NORA: Imagine, Torvald! She came all this long way just to talk to you.

HELMER: How do you mean?

MRS. LINDE: Well, it wasn't exactly—

NORA: Kristine is tremendously good at office work, and her great dream is to get a position with a really clever man—so she can improve still more, you see—

HELMER: Very sensible, Mrs. Linde.

NORA: And when she heard that you had become president of the bank—it was in the paper, you know—she started off at once; you *will* try and do something for Kristine, won't you, Torvald? For my sake?

HELMER: It's by no means impossible. You're a widow, I presume?

MRS. LINDE: Yes.

HELMER: And you've already had business experience?

MRS. LINDE: A good deal.

HELMER: Then I think it's quite likely I may be able to find a place for you.

NORA *(Clapping her hands)*: There, you see! You see!

HELMER: You have come at a good moment, Mrs. Linde.

MRS. LINDE: How can I ever thank you?

HELMER *(Smiling)*: Don't mention it. *(Puts on his overcoat)* But just now, I'm afraid you must excuse me.

RANK: I'll go with you. *(Fetches his fur coat from the hall and warms it at the stove.)*

NORA: Don't be long, Torvald dear.

HELMER: I shan't be more than an hour.

NORA: Are you going too, Kristine?

MRS. LINDE *(Putting on her outdoor things)*: Yes; I must go and find a place to live.

HELMER: We can all go out together.

NORA *(Helping her)*: How tiresome that we're so cramped for room, Kristine; otherwise—

MRS. LINDE: Oh, you mustn't think of that! Good-bye, dear Nora, and thanks for everything.

NORA: Good-bye for the present. Of course you'll come back this evening. And you too, Dr. Rank—eh? If you're well enough? But of course you'll be well enough! Wrap up warmly now! *(They go out talking, into the hall; children's voices are heard on the stairs)* Here they come! Here they come! *(She runs to the outer door and opens it. The nurse, ANNE-MARIE, enters the hall with the children)* Come in, come in—you darlings! Just look at them, Kristine. Aren't they sweet?

RANK: No chattering in this awful draft!

HELMER: Come along, Mrs. Linde; you have to be a mother to put up with this!

(RANK, HELMER, and MRS. LINDE go down the stairs; ANNE-MARIE enters the room with the children; NORA comes in too, shutting the door behind her.)

NORA: How fresh and bright you look! And what red cheeks! Like apples and roses. *(The children chatter to her during what follows)* Did you have a good time? Splendid! You gave Emmy and Bob a ride on your sled? Both at once? You *are* a clever boy, Ivar! Let me hold her for a bit, Anne-Marie. My darling little doll-baby. *(Takes the smallest from the nurse and dances with her)* All right, Bobbie!

28

Mama will dance with you too. You threw snowballs, did you? I should have been in on that! Never mind, Anne-Marie; I'll undress them myself—oh, do let me— it's such fun. Go on into the nursery, you look half frozen. There's some hot coffee in there on the stove. *(ANNE-MARIE goes into the room on the left. NORA takes off the children's things and throws them down anywhere, while the children all talk together)* Not really! You were chased by a big dog? But he didn't bite you? No, dogs don't bite tiny little doll-babies! Don't touch the packages, Ivar. What's in them? Wouldn't you like to know! No! No! Careful! It might bite! Come on, let's play. What will we play? Hide-and-seek? Let's play hide-and-seek. Bob, you hide first! Do you want me to? All right! I'll hide first then. *(She and the children play, laughing and shouting, all over the room and in the adjacent room to the left. Finally NORA hides under the table; the children come rushing in, look for her, but cannot find her, hear her half-suppressed laughter, rush to the table, lift up the cover and see her. Loud shouts of delight. She creeps out, as though to frighten them. More shouts. Meanwhile there has been a knock at the door leading into the hall. No one has heard it. Now the door is half opened and KROGSTAD appears. He waits a little—the game continues.)*

KROGSTAD: I beg your pardon, Mrs. Helmer—

NORA *(With a stifled scream, turns round and half jumps up)*: Oh! What do you want?

KROGSTAD: Excuse me. The outer door was ajar—someone must have forgotten to close it—

NORA *(Standing up)*: My husband is not at home, Mr. Krogstad.

KROGSTAD: I know that.

NORA: Then what do you want here?

KROGSTAD: I want a few words with you.

NORA: With—? *(To the children, softly)* Go in to Anne-Marie. What? No—the strange man won't do Mama any harm; when he's gone we'll go on playing. *(She leads the children into the right-hand room, and shuts the door behind them; uneasy, in suspense)* You want to speak to me?

KROGSTAD: Yes, I do.

NORA: Today? But it's not the first of the month yet—

KROGSTAD: No, it is Christmas Eve. It's up to you whether your Christmas is a merry one.

NORA: What is it you want? Today I can't possibly—

KROGSTAD: That doesn't concern me for the moment. This is about something else. You have a few minutes, haven't you?

NORA: I suppose so, although—

KROGSTAD: Good. I was sitting in the restaurant opposite, and I saw your husband go down the street—

NORA: Well?

KROGSTAD: —with a lady.

NORA: What of it?

KROGSTAD: May I ask if that lady was a Mrs. Linde?

NORA: Yes.

KROGSTAD: She's just come to town, hasn't she?

NORA: Yes. Today.

KROGSTAD: Is she a good friend of yours?

NORA: Yes, she is. But I can't imagine—

KROGSTAD: I used to know her too.

NORA: Yes, I know you did.

KROGSTAD: Then you know all about it. I thought as much. Now, tell me: is Mrs. Linde to have a place in the bank?

NORA: How dare you question me like this, Mr. Krogstad— you, one of my husband's employees! But since you ask—you might as well know. Yes, Mrs. Linde is to have a position at the bank, and it is I who recommended her. Does that satisfy you, Mr. Krogstad?

KROGSTAD: I was right, then.

NORA *(Walks up and down)*: After all, one has a little influence now and then. Even if one is only a woman it doesn't always follow that—people in subordinate positions, Mr. Krogstad, ought really to be careful how they offend anyone who—h'm—

KROGSTAD: —has influence?

NORA: Precisely.

KROGSTAD *(Taking another tone)*: Then perhaps you'll be so kind, Mrs. Helmer, as to use your influence on *my* behalf?

NORA: What? How do you mean?

KROGSTAD: Perhaps you'll be good enough to see that I *retain* my subordinate position?

NORA: But, I don't understand. Who wants to take it from you?

KROGSTAD: Oh, don't try and play the innocent! I can well understand that it would be unpleasant for your friend to associate with me; and I understand too, whom I have to thank for my dismissal.

NORA: But I assure you—

KROGSTAD: Never mind all that—there is still time. But I advise you to use your influence to prevent this.

NORA: But, Mr. Krogstad, I *have* no influence—absolutely none!

KROGSTAD: Indeed! I thought you just told me yourself—

NORA: You misunderstood me—*really* you did! You must know my husband would never be influenced by me!

KROGSTAD: Your husband and I were at the university to-gether—I know him well. I don't suppose he's any more inflexible than other married men.

NORA: Don't you dare talk disrespectfully about my husband, or I'll show you the door!

KROGSTAD: The little lady's plucky.

NORA: I'm no longer afraid of you. I'll soon be free of all this—after the first of the year.

KROGSTAD *(In a more controlled manner)*: Listen to me, Mrs. Helmer. This is a matter of life and death to me. I warn you I shall fight with all my might to keep my position at the bank.

NORA: So it seems.

KROGSTAD: It's not just the salary; that is the least important part of it—It's something else—Well, I might as well be frank with you. I suppose you know, like everyone else, that once—a long time ago—I got into quite a bit of trouble.

NORA: I have heard something about it, I believe.

KROGSTAD: The matter never came to court; but from that time on, all doors were closed to me. I then went into the business with which you are familiar. I had to do something; and I don't think I've been among the worst. But now I must get away from all that. My sons are growing up, you see; for their sake I'm determined to recapture my good name. This position in the bank was to be the first step; and now your husband wants to kick me back into the mud again.

NORA: But I tell you, Mr. Krogstad, it's not in my power to help you.

KROGSTAD: Only because you don't really want to; but I can compel you to do it, if I choose.

NORA: You wouldn't tell my husband that I owe you money?

KROGSTAD: And suppose I were to?

NORA: But that would be an outrageous thing to do! *(With tears in her voice)* My secret—that I've guarded with such pride—such joy! I couldn't bear to have him find it out in such an ugly, hateful way—to have him find it out from you! I couldn't bear it! It would be too horribly unpleasant!

KROGSTAD: Only unpleasant, Mrs. Helmer?

NORA *(Vehemently)*: But just you do it! You'll be the one to suffer; for then my husband will *really* know the kind of man you are—there'll be no chance of keeping your job then!

KROGSTAD: Didn't you hear my question? I asked if it were only unpleasantness you feared?

NORA: If my husband got to know about it, he'd naturally pay you off at once, and then we'd have nothing more to do with you.

KROGSTAD *(Takes a step toward her)*: Listen, Mrs. Helmer: Either you have a very bad memory, or you know nothing about business. I think I'd better make the position clear to you.

NORA: What do you mean?

KROGSTAD: When your husband fell ill, you came to me to borrow twelve hundred dollars.

NORA: I didn't know what else to do.

KROGSTAD: I promised to find you the money—

NORA: And you did find it.

KROGSTAD: I promised to find you the money, on certain conditions. At that time you were so taken up with your husband's illness and so anxious to procure the money for your journey, that you probably did not give much thought to details. Perhaps I'd better remind you of them. I promised to find you the amount in exchange for a note, which I drew up.

NORA: Yes, and I signed it.

KROGSTAD: Very good. But then I added a clause, stating that your father would stand sponsor for the debt. This clause your father was to have signed.

NORA: Was to—? He did sign it.

KROGSTAD: I left the date blank, so that your father himself should date his signature. You recall that?

NORA: Yes, I believe—

KROGSTAD: Then I gave you the paper, and you were to mail it to your father. Isn't that so?

NORA: Yes.

KROGSTAD: And you must have mailed it at once; for five or six days later you brought me back the document with your father's signature; and then I handed you the money.

NORA: Well? Haven't I made my payments punctually?

KROGSTAD: Fairly—yes. But to return to the point: That was a sad time for you, wasn't it, Mrs. Helmer?

NORA: It was indeed!

KROGSTAD: Your father was very ill, I believe?

NORA: Yes—he was dying.

KROGSTAD: And he did die soon after, didn't he?

NORA: Yes.

KROGSTAD: Now tell me, Mrs. Helmer: Do you happen to recollect the date of your father's death? The day of the month, I mean?

NORA: Father died on the 29th of September.

KROGSTAD: Quite correct. I have made inquiries. Now here is a strange thing, Mrs. Helmer—*(Produces a paper)* something rather hard to explain.

NORA: What do you mean? What strange thing?

KROGSTAD: The strange thing about it is, that your father seems to have signed this paper three days after his death!

NORA: I don't understand—

KROGSTAD: Your father died on the 29th of September. But look at this: his signature is dated October 2nd! Isn't that rather strange, Mrs. Helmer? *(NORA is silent)* Can you explain that to me? *(NORA continues silent)* It is curious, too, that the words "October 2nd" and the year are not in your father's handwriting, but in a handwriting I seem to know. This could easily be explained, however; your

father might have forgotten to date his signature, and
someone might have added the date at random, before
the fact of your father's death was known. There is
nothing wrong in that. It all depends on the signature
itself. It is of course genuine, Mrs. Helmer? It was your
father himself who wrote his name here?

NORA *(After a short silence, throws her head back and looks defiantly
at him)*: No, it wasn't. I wrote Father's name.

KROGSTAD: I suppose you realize, Mrs. Helmer, what a dangerous confession that is?

NORA: Why should it be dangerous? You will get your money
soon enough!

KROGSTAD: I'd like to ask you a question. Why didn't you send
the paper to your father?

NORA: It was impossible. Father was too ill. If I had asked him
for his signature, he'd have wanted to know what the
money was for. In his condition I simply could not tell
him that my husband's life was in danger. That's why it
was impossible.

KROGSTAD: Then wouldn't it have been wiser to give up the
journey?

NORA: How could I? That journey was to save my husband's
life. I simply couldn't give it up.

KROGSTAD: And it never occurred to you that you weren't
being honest with me?

NORA: I really couldn't concern myself with that. You meant
nothing to me—In fact I couldn't help disliking you for
making it all so difficult—with your cold, businesslike
clauses and conditions—when you knew my husband's
life was at stake.

KROGSTAD: You evidently haven't the faintest idea, Mrs.
Helmer, what you have been guilty of. Yet let me tell
you that it was nothing more and nothing worse that
made me an outcast from society.

NORA: You don't expect me to believe that you ever did a brave thing to save your wife's life?

KROGSTAD: The law takes no account of motives.

NORA: It must be a very bad law then!

KROGSTAD: Bad or not, if I produce this document in court, you will be condemned according to the law.

NORA: I don't believe that for a minute. Do you mean to tell me that a daughter has no right to spare her dying father worry and anxiety? Or that a wife has no right to save her husband's life? I may not know much about it—but I'm sure there must be something or other in the law that permits such things. You as a lawyer should be aware of that. You don't seem to know very much about the law, Mr. Krogstad.

KROGSTAD: Possibly not. But business—the kind of business we are concerned with—I *do* know something about. Don't you agree? Very well, then; do as you please. But I warn you: if I am made to suffer a second time, you shall keep me company. *(Bows and goes out through the hall.)*

NORA *(Stands awhile thinking, then tosses her head)*: What nonsense! He's just trying to frighten me. I'm not such a fool as all that! *(Begins folding the children's clothes. Pauses)* And yet—? No, it's impossible! After all—I only did it for love's sake.

CHILDREN *(At the door, left)*: Mama, the strange man has gone now.

NORA: Yes, yes, I know. But don't tell anyone about the strange man. Do you hear? Not even Papa!

CHILDREN: No, Mama; now will you play with us again?

NORA: No, not just now.

CHILDREN: But Mama! You promised!

NORA: But I can't just now. Run back to the nursery; I have so much to do. Run along now! Run along, my darlings! *(She pushes them gently into the inner room, and closes the door behind them. Sits on the sofa, embroiders a few stitches, but soon pauses)* No! *(Throws down the work, rises, goes to the hall door and calls out)* Helene, bring the tree in to me, will you? *(Goes to table, right, and opens the drawer; again pauses)* No, it's utterly impossible!

HELENE *(Carries in the Christmas tree)*: Where shall I put it, ma'am?

NORA: Right there; in the middle of the room.

HELENE: Is there anything else you need?

NORA: No, thanks; I have everything.

(HELENE, having put down the tree, goes out.)

NORA *(Busy dressing the tree)*: We'll put a candle here—and some flowers here—that dreadful man! But it's just nonsense! There's nothing to worry about. The tree will be lovely. I'll do everything to please you, Torvald; I'll sing for you, I'll dance for you—

(Enter HELMER by the hall door, with a bundle of documents.)

NORA: Oh! You're back already?

HELMER: Yes. Has somebody been here?

NORA: No. Nobody.

HELMER: That's odd. I just saw Krogstad leave the house.

NORA: Really? Well—as a matter of fact—Krogstad was here for a moment.

HELMER: Nora—I can tell by your manner—he came here to ask you to put in a good word for him, didn't he?

NORA: Yes, Torvald.

HELMER: And you weren't supposed to tell me he'd been here—You were to do it as if of your own accord—isn't that it?

NORA: Yes, Torvald; but—

HELMER: Nora, Nora! How could you consent to such a thing! To have dealings with a man like that—make him promises! And then to lie about it too!

NORA: Lie!

HELMER: Didn't you tell me that nobody had been here? *(Threatens with his finger)* My little bird must never do that again! A song-bird must sing clear and true! No false notes! *(Puts arm around her)* Isn't that the way it should be? Of course it is! *(Lets her go)* And now we'll say no more about it. *(Sits down before the fire)* It's so cozy and peaceful here! *(Glances through the documents.)*

NORA *(Busy with the tree, after a short silence)*: Torvald!

HELMER: Yes.

NORA: I'm so looking forward to the Stenborgs' fancy dress party, day after tomorrow.

HELMER: And I can't wait to see what surprise you have in store for me.

NORA: Oh, it's so awful, Torvald!

HELMER: *What* is?

NORA: I can't think of anything amusing. Everything seems so silly, so pointless.

HELMER: Has my little Nora come to *that* conclusion?

NORA *(Behind his chair, with her arms on the back)*: Are you very busy, Torvald?

HELMER: Well—

NORA: What are all those papers?

HELMER: Just bank business.

NORA: Already!

HELMER: The board of directors has given me full authority to do some reorganizing—to make a few necessary changes in the staff. I'll have to work on it during Christmas week. I want it all settled by the New Year.

NORA: I see. So that was why that poor Krogstad—

HELMER: H'm.

NORA *(Still leaning over the chair-back and slowly stroking his hair)*:

38

If you weren't so very busy, I'd ask you to do me a great, great favor, Torvald.

HELMER: Well, let's hear it! Out with it!

NORA: You have such perfect taste, Torvald; and I do so want to look well at the fancy dress ball. Couldn't you take me in hand, and decide what I'm to be, and arrange my costume for me?

HELMER: Well, well! So we're not so self-sufficient after all! We need a helping hand, do we?

NORA: Oh, please, Torvald! I know I shall *never* manage without your help!

HELMER: I'll think about it; we'll hit on something.

NORA: Oh, how sweet of you! *(Goes to the tree again; pause)* Those red flowers show up beautifully! Tell me, Torvald; did that Krogstad do something very wrong?

HELMER: He committed forgery. Have you any idea of what that means?

NORA: Perhaps he did it out of necessity?

HELMER: Or perhaps he was just foolhardy, like so many others. I am not so harsh as to condemn a man irrevocably for one mistake.

NORA: No, of course not!

HELMER: A man has a chance to rehabilitate himself, if he honestly admits his guilt and takes his punishment.

NORA: Punishment—

HELMER: But that wasn't Krogstad's way. He resorted to tricks and evasions, became thoroughly demoralized.

NORA: You really think it would—?

HELMER: When a man has that sort of thing on his conscience his life becomes a tissue of lies and deception. He's forced to wear a mask—even with those nearest to him—his own wife and children even. And the children—that's the worst part of it, Nora.

NORA: Why?

HELMER: Because the whole atmosphere of the home would be contaminated. The very air the children breathed would be filled with evil.

NORA *(Closer behind him)*: Are you sure of that?

HELMER: As a lawyer, I know it from experience. Almost all cases of early delinquency can be traced to dishonest mothers.

NORA: Why—only mothers?

HELMER: It usually stems from the mother's side; but of course it can come from the father too. We lawyers know a lot about such things. And this Krogstad has been deliberately poisoning his own children for years, by surrounding them with lies and hypocrisy—that is why I call him demoralized. *(Holds out both hands to her)* So my sweet little Nora must promise not to plead his cause. Shake hands on it. Well? What's the matter? Give me your hand. There! That's all settled. I assure you it would have been impossible for me to work with him. It literally gives me a feeling of physical discomfort to come in contact with such people.
*(*NORA *draws her hand away, and moves to the other side of the Christmas tree.)*

NORA: It's so warm here. And I have such a lot to do.

HELMER *(Rises and gathers up his papers)*: I must try and look through some of these papers before dinner. I'll give some thought to your costume too. Perhaps I may even find something to hang in gilt paper on the Christmas tree! *(Lays his hand on her head)* My own precious little song-bird! *(He goes into his study and closes the door after him.)*

NORA *(Softly, after a pause)*: It can't be—! It's impossible. Of course it's impossible!

ANNE-MARIE *(At the door, left)*: The babies keep begging to come in and see Mama.

NORA: No, no! Don't let them come to me! Keep them with you, Anne-Marie.

ANNE-MARIE: Very well, ma'am. *(Shuts the door.)*

NORA *(Pale with terror)*: Harm my children!—Corrupt my home! *(Short pause. She throws back her head)* It's not true! I know it's not! It could never, never be true!

CURTAIN

Act Two

SCENE: *The same room. In the corner, beside the piano, stands the Christmas tree, stripped and with the candles burnt out.* NORA'S *outdoor things lie on the sofa.* NORA, *alone, is walking about restlessly. At last she stops by the sofa and picks up her cloak.*

NORA *(Puts the cloak down again)*: Did someone come in? *(Goes to the hall and listens)* No; no one; of course no one will come today, Christmas Day; nor tomorrow either. But perhaps—*(Opens the door and looks out)* No, there's nothing in the mailbox; it's quite empty. *(Comes forward)* Oh, nonsense! He only meant to frighten me. There won't be any trouble. It's all impossible! Why, I—I have three little children!

(ANNE-MARIE: enters from the left, with a large cardboard box.)

ANNE-MARIE: Well—I found the box with the fancy dress clothes at last, Miss Nora.

NORA: Thanks; put it on the table.

ANNE-MARIE *(Does so)*: I'm afraid they're rather shabby.

NORA: If I had my way I'd tear them into a thousand pieces!

ANNE-MARIE: Good gracious! They can be repaired—just have a little patience.

NORA: I'll go and get Mrs. Linde to help me.

ANNE-MARIE: I wouldn't go out again in this awful weather! You might catch cold, Miss Nora, and get sick.

NORA: Worse things might happen—How are the children?

ANNE-MARIE: The poor little things are playing with their Christmas presents; but—

NORA: Have they asked for me?

ANNE-MARIE: They're so used to having Mama with them.

42

NORA: I know. But, you see, Anne-Marie, I won't be able to be with them as much as I used to.

ANNE-MARIE: Well, little children soon get used to anything.

NORA: You really think so? Would they forget me if I went away for good?

ANNE-MARIE: Good gracious!—for good!

NORA: Tell me something, Anne-Marie—I've so often wondered about it—how could you bear to part with your child—give it up to strangers?

ANNE-MARIE: Well, you see, I had to—when I came to nurse my little Nora.

NORA: Yes—but how could you *bear* to do it?

ANNE-MARIE: I couldn't afford to say no to such a good position. A poor girl who's been in trouble must take what comes. Of course *he* never offered to help me—the wicked sinner!

NORA: Then I suppose your daughter has forgotten all about you.

ANNE-MARIE: No—indeed she hasn't! She even wrote to me—once when she was confirmed and again when she was married.

NORA *(Embracing her)*: Dear old Anne-Marie—you were a good mother to me when I was little.

ANNE-MARIE: But then my poor little Nora *had* no mother of her own!

NORA: And if ever my little ones were left without—you'd look after them, wouldn't you?—Oh, that's just nonsense! *(Opens the box)* Go back to them. Now I must—Just you wait and see how lovely I'll look tomorrow!

ANNE-MARIE: My Miss Nora will be the prettiest person there! *(She goes into the room on the left.)*

NORA *(Takes the costume out of the box, but soon throws it down again)*: I wish I dared go out—I'm afraid someone might come. I'm afraid something might happen while I'm gone. That's just silly! No one will come. I must try not to think—This muff needs cleaning. What pretty gloves—they're lovely! I must put it out of my head! One, two, three, four, five, six—*(With a scream)* Ah! They're here!

(Goes toward the door, then stands irresolute. MRS. LINDE *enters from the hall, where she has taken off her things.)*

NORA: Oh, it's you, Kristine! There's no one else out there, is there? I'm so glad you have come!

MRS. LINDE: I got a message you'd been asking for me.

NORA: Yes, I just happened to be passing by. There's something I want you to help me with. Sit down here on the sofa. Now, listen: There's to be a fancy dress ball at the Stenborgs' tomorrow evening—they live just overhead—and Torvald wants me to go as a Neapolitan peasant girl, and dance the tarantella; I learned it while we were in Capri.

MRS. LINDE: So you're going to give a real performance, are you?

NORA: Torvald wants me to. Look, here's the costume; Torvald had it made for me down there. But it's all torn, Kristine, and I don't know whether—

MRS. LINDE: Oh, we'll soon fix that. It's only the trimming that has come loose here and there. Have you a needle and thread? Oh, yes. Here's everything I need.

NORA: It's awfully good of you!

MRS. LINDE *(Sewing)*: So you're going to be all dressed up, Nora—what fun! You know—I think I'll run in for a moment—just to see you in your costume—I haven't really thanked you for last night. I had such a happy time!

NORA *(Rises and walks across the room)*: Somehow it didn't seem as nice to me as usual. I wish you'd come to town a little earlier, Kristine. Yes—Torvald has a way of making things so gay and cozy.

MRS. LINDE: Well—so have you. That's your father coming out in you! But tell me—is Dr. Rank always so depressed?

NORA: No; last night it was worse than usual. He's terribly ill, you see—tuberculosis of the spine, or something. His father was a frightful man, who kept mistresses and all that sort of thing—that's why his son has been an invalid from birth—

MRS. LINDE (*Lets her sewing fall into her lap*): Why, Nora! what do you know about such things?

NORA (*Moving about the room*): After all—I've had three children; and those women who look after one at childbirth know almost as much as doctors; and they love to gossip.

MRS. LINDE (*Goes on sewing; a short pause*): Does Dr. Rank come here every day?

NORA: Every single day. He's Torvald's best friend, you know—always has been; and he's *my* friend too. He's almost like one of the family.

MRS. LINDE: Do you think he's quite sincere, Nora? I mean—isn't he inclined to flatter people?

NORA: Quite the contrary. What gave you that impression?

MRS. LINDE: When you introduced us yesterday he said he had often heard my name mentioned here; but I noticed afterwards that your husband hadn't the faintest notion who I was. How could Dr. Rank—?

NORA: He was quite right, Kristine. You see Torvald loves me so tremendously that he won't share me with anyone; he wants me all to himself, as he says. At first he used to get terribly jealous if I even mentioned any of my old friends back home; so naturally I gave up doing it. But I often talk to Dr. Rank about such things—he likes to hear about them.

MRS. LINDE: Listen to me, Nora! In many ways you are still a child. I'm somewhat older than you, and besides, I've had much more experience. I think you ought to put a stop to all this with Dr. Rank.

NORA: Put a stop to what?

MRS. LINDE: To the whole business. You said something yesterday about a rich admirer who was to give you money—

NORA: One who never existed, unfortunately. Go on.

MRS. LINDE: Has Dr. Rank money?

NORA: Why yes, he has.

MRS. LINDE: And he has no one dependent on him?

NORA: No, no one. But—

MRS. LINDE: And he comes here every single day?

NORA: Yes—I've just told you so.

MRS. LINDE: It's surprising that a sensitive man like that should be so importunate.

NORA: I don't understand you—

MRS. LINDE: Don't try to deceive me, Nora. Don't you suppose I can guess who lent you the twelve hundred dollars?

NORA: You must be out of your mind! How could you ever think such a thing? Why, he's a friend of ours; he comes to see us every day! The situation would have been impossible!

MRS. LINDE: So it wasn't he, then?

NORA: No, I assure you. Such a thing never even occurred to me. Anyway, he didn't have any money at that time; he came into it later.

MRS. LINDE: Perhaps that was just as well, Nora dear.

NORA: No—it would never have entered my head to ask Dr. Rank—Still—I'm sure that if I did ask him—

MRS. LINDE: But you won't, of course.

NORA: No, of course not. Anyway—I don't see why it should be necessary. But I'm sure that if I talked to Dr. Rank—

MRS. LINDE: Behind your husband's back?

NORA: I want to get that thing cleared up; after all, that's behind his back too. I must get clear of it.

MRS. LINDE: That's just what I said yesterday; but—

NORA *(Walking up and down)*: It's so much easier for a man to manage things like that—

MRS. LINDE: One's own husband, yes.

NORA: Nonsense. *(Stands still)* Surely if you pay back everything you owe—the paper is returned to you?

MRS. LINDE: Naturally.

NORA: Then you can tear it into a thousand pieces, and burn it up—the nasty, filthy thing!

MRS. LINDE *(Looks at her fixedly, lays down her work, and rises slowly)*: Nora, you are hiding something from me.

NORA: You can see it in my face, can't you?

MRS. LINDE: Something's happened to you since yesterday morning, Nora, what is it?

NORA *(Going toward her)*: Kristine—! *(Listens)* Hush! Here comes Torvald! Go into the nursery for a little while. Torvald hates anything to do with sewing. Get Anne-Marie to help you.

MRS. LINDE *(Gathers the things together)*: Very well; but I shan't leave until you have told me all about it. *(She goes out to the left, as HELMER enters from the hall.)*

NORA *(Runs to meet him)*: Oh, I've missed you so, Torvald dear!

HELMER: Was that the dressmaker—?

NORA: No, it was Kristine. She's helping me fix my costume. It's going to look so nice.

HELMER: Wasn't that a good idea of mine?

NORA: Splendid! But don't you think it was good of me to let you have your way?

HELMER: Good of you! To let your own husband have his way!

There, there, you crazy little thing; I'm only teasing. Now I won't disturb you. You'll have to try the dress on, I suppose.

NORA: Yes—and I expect you've work to do.

HELMER: I have. *(Shows her a bundle of papers)* Look. I've just come from the bank—*(Goes toward his room.)*

NORA: Torvald.

HELMER *(Stopping)*: Yes?

NORA: If your little squirrel were to beg you—with all her heart—

HELMER: Well?

NORA: Would you do something for her?

HELMER: That depends on what it is.

NORA: Be a darling and say yes, Torvald! Your squirrel would skip about and play all sorts of pretty tricks—

HELMER: Well—out with it!

NORA: Your little lark would twitter all day long—

HELMER: She does that anyway!

NORA: I'll pretend to be an elf and dance for you in the moonlight, Torvald.

HELMER: Nora—you're surely not getting back to what we talked about this morning?

NORA *(Coming nearer)*: Oh, Torvald dear, I do most humbly beg you—!

HELMER: You have the temerity to bring that up again?

NORA: You must give in to me about this, Torvald! You *must* let Krogstad keep his place!

HELMER: I'm giving his place to Mrs. Linde.

NORA: That's awfully sweet of you. But instead of Krogstad— couldn't you dismiss some other clerk?

HELMER: This is the most incredible obstinacy! Because you were thoughtless enough to promise to put in a good word for him, am I supposed to—?

NORA: That's not the reason, Torvald. It's for your own sake. Didn't you tell me yourself he writes for the most horrible newspapers? He can do you no end of harm. Oh! I'm so afraid of him—

HELMER: I think I understand; you have some unpleasant memories—that's why you're frightened.

NORA: What do you mean?

HELMER: Aren't you thinking of your father?

NORA: Oh, yes—of course! You remember how those awful people slandered poor Father in the newspapers? If you hadn't been sent to investigate the matter, and been so kind and helpful—he might have been dismissed.

HELMER: My dear Nora, there is a distinct difference between your father and me. Your father's conduct was not entirely unimpeachable. But mine is; and I trust it will remain so.

NORA: You never know what evil-minded people can think up. We could be so happy now, Torvald, in our lovely, peaceful home—you and I and the children! Oh! I implore you, Torvald—!

HELMER: The more you plead his cause the less likely I am to keep him on. It's already known at the bank that I intend to dismiss Krogstad. If I were to change my mind, people might say I'd done it at the insistence of my wife—

NORA: Well—what of that?

HELMER: Oh, nothing, of course! As long as the obstinate little woman gets her way! I'd simply be the laughingstock of the whole staff; they'd think I was weak and easily influenced—I should soon be made to feel the consequences. Besides—there is one factor that makes it quite impossible for Krogstad to work at the bank as long as I'm head there.

NORA: What could that be?

HELMER: His past record I might be able to overlook—

NORA: Yes, you might, mightn't you, Torvald—?

HELMER: And I'm told he's an excellent worker. But unfortunately we were friendly during our college days. It was one of those impetuous friendships that subsequently often prove embarrassing. He's tactless enough to call me by my first name—regardless of the circumstances—and feels quite justified in taking a familiar tone with me. At any moment he comes out with "Torvald" this, and "Torvald" that! It's acutely irritating. It would make my position at the bank intolerable.

NORA: You're surely not serious about this, Torvald?

HELMER: Why not?

NORA: But—it's all so petty.

HELMER: Petty! So you think I'm petty!

NORA: Of course not, Torvald—just the opposite; that's why—

HELMER: Never mind; you call my motives petty; so I must be petty too! Petty! Very well!—We'll put an end to this now—once and for all. (HELMER *goes to the door into the hall and calls* HELENE.)

NORA: What do you want?

HELMER (*Searching among his papers*): I want this thing settled. (HELENE *enters*) Take this letter, will you? Get a messenger and have him deliver it at once! It's urgent. Here's some money.

HELENE: Very good, sir. (*Goes with the letter.*)

HELMER (*Putting his papers together*): There, little Miss Obstinacy.

NORA (*Breathless*): Torvald—what was in that letter?

HELMER: Krogstad's dismissal.

NORA: Call her back, Torvald! There's still time. Call her back! For my sake, for your own sake, for the sake of the children, don't send that letter! Torvald, do you hear? You don't realize what may come of this!

HELMER: It's too late.

NORA: Too late, yes.

HELMER: Nora dear; I forgive your fears—though it's not exactly flattering to me to think I could ever be afraid of
any spiteful nonsense Krogstad might choose to write
about me! But I forgive you all the same—it shows how
much you love me. *(Takes her in his arms)* And that's the
way it should be, Nora darling. No matter what happens, you'll see—I have strength and courage for us both.
My shoulders are broad—I'll bear the burden.

NORA *(Terror-struck)*: How do you mean?

HELMER: The whole burden, my darling. Don't you worry any
more.

NORA *(With decision)*: No! You mustn't—I won't let you!

HELMER: Then we'll share it, Nora, as man and wife. That is as
it should be. *(Petting her)* Are you happy now? There!
Don't look at me like a frightened little dove! You're just
imagining things, you know—Now don't you think you
ought to play the tarantella through—and practice your
tambourine? I'll go into my study and close both doors,
then you won't disturb me. You can make all the noise
you like! *(Turns round in doorway)* And when Rank comes,
just tell him where I am. *(He nods to her, and goes with his
papers to his room, closing the door.)*

NORA *(Bewildered with terror, stands as though rooted to the ground,
and whispers)*: He'd do it too! He'd do it—in spite of
anything! But he mustn't—never, never! Anything but
that! There must be some way out! What shall I do? *(The
hall bell rings)* Dr. Rank—! Anything but that—anything,
anything but that!

*(NORA draws her hands over her face, pulls herself together, goes
to the door and opens it. RANK stands outside hanging up his fur
coat. During the following scene, darkness begins to fall.)*

NORA: How are you, Dr. Rank? I recognized your ring. You'd
better not go in to Torvald just now; I think he's busy.

RANK: How about you? *(Enters and closes the door.)*

NORA: You know I always have an hour to spare for you.

RANK: Many thanks. I'll make use of that privilege as long as possible.

NORA: What do you mean—as long as possible?

RANK: Does that frighten you?

NORA: No—but it's such a queer expression. Has anything happened?

RANK: I've been expecting it for a long time; but I never thought it would come quite so soon.

NORA: What is it you have found out? Dr. Rank, please tell me!

RANK *(Sitting down by the stove)*: I haven't much time left. There's nothing to do about it.

NORA *(With a sigh of relief)*: Oh! Then—it's about you—?

RANK: Of course. What did you think? It's no use lying to one's self. I am the most miserable of all my patients, Mrs. Helmer. These past few days I've been taking stock of my position—and I find myself completely bankrupt. Within a month, I shall be rotting in the churchyard.

NORA: What a ghastly way to talk!

RANK: The whole business is pretty ghastly, you see. And the worst of it is, there are so many ghastly things to be gone through before it's over. I've just one last examination to make, then I shall know approximately when the final dissolution will begin. There's something I want to say to you: Helmer's sensitive nature is repelled by anything ugly. I couldn't bear to have him near me when—

NORA: But Dr. Rank—

RANK: No, I couldn't bear it! I won't have him there—I shall bar my door against him—As soon as I am absolutely certain of the worst, I'll send you my visiting card

52

marked with a black cross; that will mean that the final horror has begun.

NORA: Dr. Rank—you're absolutely impossible today! And I did so want you to be in a good humor.

RANK: With death staring me in the face? And why should I have to expiate another's sins! What justice is there in that? Well—I suppose in almost every family there are some such debts that have to be paid.

NORA *(Stopping her ears)*: Don't talk such nonsense! Come along! Cheer up!

RANK: One might as well laugh. It's really very funny when you come to think of it—that my poor innocent spine should be made to suffer for my father's exploits!

NORA *(At table, left)*: He was much addicted to asparagus tips and paté de foie gras, wasn't he?

RANK: Yes; and truffles.

NORA: Oh, of course—truffles, yes. And I suppose oysters too?

RANK: Oh, yes! Masses of oysters, certainly!

NORA: And all the wine and champagne that went with them! It does seem a shame that all these pleasant things should be so damaging to the spine, doesn't it?

RANK: Especially when it's a poor miserable spine that never had any of the fun!

NORA: Yes, that's the biggest shame of all!

RANK *(Gives her a searching look)*: H'm—

NORA *(A moment later)*: Why did you smile?

RANK: No; you were the one who laughed.

NORA: No; you were the one who smiled, Dr. Rank!

RANK *(Gets up)*: You're more of a rogue than I thought you were.

NORA: I'm full of mischief today.

RANK: So it seems.

NORA *(With her hands on his shoulders)*: Dear, dear Dr. Rank, don't go and die and leave Torvald and me.

RANK: Oh, you won't miss me long! Those who go away—are soon forgotten.

NORA *(Looks at him anxiously)*: You really believe that?

RANK: People develop new interests, and soon—

NORA: What do you mean—new interests?

RANK: That'll happen to you and Helmer when I am gone. You seem to have made a good start already. What was that Mrs. Linde doing here last evening?

NORA: You're surely not jealous of poor old Kristine!

RANK: Yes, I am. She will be my successor in this house. When I'm gone she'll probably—

NORA: Sh—hh! She's in there.

RANK: She's here again today? You see!

NORA: She's just helping me with my costume. Good heavens, you *are* in an unreasonable mood! *(Sits on sofa)* Now do try to be good, Dr. Rank. Tomorrow you'll see how beautifully I'll dance; and then you can pretend I'm doing it all to please you—and Torvald too, of course— that's understood. *(Takes several things out of the box)* Sit down here, Dr. Rank, and I'll show you something.

RANK: What is it?

NORA: Look here—look!

RANK: Silk stockings.

NORA: Flesh-colored. Aren't they lovely? It's too dark here now to see them properly, but tomorrow—No, no no; you mustn't look above the ankle. Oh well—it doesn't matter; you can look higher if you like.

RANK: H'm—

NORA: Why do you look so critical? Perhaps you think they won't fit me?

RANK: Unfortunately, I'm in no position to express a valid opinion on that matter.

NORA (*Looks at him for a moment*): Fie on you! For shame! (*Slaps him lightly over the ear with the silk stocking*) There! That's what you get for that! (*She rolls stockings.*)

RANK: And now what other marvels am I to be allowed to see?

NORA: You shan't be allowed to see anything else. You're being very naughty! (*She hums a little as she turns over the things in the box.*)

RANK (*After a short silence*): You know—sitting here talking to you so informally—I simply can't imagine what would have become of me if I had never had this house to come to.

NORA (*Smiling*): You really *do* feel at home with us, don't you?

RANK (*In a low voice—looking straight before him*): And to be obliged to leave it all—

NORA: Nonsense! You're not going to leave anything.

RANK (*In the same tone*): And not to be able to leave behind one even the smallest proof of gratitude; at most a fleeting regret—an empty place to be filled by the first person who comes along.

NORA: And supposing I were to ask you for—? No—

RANK: For what?

NORA: For a great proof of your friendship.

RANK: Yes?—Yes?

NORA: No, I mean—if I were to ask you to do me a really tremendous favor—

RANK: You'd really, for once, give me that great happiness?

NORA: Oh, but you don't know what it is.

RANK: Then tell me.

NORA: I don't think I can, Dr. Rank. It's much too much to

ask—it's not just a favor—I need your help and advice as well—

RANK: So much the better. I've no conception of what you mean. But tell me about it. You trust me, don't you?

NORA: More than anyone. I know you are my best and truest friend—that's why I can tell you. Well then, Dr. Rank, there is something you must help me prevent. You know how deeply, how intensely Torvald loves me; he wouldn't hesitate for a moment to give up his life for my sake.

RANK *(Bending toward her)*: Nora—do you think he is the only one who—?

NORA *(With a slight start)*: Who—what?

RANK: Who would gladly give his life for you?

NORA *(Sadly)*: I see.

RANK: I was determined that you should know this before I—went away. There'll never be a better chance to tell you. Well, Nora, now you know, and you must know too that you can trust me as you can no one else.

NORA *(Standing up; simply and calmly)*: Let me get by—

RANK *(Makes way for her, but remains sitting)*: Nora—

NORA *(In the doorway)*: Bring in the lamp, Helene. *(Crosses to the stove)* Oh, dear Dr. Rank, that was really horrid of you.

RANK *(Rising)*: To love you just as deeply as—as someone else does; is that horrid?

NORA: No—but the fact of your telling me. There was no need to do that.

RANK: What do you mean? Did you know—?

(HELENE enters with the lamp; sets it on the table and goes out again.)

RANK: Nora—Mrs. Helmer—tell me, did you know?

NORA: Oh, how do I know what I knew or didn't know. I really can't say—How could you be so clumsy, Dr. Rank? It was all so nice.

RANK: Well, at any rate, you know now that I stand ready to serve you body and soul. So—tell me.

NORA *(Looking at him)*: After this?

RANK: I beg you to tell me what it is.

NORA: I can't tell you anything now.

RANK: But you must! Don't punish me like that! Let me be of use to you; I'll do anything for you—anything within human power.

NORA: You can do nothing for me now. Anyway—I don't really need help. I was just imagining things, you see. Really! That's all it was! *(Sits in the rocking chair, looks at him and smiles)* Well—you're a nice one, Dr. Rank! Aren't you a bit ashamed, now that the lamp's been lit?

RANK: No; really not. But I suppose I'd better go now—for good?

NORA: You'll do no such thing! You must come here just as you always have. Torvald could never get on without you!

RANK: But how about *you?*

NORA: You know I always love to have you here.

RANK: Yes—I suppose that's what misled me. I can't quite make you out. I've often felt you liked being with me almost as much as being with Helmer.

NORA: Well—you see—There are the people one loves best— and yet there are others one would almost rather *be* with.

RANK: Yes—there's something in that.

NORA: When I was still at home, it was of course Papa whom I loved best. And yet whenever I could, I used to slip down to the servants' quarters. I loved being with them. To begin with, they never lectured me a bit, and it was such fun to hear them talk.

RANK: I see; and now you have me instead!

NORA *(Jumps up and hurries toward him)*: Oh, dear, darling Dr. Rank. I didn't mean it like that! It's just that now,

57

Torvald comes first—the way Papa did. *You* understand—!

(HELENE *enters from the hall.*)

HELENE: I beg your pardon, ma'am—*(Whispers to* NORA, *and
gives her a card.)*

NORA *(Glancing at card)*: Ah! *(Puts it in her pocket.)*

RANK: Anything wrong?

NORA: No, nothing! It's just—it's my new costume—

RANK: Isn't that your costume—there?

NORA: Oh, that one, yes. But this is a different one. It's one
I've ordered—Torvald mustn't know—

RANK: So *that's* the great secret!

NORA: Yes, of course it is! Go in and see him, will you? He's
in his study. Be sure and keep him there as long as—

RANK: Don't worry; he shan't escape me. *(Goes into* HELMER'S
room.)

NORA *(To* HELENE*)*: He's waiting in the kitchen?

HELENE: Yes, he came up the back stairs—

NORA: Why didn't you tell him I was busy?

HELENE: I did, but he insisted.

NORA: He won't go away?

HELENE: Not until he has spoken to you, ma'am.

NORA: Very well, then; show him in; but quietly, Helene—and
don't say a word to anyone; it's about a surprise for my
husband.

HELENE: I understand, ma'am. *(She goes out.)*

NORA: It's coming! It's going to happen after all! No, no! It
can't happen. It *can't!*

(She goes to HELMER'S *door and locks it.* HELENE *opens the hall
door for* KROGSTAD, *and shuts it after him. He wears a traveling
coat, boots, and a fur cap.)*

NORA *(Goes toward him)*: Talk quietly; my husband is at home.

KROGSTAD: What's that to me?

NORA: What is it you want?

KROGSTAD: I want to make sure of something.

NORA: Well—what is it? Quickly!

KROGSTAD: I suppose you know I've been dismissed.

NORA: I couldn't prevent it, Mr. Krogstad. I did everything in my power, but it was useless.

KROGSTAD: So that's all your husband cares about you! He must realize what I can put you through, and yet, in spite of that, he dares to—

NORA: You don't imagine my husband knows about it?

KROGSTAD: No—I didn't really suppose he did. I can't imagine my friend Torvald Helmer showing that much courage.

NORA: I insist that you show respect when speaking of my husband, Mr. Krogstad!

KROGSTAD: With all due respect, I assure you! But am I right in thinking—since you are so anxious to keep the matter secret—that you have a clearer idea today than you had yesterday of what you really did?

NORA: Clearer than *you* could ever give me!

KROGSTAD: Of course! I who know so little about the law—!

NORA: What do you want of me?

KROGSTAD: I just wanted to see how you were getting on, Mrs. Helmer. I've been thinking about you all day. You see—even a mere money-lender, a cheap journalist—in short, someone like me—is not entirely without feeling.

NORA: Then prove it; think of my little children.

KROGSTAD: Did you or your husband think of mine? But that's not the point. I only wanted to tell you not to take this matter too seriously. I shan't take any action—for the present, at least.

NORA: You won't, will you? I was sure you wouldn't!

KROGSTAD: It can all be settled quite amicably. It needn't be made public. It needn't go beyond us three.

NORA: But my husband must never know.

KROGSTAD: How can you prevent it? Can you pay off the balance?

NORA: No, not immediately.

KROGSTAD: Have you any way of raising the money within the next few days?

NORA: None—that I will make use of.

KROGSTAD: And if you had, it would have made no difference. Even if you were to offer me the entire sum in cash—I still wouldn't give you back your note.

NORA: What are you going to do with it?

KROGSTAD: I shall simply keep it—I shall guard it carefully. No one, outside the three of us, shall know a thing about it. So, if you have any thought of doing something desperate—

NORA: I shall.

KROGSTAD: —of running away from home, for instance—

NORA: I shall!

KROGSTAD: —or perhaps even something worse—

NORA: How could you guess that?

KROGSTAD: —then put all such thoughts out of your head.

NORA: How did you know I had thought of *that?*

KROGSTAD: Most of us think of *that,* at first. I thought of it, too; but I didn't have the courage—

NORA *(Tonelessly)*: I haven't either.

KROGSTAD *(Relieved)*: No; you haven't the courage for it either, have you?

NORA: No! I haven't, I haven't!

KROGSTAD: Besides, it would be a very foolish thing to do. You'll just have to get through one domestic storm—and then it'll all be over. I have a letter for your husband, here in my pocket—

NORA: Telling him all about it?

KROGSTAD: Sparing you as much as possible.

NORA *(Quickly)*: He must never read that letter. Tear it up, Mr. Krogstad! I will manage to get the money somehow—

KROGSTAD: Excuse me, Mrs. Helmer, but I thought I just told you—

NORA: Oh, I'm not talking about the money I owe you. Just tell me how much money you want from my husband—I will get it somehow!

KROGSTAD: I want no money from your husband.

NORA: What *do* you want then?

KROGSTAD: Just this: I want a new start; I want to make something of myself; and your husband shall help me do it. For the past eighteen months my conduct has been irreproachable. It's been a hard struggle—I've lived in abject poverty; still, I was content to work my way up gradually, step by step. But now I've been kicked out, and now I shall not be satisfied to be merely reinstated—taken back on sufferance. I'm determined to make something of myself, I tell you. I intend to continue working in the bank—but I expect to be promoted. Your husband shall create a new position for me—

NORA: He'll never do it!

KROGSTAD: Oh, yes he will; I know him—he'll do it without a murmur; he wouldn't dare do otherwise. And then—you'll see! Within a year I'll be his right-hand man. It'll be Nils Krogstad, not Torvald Helmer, who'll run the Joint Stock Bank.

NORA: That will never happen.

KROGSTAD: No? Would you, perhaps—?

NORA: Yes! I have the courage for it now.

KROGSTAD: You don't frighten me! A dainty, pampered little lady such as you—

NORA: You'll see, you'll see!

KROGSTAD: Yes, I dare say! How would you like to lie there

under the ice—in that freezing, pitch-black water? And in the spring your body would be found floating on the surface—hideous, hairless, unrecognizable—

NORA: You can't frighten me!

KROGSTAD: You can't frighten me either. People don't do that sort of thing, Mrs. Helmer. And, anyway, what would be the use? I'd still have your husband in my power.

NORA: You mean—afterward? Even if I were no longer—?

KROGSTAD: Remember—I'd still have your reputation in my hands! *(NORA stands speechless and looks at him)* Well, I've given you fair warning. I wouldn't do anything foolish, if I were you. As soon as Helmer receives my letter, I shall expect to hear from him. And just remember this: I've been forced back into my former way of life—and your husband is responsible. I shall never forgive him for it. Good-bye, Mrs. Helmer.

(Goes out through the hall. NORA *hurries to the door, opens it a little, and listens.)*

NORA: He's gone. He didn't leave the letter. Of course he didn't—that would be impossible! *(Opens the door wider and wider)* What's he doing? He's stopped outside the door. He's not going down the stairs. Has he changed his mind? Is he—? *(A letter falls into the box.* KROGSTAD's *footsteps are heard gradually receding down the stairs.* NORA *utters a suppressed shriek, and rushes forward toward the sofa table; pause)* It's in the letter box! *(Slips shrinkingly up to the hall door)* It's there!—Torvald, Torvald—now we are lost!

(MRS. LINDE enters from the left with the costume.)

MRS. LINDE: There, I think it's all right now. If you'll just try it on—?

NORA *(Hoarsely and softly)*: Come here, Kristine.

MRS. LINDE *(Throws down the dress on the sofa)*: What's the matter with you? You look upset.

NORA: Come here. Do you see that letter? Do you see it—in the letter box?

MRS. LINDE: Yes, yes, I see it.

NORA: It's from Krogstad—

MRS. LINDE: Nora—you don't mean Krogstad lent you the money!

NORA: Yes; and now Torvald will know everything.

MRS. LINDE: It'll be much the best thing for you both, Nora.

NORA: But you don't know everything. I committed forgery—

MRS. LINDE: Good heavens!

NORA: Now, listen to me, Kristine; I want you to be my witness—

MRS. LINDE: How do you mean "witness"? What am I to—?

NORA: If I should go out of my mind—that might easily happen—

MRS. LINDE: Nora!

NORA: Or if something should happen to me—something that would prevent my being here—!

MRS. LINDE: Nora, Nora, you're quite beside yourself!

NORA: In case anyone else should insist on taking all the blame upon himself—the whole blame—you understand—

MRS. LINDE: Yes, but what makes you think—?

NORA: Then you must bear witness to the fact that that isn't true. I'm in my right mind now; I know exactly what I'm saying; and I tell you nobody else knew anything about it; I did the whole thing on my own. Just remember that.

MRS. LINDE: Very well—I will. But I don't understand at all.

NORA: No—of course—you couldn't. It's the wonderful thing—It's about to happen, don't you see?

MRS. LINDE: What "wonderful thing"?

NORA: The wonderful—wonderful thing! But it must never be allowed to happen—never. It would be too terrible.

MRS. LINDE: I'll go and talk to Krogstad at once.

NORA: No, don't go to him! He might do you some harm.

MRS. LINDE: There was a time—he would have done anything in the world for me.

NORA: He?

MRS. LINDE: Where does he live?

NORA: How do I know—? Yes—*(Feels in her pocket)* Here's his card. But the letter, the letter—!

HELMER *(From his study; knocking on the door)*: Nora!

NORA *(Shrieks in terror)*: Oh! What is it? What do you want?

HELMER: Don't be frightened! We're not coming in! Anyway, you've locked the door. Are you trying on?

NORA: Yes, yes, I'm trying on. I'm going to look so pretty, Torvald.

MRS. LINDE *(Who has read the card)*: He lives just around the corner.

NORA: But it won't do any good. It's too late now. The letter is in the box.

MRS. LINDE: I suppose your husband has the key?

NORA: Of course.

MRS. LINDE: Krogstad must ask for his letter back, unread. He must make up some excuse—

NORA: But this is the time that Torvald usually—

MRS. LINDE: Prevent him. Keep him occupied. I'll come back as quickly as I can. *(She goes out hastily by the hall door.)*

NORA *(Opens HELMER's door and peeps in)*: Torvald!

HELMER *(In the study)*: Well? May one venture to come back into one's own living room? Come along, Rank—now we shall see—*(In the doorway)* Why—what's this?

NORA: What, Torvald, dear?

HELMER: Rank led me to expect some wonderful disguise.

RANK *(In the doorway)*: That's what I understood. I must have been mistaken.

NORA: Not till tomorrow evening! Then I shall appear in all my splendor!

HELMER: But you look quite tired, Nora dear. I'm afraid you've been practicing too hard.

NORA: Oh, I haven't practiced at all yet.

HELMER: You ought to though—

NORA: Yes—I really should, Torvald! But I can't seem to manage without your help. I'm afraid I've forgotten all about it.

HELMER: Well—we'll see what we can do. It'll soon come back to you.

NORA: You will help me, won't you, Torvald? Promise! I feel so nervous—all those people! You must concentrate on me this evening—forget all about business. *Please,* Torvald dear—promise me you will!

HELMER: I promise. This evening I'll be your slave—you sweet, helpless little thing—! Just one moment though—I want to see—*(Going to hall door.)*

NORA: What do you want out there?

HELMER: I just want to see if there are any letters.

NORA: Oh, don't, Torvald! Don't bother about that now!

HELMER: Why not?

NORA: *Please* don't, Torvald! There aren't any.

HELMER: Just let me take a look—*(Starts to go.)*
    *(*NORA*, at the piano, plays the first bars of the tarantella.)*

HELMER *(Stops in the doorway)*: Aha!

NORA: I shan't be able to dance tomorrow if I don't rehearse with you!

HELMER *(Going to her)*: Are you really so nervous, Nora dear?

NORA: Yes, I'm terrified! Let's rehearse right away. We've plenty of time before dinner. Sit down and play for me, Torvald dear; direct me—guide me; you know how you do!

HELMER: With pleasure, my darling, if you wish me to. *(Sits at piano.)*

(NORA *snatches the tambourine out of the box, and hurriedly drapes herself in a long particolored shawl; then, with a bound, stands in the middle of the floor and cries out.*)

NORA: Now play for me! Now I'll dance!

(HELMER *plays and* NORA *dances.* RANK *stands at the piano behind* HELMER *and looks on.*)

HELMER *(Playing)*: Too fast! Too fast!

NORA: I can't help it!

HELMER: Don't be so violent, Nora!

NORA: That's the way it *should* be!

HELMER *(Stops)*: No, no; this won't do at all!

NORA *(Laughs and swings her tambourine)*: You see? What did I tell you?

RANK: I'll play for her.

HELMER *(Rising)*: Yes, do—then I'll be able to direct her.

(RANK *sits down at the piano and plays;* NORA *dances more and more wildly.* HELMER *stands by the stove and addresses frequent corrections to her; she seems not to hear. Her hair breaks loose, and falls over her shoulders. She does not notice it, but goes on dancing.* MRS. LINDE *enters and stands spellbound in the doorway.*)

MRS. LINDE: Ah—!

NORA *(Dancing)*: We're having such fun, Kristine!

HELMER: Why, Nora dear, you're dancing as if your life were at stake!

NORA: It is! It is!

HELMER: Rank, stop! This is absolute madness. Stop, I say!

(RANK *stops playing, and* NORA *comes to a sudden standstill.*)

HELMER *(Going toward her)*: I never would have believed it. You've forgotten everything I ever taught you.

NORA *(Throws the tambourine away)*: I told you I had!

HELMER: This needs an immense amount of work.

NORA: That's what I said; you see how important it is! You must work with me up to the very last minute. Will you promise me, Torvald?

HELMER: I most certainly will!

NORA: This evening and all day tomorrow you must think of nothing but me. You mustn't open a single letter— mustn't even *look* at the mailbox.

HELMER: Nora! I believe you're still worried about that wretched man—

NORA: Yes—yes, I am!

HELMER: Nora—Look at me—there's a letter from him in the box, isn't there?

NORA: Maybe—I don't know; I believe there is. But you're not to read anything of that sort now; nothing must come between us until the party's over.

RANK (*Softly, to* HELMER): Don't go against her.

HELMER (*Putting his arm around her*): Very well! The child shall have her way. But tomorrow night, when your dance is over—

NORA: Then you'll be free.

(HELENE *appears in the doorway, right.*)

HELENE: Dinner is served, ma'am.

NORA: We'll have champagne, Helene.

HELENE: Very good, ma'am. (*Goes out.*)

HELMER: Quite a feast, I see!

NORA: Yes—a real feast! We'll stay up till dawn drinking champagne! (*Calling out*) Oh, and we'll have macaroons, Helene—lots of them! Why not—for once!

HELMER (*Seizing her hand*): Come, come! Not so violent! Be my own little lark again.

NORA: I will, Torvald. But now—both of you go in—while Kristine helps me with my hair.

RANK (*Softly, as they go*): Is anything special the matter? I mean—anything—?

HELMER: No, no; nothing at all. It's just this childish fear I was telling you about. (*They go out to the right.*)

NORA: Well?

MRS. LINDE: He's gone out of town.

NORA: I saw it in your face.

MRS. LINDE: He'll be back tomorrow evening. I left a note for him.

NORA: You shouldn't have bothered. You couldn't prevent it anyway. After all, there's a kind of joy in waiting for the wonderful thing to happen.

MRS. LINDE: I don't understand. What *is* this thing you're waiting for?

NORA: I can't explain. Go in and join them. I'll be there in a moment.

(MRS. LINDE *goes into the dining room.* NORA *stands for a moment as though pulling herself together; then looks at her watch.*)

NORA: Five o'clock. Seven hours till midnight. Twenty-four hours till the next midnight and then the tarantella will be over. Twenty-four and seven? I've thirty-one hours left to live.

(HELMER *appears at the door, right.*)

HELMER: Well! What has become of the little lark?

NORA (*Runs to him with open arms*): Here she is!

CURTAIN

Act Three

SCENE: *The same room. The table, with the chairs around it, has been moved to stage center. A lighted lamp on the table. The hall door is open. Dance music is heard from the floor above.* MRS. LINDE *sits by the table absentmindedly turning the pages of a book. She tries to read, but seems unable to keep her mind on it. Now and then she listens intently and glances toward the hall door.*

MRS. LINDE *(Looks at her watch)*: Where can he be? The time is nearly up. I hope he hasn't—*(Listens again)* Here he is now. *(She goes into the hall and cautiously opens the outer door; cautious footsteps are heard on the stairs; she whispers)* Come in; there is no one here.

KROGSTAD *(In the doorway)*: I found a note from you at home. What does it mean?

MRS. LINDE: I simply *must* speak to you.

KROGSTAD: Indeed? But why here? Why in this house?

MRS. LINDE: I couldn't see you at my place. My room has no separate entrance. Come in; we're quite alone. The servants are asleep, and the Helmers are upstairs at a party.

KROGSTAD *(Coming into the room)*: Well, well! So the Helmers are dancing tonight, are they?

MRS. LINDE: Why shouldn't they?

KROGSTAD: Well—why not!

MRS. LINDE: Let's have a talk, Krogstad.

KROGSTAD: Have we two anything to talk about?

MRS. LINDE: Yes. A great deal.

KROGSTAD: I shouldn't have thought so.

MRS. LINDE: But then, you see—you have never really understood me.

KROGSTAD: There wasn't much to understand, was there? A woman is heartless enough to break off with a man, when a better match is offered; it's quite an ordinary occurrence.

MRS. LINDE: You really think me heartless? Did you think it was so easy for me?

KROGSTAD: Wasn't it?

MRS. LINDE: You really believed that, Krogstad?

KROGSTAD: If not, why should you have written to me as you did?

MRS. LINDE: What else could I do? Since I was forced to break with you, I felt it was only right to try and kill your love for me.

KROGSTAD *(Clenching his hands together)*: So that was it! And you did this for money!

MRS. LINDE: Don't forget I had my mother and two little brothers to think of. We couldn't wait for you, Krogstad; things were so unsettled for you then.

KROGSTAD: That may be; but, even so, you had no right to throw me over—not even for their sake.

MRS. LINDE: Who knows? I've often wondered whether I did right or not.

KROGSTAD *(More softly)*: When I had lost you, I felt the ground crumble beneath my feet. Look at me. I'm like a ship-wrecked man clinging to a raft.

MRS. LINDE: Help may be nearer than you think.

KROGSTAD: Help was here! Then you came and stood in the way.

MRS. LINDE: I knew nothing about it, Krogstad. I didn't know until today that I was to replace *you* at the bank.

KROGSTAD: Very well—I believe you. But now that you do know, will you withdraw?

MRS. LINDE: No; I'd do you no good by doing that.

KROGSTAD: "Good" or not—I'd withdraw all the same.

MRS. LINDE: I have learned to be prudent, Krogstad—I've had to. The bitter necessities of life have taught me that.

KROGSTAD: And life has taught me not to believe in phrases.

MRS. LINDE: Then life has taught you a very wise lesson. But what about deeds? Surely you must still believe in them?

KROGSTAD: How do you mean?

MRS. LINDE: You just said you were like a shipwrecked man, clinging to a raft.

KROGSTAD: I have good reason to say so.

MRS. LINDE: Well—I'm like a shipwrecked *woman* clinging to a raft. I have no one to mourn for, no one to care for.

KROGSTAD: You made your choice.

MRS. LINDE: I *had* no choice, I tell you!

KROGSTAD: What then?

MRS. LINDE: Since we're both of us shipwrecked, couldn't we join forces, Krogstad?

KROGSTAD: You don't mean—?

MRS. LINDE: Two people on a raft have a better chance than one.

KROGSTAD: Kristine!

MRS. LINDE: Why do you suppose I came here to the city?

KROGSTAD: You mean—you thought of me?

MRS. LINDE: I can't live without work; all my life I've worked, as far back as I can remember; it's always been my one great joy. Now I'm quite alone in the world; my life is empty—aimless. There's not much joy in working for one's self. You could help me, Nils; you could give me something and someone to work for.

KROGSTAD: I can't believe all this. It's an hysterical impulse—a woman's exaggerated craving for self-sacrifice.

MRS. LINDE: When have you ever found me hysterical?

KROGSTAD: You'd really be willing to do this? Tell me honestly—do you quite realize what my past has been?

MRS. LINDE: Yes.

KROGSTAD: And you know what people think of me?

MRS. LINDE: Didn't you just say you'd have been a different person if you'd been with me?

KROGSTAD: I'm sure of it.

MRS. LINDE: Mightn't that still be true?

KROGSTAD: You really mean this, Kristine, don't you? I can see it in your face. Are you sure you have the courage—?

MRS. LINDE: I need someone to care for, and your children need a mother. We two need each other, Nils. I have faith in your fundamental goodness. I'm not afraid.

KROGSTAD *(Seizing her hands)*: Thank you—thank you, Kristine. I'll make others believe in me too—I won't fail you! But—I'd almost forgotten—

MRS. LINDE *(Listening)*: Hush! The tarantella! You must go!

KROGSTAD: Why? What is it?

MRS. LINDE: Listen! She's begun her dance; as soon as she's finished dancing, they'll be down.

KROGSTAD: Yes—I'd better go. There'd have been no need for all that—but, of course, you don't know what I've done about the Helmers.

MRS. LINDE: Yes, I do, Nils.

KROGSTAD: And yet you have the courage to—?

MRS. LINDE: I know you were desperate—I understand.

KROGSTAD: I'd give anything to undo it!

MRS. LINDE: You can. Your letter's still in the mailbox.

KROGSTAD: Are you sure?

MRS. LINDE: Quite, but—

KROGSTAD *(Giving her a searching look)*: Could that be it? You're doing all this to save your friend? You might as well be honest with me! Is that it?

MRS. LINDE: I sold myself once for the sake of others, Nils; I'm not likely to do it again.

KROGSTAD: I'll ask for my letter back unopened.

MRS. LINDE: No, no.

KROGSTAD: Yes, of course. I'll wait till Helmer comes; I'll tell him to give me back the letter—I'll say it refers to my dismissal—and ask him not to read it—

MRS. LINDE: No, Nils; don't ask for it back.

KROGSTAD: But wasn't that actually your reason for getting me to come here?

MRS. LINDE: Yes, in my first moment of fear. But that was twenty-four hours ago, and since then I've seen incredible things happening here. Helmer must know the truth; this wretched business must no longer be kept secret; it's time those two came to a thorough understanding; there's been enough deceit and subterfuge.

KROGSTAD: Very well, if you like to risk it. But there's one thing I can do, and at once—

MRS. LINDE *(Listening)*: You must go now. Make haste! The dance is over; we're not safe here another moment.

KROGSTAD: I'll wait for you downstairs.

MRS. LINDE: Yes, do; then you can see me home.

KROGSTAD: Kristine! I've never been so happy! *(KROGSTAD goes out by the outer door. The door between the room and the hall remains open.)*

MRS. LINDE *(Arranging the room and getting her outdoor things together)*: How different things will be! Someone to work for, to live for; a home to make happy! How wonderful it will be to try!—I wish they'd come—(Listens) Here they are! I'll get my coat—*(Takes bonnet and cloak.* HELMER'S *and* NORA'S *voices are heard outside, a key is turned in the lock, and* HELMER *drags* NORA *almost by force into the hall. She wears the Italian costume with a large black shawl over it. He is in evening dress and wears a black domino, open.)*

NORA *(Struggling with him in the doorway)*: No, no! I don't want to come home; I want to go upstairs again; I don't want to leave so early!

HELMER: Come—Nora dearest!

NORA: I beg you, Torvald! Please, *please*—just one hour more!

HELMER: Not one single minute more, Nora darling; don't you remember our agreement? Come along in now; you'll catch cold. *(He leads her gently into the room in spite of her resistance.)*

MRS. LINDE: Good evening.

NORA: Kristine!

HELMER: Why, Mrs. Linde! What are you doing here so late?

MRS. LINDE: Do forgive me. I did so want to see Nora in her costume.

NORA: Have you been waiting for me all this time?

MRS. LINDE: Yes; I came too late to catch you before you went upstairs, and I didn't want to go away without seeing you.

HELMER *(Taking* NORA's *shawl off)*: And you *shall* see her, Mrs. Linde! She's worth looking at I can tell you! Isn't she lovely?

MRS. LINDE: Oh, Nora! How perfectly—!

HELMER: Absolutely exquisite, isn't she? That's what everybody said. But she's obstinate as a mule, is my sweet little thing! I don't know what to do with her! Will you believe it, Mrs. Linde, I had to drag her away by force?

NORA: You'll see—you'll be sorry, Torvald, you didn't let me stay, if only for another half hour.

HELMER: Do you hear that, Mrs. Linde? Now, listen to this: She danced her tarantella to wild applause, and she deserved it, too, I must say—though, perhaps, from an artistic point of view, her interpretation was a bit too realistic. But never mind—the point is, she made a great success, a phenomenal success. Now—should I have allowed her to stay on and spoil the whole effect? Certainly not! I took my sweet little Capri girl—my capricious little Capri girl, I might say—in my arms; a rapid whirl round the room, a low curtsy to all sides, and—as they say in novels—the lovely apparition vanished! An exit should always be effective, Mrs. Linde; but I can't get Nora to see that. Phew! It's warm here. *(Throws his domino on a chair and opens the door to his room)* Why—there's no light on in here! Oh; no, of course—Excuse me—*(Goes in and lights candles.)*

NORA *(Whispers breathlessly)*: Well?

MRS. LINDE *(Softly)*: I've spoken to him.

NORA: And—?

MRS. LINDE: Nora—you must tell your husband everything—

NORA *(Tonelessly)*: I knew it!

MRS. LINDE: You have nothing to fear from Krogstad; but you must speak out.

NORA: I shan't.

MRS. LINDE: Then the letter will.

NORA: Thank you, Kristine. Now I know what I must do. Hush—!

HELMER *(Coming back)*: Well, have you finished admiring her, Mrs. Linde?

MRS. LINDE: Yes, and now I must say good night.

HELMER: Oh—must you be going already? Does this knitting belong to you?

MRS. LINDE *(Takes it)*: Oh, thank you; I almost forgot it.

HELMER: So you knit, do you?

MRS. LINDE: Yes.

HELMER: Why don't you do embroidery instead?

MRS. LINDE: Why?

HELMER: Because it's so much prettier. Now watch! You hold the embroidery in the left hand—so—and then, in the right hand, you hold the needle, and guide it—so—in a long graceful curve—isn't that right?

MRS. LINDE: Yes, I suppose so—

HELMER: Whereas, knitting can never be anything but ugly. Now, watch! Arms close to your sides, needles going up and down—there's something Chinese about it!—That really was splendid champagne they gave us.

MRS. LINDE: Well, good night, Nora; don't be obstinate any more.

HELMER: Well said, Mrs. Linde!

MRS. LINDE: Good night, Mr. Helmer.

HELMER *(Accompanying her to the door)*: Good night, good night; I hope you get home safely. I'd be only too glad to—but you've such a short way to go. Good night, good night. *(She goes;* HELMER *shuts the door after her and comes forward again)* Well—thank God we've got rid of her; she's a dreadful bore, that woman.

NORA: You must be tired, Torvald.

HELMER: Me? Not in the least.

NORA: But aren't you sleepy?

HELMER: Not a bit. On the contrary, I feel exceedingly lively. But what about you? You seem to be very tired and sleepy.

NORA: Yes, I am very tired. But I'll soon sleep now.

HELMER: You see! I was right not to let you stay there any longer.

NORA: Everything you do is always right, Torvald.

HELMER *(Kissing her forehead)*: There's my sweet, sensible little lark! By the way, did you notice how gay Rank was this evening?

NORA: Was he? I didn't get a chance to speak to him.

HELMER: I didn't either, really; but it's a long time since I've seen him in such a jolly mood. *(Gazes at* NORA *for a while, then comes nearer her)* It's so lovely to be home again—to be here alone with you. You glorious, fascinating creature!

NORA: Don't look at me like that, Torvald.

HELMER: Why shouldn't I look at my own dearest treasure?—at all this loveliness that is mine, wholly and utterly mine—mine alone!

NORA *(Goes to the other side of the table)*: You mustn't talk to me like that tonight.

HELMER *(Following)*: You're still under the spell of the tarantella—and it makes you even more desirable. Listen! The other guests are leaving now. *(More softly)* Soon the whole house will be still, Nora.

NORA: I hope so.

HELMER: Yes, you do, don't you, my beloved? Do you know something—when I'm out with you among a lot of people—do you know why it is I hardly speak to you, why I keep away from you, and only occasionally steal a quick glance at you; do you know why that is? It's because I pretend that we love each other in secret, that we're secretly engaged, and that no one suspects there is anything between us.

NORA: Yes, yes; I know your thoughts are always around me.

HELMER: Then, when it's time to leave, and I put your shawl around your smooth, soft, young shoulders—around that beautiful neck of yours—I pretend that you are my young bride, that we've just come from the wedding, and that I'm taking you home for the first time—that for the first time I shall be alone with you—quite alone with you, in all your tremulous beauty. All evening I have been filled with longing for you. As I watched you swaying and whirling in the tarantella—my pulses began to throb until I thought I should go mad; that's why I carried you off—made you leave so early—

NORA: Please go, Torvald! Please leave me. I don't want you like this.

HELMER: What do you mean? You're teasing me, aren't you, little Nora? Not want me—! Aren't I your husband—? *(A knock at the outer door.)*

NORA *(Starts)*: Listen—!

HELMER *(Going toward the hall)*: Who is it?

RANK *(Outside)*: It is I; may I come in a moment?

HELMER *(In a low tone, annoyed)*: Why does he have to bother us now! *(Aloud)* Just a second! *(Opens door)* Well! How nice of you to look in.

RANK: I heard your voice, and I thought I'd like to stop in a minute. *(Looks around)* These dear old rooms! You must be so cozy and happy here, you two!

HELMER: I was just saying how gay and happy you seemed to be upstairs.

RANK: Why not? Why shouldn't I be? One should get all one can out of life; all one can, for as long as one can. That wine was excellent—

HELMER: Especially the champagne.

RANK: You noticed that, did you? It's incredible how much I managed to get down.

NORA: Torvald drank plenty of it too.

RANK: Oh?

NORA: It always puts him in such a jolly mood.

RANK: Well, why shouldn't one have a jolly evening after a well-spent day?

HELMER: Well-spent! I'm afraid mine wasn't much to boast of!

RANK *(Slapping him on the shoulder)*: But mine was, you see?

NORA: Did you by any chance make a scientific investigation, Dr. Rank?

RANK: Precisely.

HELMER: Listen to little Nora, talking about scientific investigations!

NORA: Am I to congratulate you on the result?

RANK: By all means.

NORA: It was good then?

RANK: The best possible, both for the doctor and the patient—certainty.

NORA *(Quickly and searchingly)*: Certainty?

RANK: Absolute certainty. Wasn't I right to spend a jolly evening after that?

NORA: You were quite right, Dr. Rank.

HELMER: I quite agree! Provided you don't have to pay for it tomorrow.

RANK: You don't get anything for nothing in this life.

NORA: You like masquerade parties, don't you, Dr. Rank?

RANK: Very much—when there are plenty of amusing disguises—

NORA: What shall we two be at our next masquerade?

HELMER: Listen to her! Thinking of the next party already!

RANK: We two? I'll tell you. You must go as a precious talisman.

HELMER: How on earth would you dress that!

RANK: That's easy. She'd only have to be herself.

HELMER: Charmingly put. But what about you? Have you decided what you'd be?

RANK: Oh, definitely.

HELMER: Well?

RANK: At the next masquerade party I shall be invisible.

HELMER: That's a funny notion!

RANK: There's a large black cloak—you've heard of the invisible cloak, haven't you? You've only to put it around you and no one can see you any more.

HELMER *(With a suppressed smile)*: Quite true!

RANK: But I almost forgot what I came for. Give me a cigar, will you, Helmer? One of the dark Havanas.

HELMER: Of course—with pleasure. *(Hands cigar case.)*

RANK *(Takes one and cuts the end off)*: Thanks.

NORA *(Striking a wax match)*: Let me give you a light.

RANK: I thank you. *(She holds the match. He lights his cigar at it)* And now, I'll say good-bye!

HELMER: Good-bye, good-bye, my dear fellow.

NORA: Sleep well, Dr. Rank.

RANK: Thanks for the wish.

NORA: Wish me the same.

RANK: You? Very well, since you ask me—Sleep well. And thanks for the light. *(He nods to them both and goes out.)*

HELMER *(In an undertone)*: He's had a lot to drink.

NORA *(Absently)*: I dare say. (HELMER *takes his bunch of keys from his pocket and goes into the hall)* Torvald! What do you want out there?

HELMER: I'd better empty the mailbox; it's so full there won't be room for the papers in the morning.

NORA: Are you going to work tonight?

HELMER: No—you know I'm not! Why, what's this? Someone has been at the lock.

NORA: The lock—?

HELMER: Yes—that's funny! I shouldn't have thought that the maids would—Here's a broken hairpin. Why—it's one of yours, Nora.

NORA *(Quickly)*: It must have been the children—

HELMER: You'll have to stop them doing that—There! I got it open at last. *(Takes contents out and calls out toward the kitchen)* Helene?—Oh, Helene; put out the lamp in the hall, will you? (*He returns with letters in his hand, and shuts*

the door to the hall) Just look how they've stacked up.
(Looks through them) Why, what's this?

NORA *(At the window):* The letter! Oh, Torvald! No!

HELMER: Two visiting cards—from Rank.

NORA: From Dr. Rank?

HELMER *(Looking at them):* Dr. Rank, physician. They were right
on top. He must have stuck them in just now, as he left.

NORA: Is there anything on them?

HELMER: There's a black cross over his name. Look! What a
gruesome thought. Just as if he were announcing his
own death.

NORA: And so he is.

HELMER: What do you mean? What do you know about it?
Did he tell you anything?

NORA: Yes. These cards mean that he has said good-bye to us
for good. Now he'll lock himself up to die.

HELMER: Oh, my poor friend! I always knew he hadn't long to
live, but I never dreamed it would be quite so soon—!
And to hide away like a wounded animal—

NORA: When the time comes, it's best to go in silence. Don't
you think so, Torvald?

HELMER *(Walking up and down):* He'd become so much a part of
us. I can't imagine his having gone for good. With his
suffering and loneliness he was like a dark, cloudy
background to our lives—it made the sunshine of our
happiness seem even brighter—Well, I suppose it's for
the best—for him at any rate. *(Stands still)* And perhaps
for us too, Nora. Now we are more than ever dependent
on each other. *(Takes her in his arms)* Oh, my beloved
wife! I can't seem to hold you close enough. Do you
know something, Nora? I often wish you were in some
great danger—so I could risk body and soul—my whole
life—everything, everything, for your sake.

NORA *(Tears herself from him and says firmly)*: Now you must read your letters, Torvald.

HELMER: No, no; not tonight. I want to be with you, my beloved wife.

NORA; With the thought of your dying friend—?

HELMER: Of course—You are right. It's been a shock to both of us. A hideous shadow has come between us—thoughts of death and decay. We must try and throw them off. Until then—we'll stay apart.

NORA *(Her arms around his neck)*: Torvald! Good night! Good night!

HELMER *(Kissing her forehead)*: Good night, my little song-bird; Sleep well! Now I'll go and read my letters. *(He goes with the letters in his hand into his room and shuts the door.)*

NORA *(With wild eyes, gropes about her, seizes* HELMER's *domino, throws it around her, and whispers quickly, hoarsely, and brokenly)*: I'll never see him again. Never, never, never. *(Throws her shawl over her head)* I'll never see the children again. I'll never see them either—Oh, the thought of that black, icy water! That fathomless—! If it were only over! He has it now; he's reading it. Oh, not yet—please! Not yet! Torvald, good-bye! Good-bye to you and the children!
(She is rushing out by the hall; at the same moment HELMER *flings his door open, and stands there with an open letter in his hand.)*

HELMER: Nora!

NORA *(Shrieks)*: Ah—!

HELMER: What does this mean? Do you know what is in this letter?

NORA: Yes, yes, I know. Let me go! Let me out!

HELMER *(Holds her back)*: Where are you going?

NORA *(Tries to break away from him)*: Don't try to save me, Torvald!

HELMER *(Falling back)*: So it's true! It's true what he writes? It's too horrible! It's impossible—it can't be true.

NORA: It *is* true. I've loved you more than all the world.

HELMER: Oh, come now! Let's have no silly nonsense!

NORA *(A step nearer him)*: Torvald—!

HELMER: Do you realize what you've done?

NORA: Let me go—I won't have you suffer for it! I won't have you take the blame!

HELMER: Will you stop this play-acting! *(Locks the outer door)* You'll stay here and give an account of yourself. Do you understand what you have done? Answer me! Do you understand it?

NORA *(Looks at him fixedly, and says with a stiffening expression)*: I think I'm beginning to understand for the first time.

HELMER *(Walking up and down)*: God! What an awakening! After eight years to discover that you who have been my pride and joy—are no better than a hypocrite, a liar—worse than that—a criminal! It's too horrible to think of! *(NORA says nothing, and continues to look fixedly at him)* I might have known what to expect. I should have foreseen it. You've inherited all your father's lack of principle—be silent!—all of your father's lack of principle, I say!—no religion, no moral code, no sense of duty. This is my punishment for shielding him! I did it for your sake; and this is my reward!

NORA: I see.

HELMER: You've destroyed my happiness. You've ruined my whole future. It's ghastly to think of! I'm completely in the power of this scoundrel; he can force me to do whatever he likes, demand whatever he chooses; order me about at will; and I shan't dare open my mouth! My entire career is to be wrecked and all because of a lawless, unprincipled woman!

NORA: If I were no longer alive, then you'd be free.

HELMER: Oh, yes! You're full of histrionics! Your father was just the same. Even if you "weren't alive," as you put it, what good would that do me? None whatever! He could publish the story all the same; I might even be suspected of collusion. People might say I was behind it all—that I had prompted you to do it. And to think I have you to thank for all this—you whom I've done nothing but pamper and spoil since the day of our marriage. Now do you realize what you've done to me?

NORA *(With cold calmness)*: Yes.

HELMER: It's all so incredible, I can't grasp it. But we must try and come to some agreement. Take off that shawl. Take it off, I say! Of course, we must find some way to appease him—the matter must be hushed up at any cost. As far as we two are concerned, there must be no change in our way of life—in the eyes of the world, I mean. You'll naturally continue to live here. But you won't be allowed to bring up the children—I'd never dare trust them to you—God! to have to say this to the woman I've loved so tenderly—There can be no further thought of happiness between us. We must save what we can from the ruins—we can save appearances, at least—*(A ring;* HELMER *starts)* Who can that be? At this hour! You don't suppose he—! Could he—? Hide yourself, Nora; say you are ill.

*(*NORA *stands motionless.* HELMER *goes to the door and opens it.)*

HELENE *(Half-dressed, in the hall)*: It's a letter for Mrs. Helmer.

HELMER: Give it to me. *(Seizes the letter and shuts the door)* It's from him. I shan't give it to you. I'll read it myself.

NORA: Very well.

HELMER *(By the lamp)*: I don't dare open it; this may be the end—for both of us. Still—I must know. *(Hastily tears the letter open; reads a few lines, looks at an enclosure; with a cry of joy)* Nora! *(*NORA *looks inquiringly at him)* Nora!—I can't believe it—I must read it again. But it's true—it's really true! Nora, I am saved! I'm saved!

NORA: What about me?

HELMER: You too, of course; we are both of us saved, both of us. Look!—he's sent you back your note—he says he's sorry for what he did and apologizes for it—that due to a happy turn of events he—Oh, what does it matter what he says! We are saved, Nora! No one can harm you now. Oh, Nora, Nora! But let's get rid of this hateful thing. I'll just see—*(Glances at the I.O.U.)* No, no—I won't even look at it; I'll pretend it was all a horrible dream. *(Tears the I.O.U. and both letters in pieces. Throws them into the fire and watches them burn)* There! Now it's all over—He said in his letter you've known about this since Christmas Eve—you must have had three dreadful days, Nora!

NORA: Yes. It's been very hard.

HELMER: How you must have suffered! And you saw no way out but—No! We'll forget the whole ghastly business. We'll just thank God and repeat again and again: It's over; all over! Don't you understand, Nora? You don't seem to grasp it: It's over. What's the matter with you? Why do you look so grim? My poor, darling little Nora, I understand; but you mustn't worry—because I've forgiven you, Nora; I swear I have; I've forgiven everything. You did what you did because you loved me—I see that now.

NORA: Yes—that's true.

HELMER: You loved me as a wife should love her husband. You didn't realize what you were doing—you weren't able to judge how wrong it was. Don't think this makes you any less dear to me. Just you lean on me; let me guide you and advise you; I'm not a man for nothing! There's something very endearing about a woman's helplessness. And try and forget those harsh things I said just now. I was frantic; my whole world seemed to be tumbling about my ears. Believe me, I've forgiven you, Nora—I swear it—I've forgiven everything.

NORA: Thank you for your forgiveness, Torvald. *(Goes out, to the right.)*

HELMER: No! Don't go. *(Looking through the doorway)* Why do you have to go in there?

NORA *(Inside)*: I want to get out of these fancy dress clothes.

HELMER *(In the doorway)*: Yes, do, my darling. Try to calm down now, and get back to normal, my poor, frightened little song-bird. Don't you worry—you'll be safe under my wings—they'll protect you. *(Walking up and down near the door)* How lovely our home is, Nora! You'll be sheltered here; I'll cherish you as if you were a little dove I'd rescued from the claws of some dreadful hawk. You'll see—your poor fluttering little heart will soon grow calm again. Tomorrow all this will appear in quite a different light—things will be just as they were. I won't have to keep on saying I've forgiven you—you'll be able to sense it. You don't really think I could ever drive you away, do you? That I could even so much as reproach you for anything? You'd understand if you could see into my heart. When a man forgives his wife wholeheartedly—as I have you—it fills him with such tenderness, such peace. She seems to belong to him in a double sense; it's as though he'd brought her to life again; she's become more than his wife—she's become his child as well. That's how it will be with us, Nora—my own bewildered, helpless little darling. From now on you mustn't worry about anything; just open your heart to me; just let me be both will and conscience to you. *(NORA enters in everyday dress)* What's all this? I thought you were going to bed. You've changed your dress?

NORA: Yes, Torvald; I've changed my dress.

HELMER: But what for? At this hour?

NORA: I shan't sleep tonight.

HELMER: But, Nora dear—

NORA *(Looking at her watch)*: It's not so very late—Sit down, Torvald; we have a lot to talk about. *(She sits at one side of the table.)*

HELMER: Nora—what does this mean? Why that stern expression?

NORA: Sit down. It'll take some time. I have a lot to say to you.

(HELMER sits at the other side of the table.)

HELMER: You frighten me, Nora. I don't understand you.

NORA: No, that's just it. You don't understand me; and I have never understood you either—until tonight. No, don't interrupt me. Just listen to what I have to say. This is to be a final settlement, Torvald.

HELMER: How do you mean?

NORA *(After a short silence)*: Doesn't anything special strike you as we sit here like this?

HELMER: I don't think so—why?

NORA: It doesn't occur to you, does it, that though we've been married for eight years, this is the first time that we two—man and wife—have sat down for a serious talk?

HELMER: What do you mean by serious?

NORA: During eight whole years, no—more than that—ever since the first day we met—we have never exchanged so much as one serious word about serious things.

HELMER: Why should I perpetually burden you with all my cares and problems? How could you possibly help me to solve them?

NORA: I'm not talking about cares and problems. I'm simply saying we've never once sat down seriously and tried to get to the bottom of anything.

HELMER: But, Nora, darling—why should you be concerned with serious thoughts?

NORA: That's the whole point! You've never understood me—A great injustice has been done me, Torvald; first by Father, and then by you.

HELMER: What a thing to say! No two people on earth could ever have loved you more than we have!

NORA *(Shaking her head)*: You never loved me. You just thought it was fun to be in love with me.

HELMER: This is fantastic!

NORA: Perhaps. But it's true all the same. While I was still at home I used to hear Father airing his opinions and they became my opinions; or if I didn't happen to agree, I kept it to myself—he would have been displeased otherwise. He used to call me his doll-baby, and played with me as I played with my dolls. Then I came to live in your house—

HELMER: What an expression to use about our marriage!

NORA *(Undisturbed)*: I mean—from Father's hands I passed into yours. You arranged everything according to your tastes, and I acquired the same tastes, or I pretended to—I'm not sure which—a little of both, perhaps. Looking back on it all, it seems to me I've lived here like a beggar, from hand to mouth. I've lived by performing tricks for you, Torvald. But that's the way you wanted it. You and Father have done me a great wrong. You've prevented me from becoming a real person.

HELMER: Nora, how can you be so ungrateful and unreasonable! Haven't you been happy here?

NORA: No, never. I thought I was; but I wasn't really.

HELMER: Not—not happy!

NORA: No; only merry. You've always been so kind to me. But our home has never been anything but a playroom. I've been your doll-wife, just as at home I was Papa's doll-child. And the children in turn, have been my dolls. I thought it fun when you played games with me, just as they thought it fun when I played games with them. And that's been our marriage, Torvald.

HELMER: There may be a grain of truth in what you say, even though it is distorted and exaggerated. From now on things will be different. Play-time is over now; tomorrow lessons begin!

NORA: Whose lessons? Mine, or the children's?

HELMER: Both, if you wish it, Nora dear.

NORA: Torvald, I'm afraid you're not the man to teach me to be a real wife to you.

HELMER: How can you say that?

NORA: And I'm certainly not fit to teach the children.

HELMER: Nora!

NORA: Didn't you just say, a moment ago, you didn't dare trust them to me?

HELMER: That was in the excitement of the moment! You mustn't take it so seriously!

NORA: But you were quite right, Torvald. That job is beyond me; there's another job I must do first: I must try and educate myself. You could never help me to do that; I must do it quite alone. So, you see—that's why I'm going to leave you.

HELMER *(Jumping up)*: What did you say—?

NORA: I shall never get to know myself—I shall never learn to face reality—unless I stand alone. So I can't stay with you any longer.

HELMER: Nora! Nora!

NORA: I am going at once. I'm sure Kristine will let me stay with her tonight—

HELMER: But, Nora—this is madness! I shan't allow you to do this. I shall forbid it!

NORA: You no longer have the power to forbid me anything. I'll only take a few things with me—those that belong to me. I shall never again accept anything from you.

HELMER: Have you lost your senses?

NORA: Tomorrow I'll go home—to what *was* my home, I mean. It might be easier for me there, to find something to do.

HELMER: You talk like an ignorant child, Nora—!

NORA: Yes. That's just why I must educate myself.

HELMER: To leave your home—to leave your husband, and your children! What do you suppose people would say to that?

NORA: It makes no difference. This is something I *must* do.

HELMER: It's inconceivable! Don't you realize you'd be betraying your most sacred duty?

NORA: What do you consider that to be?

HELMER: Your duty toward your husband and your children—I surely don't have to tell you that!

NORA: I've another duty just as sacred.

HELMER: Nonsense! What duty do you mean?

NORA: My duty toward myself.

HELMER: Remember—before all else you are a wife and mother.

NORA: I don't believe that anymore. I believe that before all else I am a human being, just as you are—or at least that I should try and become one. I know that most people would agree with you, Torvald—and that's what they say in books. But I can no longer be satisfied with what most people say—or what they write in books. I must think things out for myself—get clear about them.

HELMER: Surely your position in your home is clear enough? Have you no sense of religion? Isn't that an infallible guide to you?

NORA: But don't you see, Torvald—I don't really know what religion is.

HELMER: Nora! How *can* you!

NORA: All I know about it is what Pastor Hansen told me

when I was confirmed. He taught me what he thought religion was—said it was *this* and *that*. As soon as I get away by myself, I shall have to look into that matter too, try and decide whether what he taught me was right—or whether it's right for *me*, at least.

HELMER: A nice way for a young woman to talk! It's unheard of! If religion means nothing to you, I'll appeal to your conscience; you must have some sense of ethics, I suppose? Answer me! Or have you none?

NORA: It's hard for me to answer you, Torvald. I don't think I know—all these things bewilder me. But I *do* know that I think quite differently from you about them. I've discovered that the law, for instance, is quite different from what I had imagined; but I find it hard to believe it can be right. It seems it's criminal for a woman to try and spare her old, sick, father, or save her husband's life! I can't agree with that.

HELMER: You talk like a child. You have no understanding of the society we live in.

NORA: No, I haven't. But I'm going to try and learn. I want to find out which of us is right—society or I.

HELMER: You are ill, Nora; you have a touch of fever; you're quite beside yourself.

NORA: I've never felt so sure—so clear-headed—as I do tonight.

HELMER: "Sure and clear-headed" enough to leave your husband and your children?

NORA: Yes.

HELMER: Then there is only one explanation possible.

NORA: What?

HELMER: You don't love me any more.

NORA: No; that is just it.

HELMER: Nora!—What are you saying!

NORA: It makes me so unhappy, Torvald; for you've always

been so kind to me. But I can't help it. I don't love you any more.

HELMER *(Mastering himself with difficulty)*: You feel "sure and clear-headed" about this too?

NORA: Yes, utterly sure. That's why I can't stay here any longer.

HELMER: And can you tell me how I lost your love?

NORA: Yes, I can tell you. It was tonight—when the wonderful thing didn't happen; I knew then you weren't the man I always thought you were.

HELMER: I don't understand.

NORA: For eight years I've been waiting patiently; I knew, of course, that such things don't happen every day. Then, when this trouble came to me—I thought to myself: Now! Now the wonderful thing will happen! All the time Krogstad's letter was out there in the box, it never occurred to me for a single moment that you'd think of submitting to his conditions. I was absolutely convinced that you'd defy him—that you'd tell him to publish the thing to all the world; and that then—

HELMER: You mean you thought I'd let my wife be publicly dishonored and disgraced?

NORA: No. What I thought you'd do, was to take the blame upon yourself.

HELMER: Nora—!

NORA: I know! You think I never would have accepted such a sacrifice. Of course I wouldn't! But my word would have meant nothing against yours. That was the wonderful thing I hoped for, Torvald, hoped for with such terror. And it was to prevent that, that I chose to kill myself.

HELMER: I'd gladly work for you day and night, Nora—go through suffering and want, if need be—but one doesn't sacrifice one's honor for love's sake.

NORA: Millions of women have done so.

HELMER: You think and talk like a silly child.

NORA: Perhaps. But you neither think nor talk like the man I want to share my life with. When you'd recovered from your fright—and you never thought of me, only of yourself—when you had nothing more to fear—you behaved as though none of this had happened. I was your little lark again, your little doll—whom you would have to guard more carefully than ever, because she was so weak and frail. *(Stands up)* At that moment it suddenly dawned on me that I had been living here for eight years with a stranger and that I'd borne him three children. I can't bear to think about it! I could tear myself to pieces!

HELMER *(Sadly)*: I see, Nora—I understand; there's suddenly a great void between us—Is there no way to bridge it?

NORA: Feeling as I do now, Torvald—I could never be a wife to you.

HELMER: But, if I were to change? Don't you think I'm capable of that?

NORA: Perhaps—when you no longer have your doll to play with.

HELMER: It's inconceivable! I *can't* part with you, Nora. I can't endure the thought.

NORA *(Going into room on the right)*: All the more reason it should happen. *(She comes back with outdoor things and a small traveling-bag, which she places on a chair.)*

HELMER: But not at once, Nora—not now! At least wait till tomorrow.

NORA *(Putting on cloak)*: I can't spend the night in a strange man's house.

HELMER: Couldn't we go on living here together? As brother and sister, if you like—as friends.

NORA *(Fastening her hat)*: You know very well that wouldn't last, Torvald. *(Puts on the shawl)* Good-bye. I won't go in and see the children. I know they're in better hands than mine. Being what I am—how can I be of any use to them?

HELMER: But surely, some day, Nora—?

NORA: How can I tell? How do I know what sort of person I'll become?

HELMER: You are my wife, Nora, now and always!

NORA: Listen to me, Torvald—I've always heard that when a wife deliberately leaves her husband as I am leaving you, he is legally freed from all responsibility toward her. At any rate, I release you now from all responsibility. You mustn't feel yourself bound, any more than I shall. There must be complete freedom on both sides. Here is your ring. Now give me mine.

HELMER: That too?

NORA: That too.

HELMER: Here it is.

NORA: So—it's all over now. Here are the keys. The servants know how to run the house—better than I do. I'll ask Kristine to come by tomorrow, after I've left town; there are a few things I brought with me from home; she'll pack them up and send them on to me.

HELMER: You really mean it's over, Nora? *Really* over? You'll never think of me again?

NORA: I expect I shall often think of you; of you—and the children, and this house.

HELMER: May I write to you?

NORA: No—never. You mustn't! Please!

HELMER: At least, let me send you—

NORA: Nothing!

HELMER: But, you'll let me help you, Nora—

NORA: No, I say! I can't accept anything from strangers.

HELMER: Must I always be a stranger to you, Nora?

NORA *(Taking her traveling-bag)*: Yes. Unless it were to happen—the most wonderful thing of all—

HELMER: What?

NORA: Unless we both could change so that—Oh, Torvald! I no longer *believe* in miracles, you see!

HELMER: Tell me! Let *me* believe! Unless we both could change so that—?

NORA: —So that our life together might truly be a marriage. Good-bye. *(She goes out by the hall door.)*

HELMER *(Sinks into a chair by the door with his face in his hands)*: Nora! Nora! *(He looks around the room and rises)* She is gone! How empty it all seems! *(A hope springs up in him)* The most wonderful thing of all—?

(From below is heard the reverberation of a heavy door closing.)

CURTAIN

Ghosts

*A Domestic Tragedy
in Three Acts*

Characters

MRS. HELENE ALVING,
the widow of Captain (Chamberlain) Alving

OSVALD ALVING,
her son; a painter

MANDERS,
the pastor of the parish

JAKOB ENGSTRAND,
a carpenter

REGINE ENGSTRAND,
his daughter; in Mrs. Alving's service

The action takes place on MRS. ALVING'S *country
estate on one of the large fjords in the west of Norway.*

Act One

SCENE: *A spacious garden room; in the left wall a door, and in the right wall two doors. In the center of the room a round table, with chairs about it. On the table lie books, periodicals and newspapers. In the foreground to the left a window, and by it a small sofa, with a work table in front of it. In the background, the room is continued into a somewhat narrower conservatory, the walls of which are formed by large panes of glass. In the right-hand wall of the conservatory is a door leading down into the garden. Through the glass wall a gloomy fjord landscape is faintly visible, veiled by steady rain.*

ENGSTRAND, the carpenter, stands by the garden door. His left leg is somewhat bent; he has a clump of wood under the sole of his boot. REGINE, with an empty plant sprayer in her hand, hinders him from advancing.

REGINE *(In a low voice)*: Well—what is it you want? No!—stay where you are—you're dripping wet!

ENGSTRAND: It's only God's rain, my child.

REGINE: It's the devil's rain, that's what it is!

ENGSTRAND: Lord, how you talk, Regine! *(Limping a few steps into the room)* But, here's what I want to tell you—

REGINE: Don't go clumping about with that foot of yours! The young master's upstairs asleep.

ENGSTRAND: Asleep at this hour—in broad daylight?

REGINE: It's none of your business.

ENGSTRAND: Now—look at *me*—I was on a bit of a spree last night—

REGINE: That's nothing new!

ENGSTRAND: Well—we're all frail creatures, my child—

REGINE: We are that!

ENGSTRAND: And temptations are manifold in this world, you see—but that didn't prevent me from going to work at half past five as usual!

103

REGINE: That's as it may be—and now, get out! I can't stand here having a rendezvous with you.

ENGSTRAND: What's that?

REGINE: I don't want anyone to see you here—so get out!

ENGSTRAND *(Comes a few steps nearer)*: Damned if I go till I've had a talk with you. Listen—I'll be through with my work at the schoolhouse this afternoon—then I'm going right back to town by the night boat—

REGINE *(Mutters)*: A pleasant journey to you!

ENGSTRAND: Thank you, my child! Tomorrow's the opening of the orphanage, they'll all be celebrating—sure to be a lot of drinking too—I'll prove to them that Jakob Engstrand can keep out of the way of temptation—

REGINE: Ha! . . .

ENGSTRAND: Lots of grand people'll be here—Pastor Manders is expected from town—

REGINE: He gets here today.

ENGSTRAND: There—you see! Damned if I give *him* a chance to say anything against me!

REGINE: So that's it, is it?

ENGSTRAND: That's what?

REGINE *(Gives him a searching look)*: What are you going to try and put over on him this time?

ENGSTRAND: Are you crazy? As if I'd try and put anything over on *him.* No—Pastor Manders has been too good a friend to me—and that's just what I want to talk to you about. As I was saying, I'm going back home tonight—

REGINE: You can't go soon enough to please me!

ENGSTRAND: But I want you to come with me, Regine.

REGINE *(Open-mouthed)*: I, go with *you?*

ENGSTRAND: Yes—I want you to come home with me.

REGINE *(Scornfully)*: You'll never get me to do that!

ENGSTRAND: Well—we'll see.

REGINE: Yes! You'll see all right! After being brought up here by Mrs. Alving—treated almost like one of the family—do you suppose I'd go home with you—back to that kind of a house? You're crazy!

ENGSTRAND: What kind of talk's that! You'd defy your own father, would you?

REGINE *(Mutters, without looking at him)*: You've said often enough I'm no concern of yours—

ENGSTRAND: Never mind about that—

REGINE: Many's the time you've cursed at me and called me a—*Fi donc!*

ENGSTRAND: When did I ever use a foul word like that?

REGINE: I know well enough what word you used!

ENGSTRAND: Well—maybe—when I wasn't feeling quite my-self—hm. Temptations are manifold in this world, Regine!

REGINE: Pah! . . .

ENGSTRAND: And then your mother used to drive me crazy—I had to find some way to get back at her. She put on so many airs: *(Mimicking her)* "Let me go, Engstrand! Leave me alone! Don't forget I spent three years in Chamber-lain Alving's house at Rosenvold!" *(Laughs)* God Al-mighty! She never got over the Captain being made Chamberlain while she was working here!

REGINE: Poor Mother! You certainly hounded her into her grave!

ENGSTRAND *(Shrugging his shoulders)*: Oh, of course! I'm to blame for everything!

REGINE *(Under her breath as she turns away)*: Ugh! And then that leg of yours!

ENGSTRAND: What did you say, my child?

REGINE: *Pied de mouton!*

ENGSTRAND: What's that? English?*

REGINE: Yes.

ENGSTRAND: Yes—well; you've certainly got educated here— and that may come in handy too.

REGINE *(After a short silence)*: Why do you want me to go back with you?

ENGSTRAND: Why wouldn't a father want his only child with him? Aren't I a lonely, deserted widower?

REGINE: Oh, don't talk rubbish to me! Why do you want me with you?

ENGSTRAND: Well—I'll tell you—I'm thinking of setting up in a new line of business—

REGINE *(Whistles)*: What, again! What is it this time?

ENGSTRAND: You'll see—this time it'll be different. Christ Almighty!

REGINE: Stop your swearing! *(She stamps her foot.)*

ENGSTRAND: Sh! You're right, my child. Well—what I wanted to say was—I've managed to save quite a bit of money— from this work on the orphanage—

REGINE: You have, have you? So much the better for you.

ENGSTRAND: There's nothing to spend your money on in this Godforsaken hole—

REGINE: Well?

ENGSTRAND: So I thought I'd invest it in a paying concern. I thought of starting a sort of tavern—for seamen—

REGINE: Ugh!

ENGSTRAND: A really high-class tavern, you know—none of your cheap dives. No—by God! I'd cater to captains and first-mates—really high-class people.

REGINE: And I suppose I'd be expected to—

ENGSTRAND: Oh, you could be a great help, Regine. You

* In performance this should be changed to "German," since the characters are speaking in English.

wouldn't have to do anything—it wouldn't be hard on you, my child—you'd have everything your own way!

REGINE: Oh, yes, of course!

ENGSTRAND: After all there must be some women in the house—that goes without saying. We'd have to have a bit of fun in the evenings, singing and dancing—and that sort of thing. You've got to remember—these poor fellows are sailors—wanderers on the seas of the world. *(Comes nearer to her)* Don't be a fool and stand in your own way. What future is there for you out here? What good's all this education the Mrs. has paid for? You're to look after the kids in the new orphanage I hear—is that a job for you? Do you want to wear yourself to the bone looking after a lot of dirty brats?

REGINE: If things turn out as I hope—well—it could be—it could be—

ENGSTRAND: What "could be"?

REGINE: You keep your nose out of that! How much money did you save?

ENGSTRAND: I'd say—in all—close to two hundred dollars.

REGINE: Not so bad!

ENGSTRAND: Enough to get me started, my child.

REGINE: Do I get any of it?

ENGSTRAND: You do not!

REGINE: Not even enough to buy myself a new dress?

ENGSTRAND: You come with me—you'll get plenty of new dresses then!

REGINE: I can get them myself, if I set my mind to it.

ENGSTRAND: But a father's guiding hand is a good thing, Regine. There's a nice little house right on Harbor Street—not much money down either—it'd be like a kind of seamen's home, you know.

REGINE: But I don't want to live with you! I don't want to have anything to do with you! So now—get out!

ENGSTRAND: You wouldn't be with me for long, my child—I know that well enough. All you've got to do is use your wits—you've turned into a handsome wench—do you know that?

REGINE: Well—what of it?

ENGSTRAND: Before you know it, some first-mate'll come along—maybe even a captain.

REGINE: I don't intend to marry any such trash. Sailors have no *savoir vivre.*

ENGSTRAND: Well—I couldn't say about that—

REGINE: I tell you I know all about sailors. I wouldn't think of marrying one of them!

ENGSTRAND: Who says you'd have to marry? You can make it pay just the same. *(More confidentially)* That English-man—the one with the yacht—he gave three hundred dollars, he did—and she wasn't any better looking than you are.

REGINE *(Goes toward him)*: Get out of here!

ENGSTRAND *(Retreating)*: Now, now! You wouldn't hit me, would you?

REGINE: You just say anything against Mother, and you'll see whether I'd hit you or not! Get out, I say! *(She pushes him toward the garden door)* And don't bang the door; young Master Alving—

ENGSTRAND: Is asleep—I know! Why should you be so worried about him? *(In a lower tone)* God—Almighty! You don't mean to tell me that *he—*?

REGINE: You must be out of your head—you fool! Go on now—get out this minute. No—not that way—here comes Pastor Manders; the back stairs for you!

ENGSTRAND *(Goes toward door right)*: All right—I'll go. But lis-ten—you have a talk with him—he'll tell you what you owe your father—for I am your father after all, you know; I can prove that by the Church Register.

(He goes out through the other door that REGINE *has opened for him and closes after him. She glances at herself quickly in the mirror, fans herself with her handkerchief and straightens her collar; then she sets about tending the flowers.* MANDERS *enters the conservatory by the garden door. He wears an overcoat, carries an umbrella and has a small traveling-bag slung over his shoulder.)*

MANDERS: Good-day, Miss Engstrand.

REGINE *(Turning in glad surprise)*: Well! Good-day, Mr. Manders! Fancy! So the steamer's in, is it?

MANDERS *(He comes into the room)*: Yes—just docked. Dreadful weather we've had these last few days.

REGINE *(Following him)*: It's a blessing for the farmers, Mr. Manders.

MANDERS: Quite right, Miss Engstrand! We city folk never think of that. *(He begins taking off his overcoat.)*

REGINE: Do let me help you! My goodness! It's soaking wet! I'll just hang it in the hall—and, let me take your umbrella—I'll open it up—so it'll dry quicker.
(She goes out with the things by the second door on the right. MANDERS *puts his traveling-bag on a chair with his hat. Meanwhile,* REGINE *comes in again.)*

MANDERS: It's very pleasant to be indoors. And how are things going here? All well, I trust?

REGINE: Yes—many thanks.

MANDERS: I expect you've been very busy with tomorrow's preparations.

REGINE: Yes—there's been so much to do!

MANDERS: And Mrs. Alving is at home, I hope?

REGINE: Oh, yes, indeed. She just went upstairs to give the young master his hot chocolate.

MANDERS: Tell me—I heard down at the pier that Osvald had come home—

REGINE: He arrived the day before yesterday—we didn't expect him until today.

MANDERS: In good health and spirits, I trust?

REGINE: Yes, thank you, he seems to be—but dreadfully tired after his journey. He came straight through from Paris—without a stop; I mean, he came the whole way without a break. I think he's taking a little nap—so we must talk very quietly.

MANDERS: Sh! We'll be still as mice!

REGINE *(She moves an armchair up to the table)*: Do sit down, Mr. Manders, and make yourself comfortable. *(He sits; she places a footstool under his feet)* There! How does that feel?

MANDERS: Most comfortable, thank you! *(He looks at her)* Do you know, Miss Engstrand, I really believe you've grown since I saw you last.

REGINE: Do you think so, Mr. Manders? Mrs. Alving says I've filled out too.

MANDERS: Filled out, eh? Yes, yes—perhaps a little—just suitably.
(Short pause.)

REGINE: Shall I tell Mrs. Alving you're here?

MANDERS: Thank you—there's no hurry, my dear child— Well—tell me, my dear Regine, how is your father getting on out here?

REGINE: Pretty well, thank you, Mr. Manders.

MANDERS: He came in to see me last time he was in town.

REGINE: Did he really? He's always so grateful for a talk with you, Mr. Manders.

MANDERS: I suppose you see him regularly, every day?

REGINE: I?—Oh, yes—of course. Whenever I have time—that is—

MANDERS: I'm afraid your father is not a very strong character, Miss Engstrand. He badly needs a guiding hand.

REGINE: Yes, I dare say he does, Mr. Manders.

MANDERS: He needs someone near him—someone he can lean on—whose judgment he respects. He admitted as much, quite candidly, last time he came to see me.

REGINE: Yes—he said something of the sort to me. But I don't know if Mrs. Alving would want to let me go—especially now that we'll have the orphanage to manage. And I really couldn't bear to leave Mrs. Alving—she's always been so good to me.

MANDERS: But a daughter's duty, my dear child—of course, we would first have to gain Mrs. Alving's consent.

REGINE: But would it be quite the thing, at my age, to keep house for a single man?

MANDERS: What do you mean? My dear Miss Engstrand, it's a question of your own father!

REGINE: Yes, I know—but all the same—of course if it were a *proper* kind of house—belonging to a real gentleman—

MANDERS: Why—my dear Regine—!

REGINE: Oh, I mean a man I could look up to—respect—become attached to—as though I were really his daughter—

MANDERS: But, my dear child—

REGINE: Then I'd gladly live in town again—for I'm often very lonely here—and you know yourself, Mr. Manders, what it is to be all alone in the world. And I'm capable and willing—though I say it myself as shouldn't. Mr. Manders—I suppose you couldn't find me a position of that sort?

MANDERS: I? No—I'm really afraid I can't.

REGINE: But, you will think of me, dear, dear Mr. Manders—you'll keep me in mind in case—

MANDERS *(Gets up)*: Yes, yes—of course, Miss Engstrand—

REGINE: Because, you see—if I could only—

MANDERS: Would you be so kind as to tell Mrs. Alving I am here?

REGINE: I'll go and call her at once, Mr. Manders.

(She goes out left. MANDERS *paces up and down the room a couple of times, then stands for a moment upstage with his hands behind his back looking out into the garden. Then he comes back to the table, picks up a book and glances at the title page. He gives a start and examines some of the others.)*

MANDERS: Hm!—Well—well! Really!

(MRS. ALVING comes in by the door left followed by REGINE, who immediately goes out by the first door on the right.)

MRS. ALVING *(With outstretched hand)*: Welcome, dear Mr. Manders!

MANDERS: Good-day, Mrs. Alving. Well—here I am—as I promised.

MRS. ALVING: And punctual as usual!

MANDERS: I had great trouble getting away. As you know—I'm chairman of so many organizations—and what with my committee meetings—

MRS. ALVING: I'm all the more grateful to you for coming so promptly. Now we shall be able to get all our business settled before dinner. But, where is your luggage?

MANDERS *(Hastily)*: I left my things down at the inn—I'll put up there for the night.

MRS. ALVING *(Repressing a smile)*: Can't I really persuade you to spend the night here this time?

MANDERS: No, no, Mrs. Alving—thank you all the same—but I prefer to stay there as usual. It's so convenient—right by the pier, you know.

MRS. ALVING: Well—just as you wish! I should have thought, that perhaps, at our age—!

MANDERS: Ah—yes, of course—you will have your little joke! Well—I suppose you're radiantly happy today—what

112

with tomorrow's ceremony—and having Osvald home again—

MRS. ALVING: Yes—isn't it wonderful! He hasn't been home for over two years, you know. And he's promised to spend the whole winter with me!

MANDERS: Has he really? That's a nice filial gesture—for I'm sure his life in Rome and Paris must offer many attractions.

MRS. ALVING: Yes, no doubt—but after all, he has his mother here. God bless him—he still has a place in his heart for me.

MANDERS: It would be regrettable indeed if separation and his interest in such a thing as art were to interfere with his natural affections.

MRS. ALVING: That's true. But fortunately, there's no danger of that with him. I'll be curious to see if you recognize him after all these years—he'll be down presently—he's just having a little rest upstairs. But—do sit down, dear Mr. Manders.

MANDERS: Thank you. You're sure I'm not disturbing you?

MRS. ALVING *(Sits by table)*: Of course not!

MANDERS: Splendid—then suppose we get down to business. *(He goes to the chair and takes a bundle of papers out of his traveling-bag. Then sits down at the table opposite MRS. ALVING. He tries to arrange a space on which to lay out the papers)* Now first of all there's the question of—*(Breaks off)* Tell me, Mrs. Alving—what are those books doing here?

MRS. ALVING: These? I happen to be reading them.

MANDERS: You really read this sort of thing?

MRS. ALVING: Of course I do.

MANDERS: Do you feel that this type of reading makes you any better—any happier?

MRS. ALVING: It gives me a certain confidence.

MANDERS: Extraordinary! How do you mean?

MRS. ALVING: It seems to clarify and confirm many things I've thought about myself. The strange thing is, Mr. Manders, there's really nothing new in any of these books; they deal with subjects that most of us think about and believe in; though I dare say most people don't take the trouble to look into them very deeply—or face them very honestly.

MANDERS: But, good heavens—you don't seriously believe that most people—?

MRS. ALVING: I most emphatically do.

MANDERS: But surely not here—surely not *our* kind of people—

MRS. ALVING: Yes! "Our kind of people" too.

MANDERS: Well—I really must say—!

MRS. ALVING: But what precisely do you object to in these books?

MANDERS: Object to? You don't imagine I waste my time delving into such subjects!

MRS. ALVING: Then you're condemning them without knowing them?

MANDERS: I've read quite enough about these books to disapprove of them.

MRS. ALVING: But how can you form an opinion if you haven't—?

MANDERS: My dear Mrs. Alving—in some things it is wiser to depend on the opinion of others. That is the way our world functions—and it is best that it should be so. Otherwise, what would become of society?

MRS. ALVING: Well—you may be right.

MANDERS: I don't deny that such books may have a certain fascination. And I don't blame you for wishing to familiarize yourself with certain intellectual trends which, I understand, are current in the sophisticated world where your son has been allowed to roam so freely. But—

MRS. ALVING: But?

MANDERS *(Lowering his voice)*: But one doesn't discuss such things openly, Mrs. Alving. There is no reason to give an account to all and sundry of what one reads, or thinks, in the privacy of one's own room.

MRS. ALVING: Certainly not—I agree with you—

MANDERS: Think of your new responsibilities toward the orphanage. When you decided to found it, your feelings on certain subjects were decidedly at variance with those you now entertain—unless I am greatly mistaken.

MRS. ALVING: I grant you that. But let's get back to the orphanage, Mr. Manders.

MANDERS: By all means—only, remember: caution, my dear Mrs. Alving! And now—to work! *(Opens an envelope and takes out some papers)* You see these papers—?

MRS. ALVING: The deeds?

MANDERS: Yes—all in order at last! I had great trouble in getting them in time. I had to bring strong pressure to bear on the authorities; they are painfully conscientious when it comes to property settlements of any kind, but here they are at last. *(Turns over the papers)* This is the deed of conveyance for that part of the Rosenvold estate known as the Solvik property, together with all the newly erected buildings, the school, the teacher's house and the chapel. And here is the Charter of the Institution: "Charter of the Orphanage in Memory of Captain Alving."

MRS. ALVING *(After examining the papers at some length)*: That all seems clear—

MANDERS: I used the title "Captain" instead of "Court Chamberlain"—it seemed less ostentatious.

MRS. ALVING: Whatever you think best.

MANDERS: Here is the bankbook controlling the invested capital—the interest on which will be used to defray the running expenses of the institution.

MRS. ALVING: Thank you—you'll take charge of that, won't you?

MANDERS: Certainly, if you wish. For the time being, I think it would be wise to leave the entire sum in the bank—the interest is not very attractive it's true—but we could then take our time and later on find a good mortgage—it would of course have to be a first mortgage and on unexceptionable security—we can afford to take no risks—but we can discuss that matter at a later date.

MRS. ALVING: Yes, dear Mr. Manders—I leave all that to you.

MANDERS: I'll keep a sharp lookout. Now, there's something else—I've meant to take it up with you several times.

MRS. ALVING: And what is that?

MANDERS: The question of insurance. Do you wish me to take out insurance on the orphanage or not?

MRS. ALVING: Well of course it must be insured!

MANDERS: Just a moment, Mrs. Alving—let us examine the matter more carefully.

MRS. ALVING: But everything I own is insured—my house and its contents—the livestock—everything.

MANDERS: Your personal property, of course. All my things are insured too. But this is quite a different matter. The orphanage is dedicated to a high spiritual purpose—

MRS. ALVING: Yes, but—

MANDERS: As far as I am personally concerned, I can't see the slightest objection to safeguarding ourselves against all possible risks—

MRS. ALVING: I quite agree—

MANDERS: But what about public opinion?

MRS. ALVING: Public opinion—?

MANDERS: Are there any groups of people here—people who matter, I mean—who might take exception to it?

MRS. ALVING: What do you mean by "people who matter"?

MANDERS: I mean men of wealth and influence whose opinion it might be unwise to overlook.

MRS. ALVING: I see what you mean—yes, there may be a few people here who might object—

MANDERS: There, you see! In town I think there might be a strong feeling against it—among my colleagues for instance, and some of the more influential members of their congregations; it could be implied that we hadn't sufficient faith in Divine Providence.

MRS. ALVING: But, surely, Mr. Manders, you have no such feeling—

MANDERS: Oh, as far as I am personally concerned, I have no qualms in the matter; but we might not be able to prevent our action from being interpreted in an erroneous and unfortunate light—and this in turn might reflect on the work of the orphanage.

MRS. ALVING: Of course, if that were to be the case—

MANDERS: And I admit, I can't quite overlook the embarrassing—I might even say difficult position—I should find myself in. In town this orphanage has been much discussed by the leading citizens. They are well aware of the benefits that would accrue to the town from such an institution—its existence would undoubtedly reduce to an important degree the yearly sums they are expected to donate to charitable works. And, since I have been your adviser in this matter—your business representative from the beginning—most of the blame and criticism would inevitably fall on me—

MRS. ALVING: I wouldn't want you to be exposed to that.

MANDERS: Not to speak of the attacks that would unquestionably be made against me by certain newspapers—

MRS. ALVING: That settles it, Mr. Manders—we'll say no more about it!

MANDERS: Then, we decide against insurance?

MRS. ALVING: Yes—we'll let that go.

MANDERS *(Leaning back in his chair)*: But on the other hand, Mrs. Alving, suppose there *should* be an accident—one never knows—would you be prepared to make good the damage?

MRS. ALVING: No, I must tell you quite frankly, that would be out of the question.

MANDERS: In that case we are assuming a very grave responsibility.

MRS. ALVING: Well—do you see anything else to do?

MANDERS: I'm afraid not—I don't really see that there's anything else we *can* do; we don't want to be placed in a false position—and we have no right to arouse the antagonism of the community.

MRS. ALVING: Especially you—as a clergyman.

MANDERS: We must simply have faith that our institution will be under the special protection of Providence.

MRS. ALVING: Let us hope so, Mr. Manders.

MANDERS: Then—we'll let it go?

MRS. ALVING: By all means.

MANDERS: As you wish. *(Makes a note)* No insurance.

MRS. ALVING: It's strange you should happen to bring this up today—

MANDERS: I've often meant to discuss it with you—

MRS. ALVING: Because only yesterday we nearly had a fire down there.

MANDERS: What!

MRS. ALVING: Nothing came of it, fortunately—some wood-shavings caught fire—in the carpenter's shop—

MANDERS: Where Engstrand works?

MRS. ALVING: Yes. They say he's often very careless with matches—

MANDERS: Poor man—he has so much on his mind—so many

worries. I'm happy to say he's decided to turn over a new leaf.

MRS. ALVING: Indeed? Who told you that?

MANDERS: He assured me so himself. I'm very glad—he's such an excellent worker.

MRS. ALVING: Yes—when he's sober.

MANDERS: That unfortunate weakness! He tells me it relieves the pain in that poor leg of his. Last time he came to see me in town, he was really very touching. He was so grateful to me for getting him this work here—where he could be near Regine.

MRS. ALVING: I don't think he sees much of her.

MANDERS: Oh, yes, he sees her every day—he told me so himself.

MRS. ALVING: Well—it's possible.

MANDERS: He realizes the need of someone near him, to help him when temptation gets too strong for him. That's what is so endearing about Jakob Engstrand—he admits how weak he is—and is so anxious to reform. Mrs. Alving—suppose it should become a real necessity for him to have Regine home with him again—?

MRS. ALVING *(Rises quickly)*: Regine—?

MANDERS: I urge you not to oppose it.

MRS. ALVING: I most certainly would oppose it! And besides— Regine is to work at the orphanage.

MANDERS: But—he *is* her father after all—

MRS. ALVING: I know only too well the kind of father he is! No! She shall never go back to him while I have anything to say in the matter!

MANDERS *(Gets up)*: But, my dear Mrs. Alving, why be so violent about it! It's a great pity that you misjudge Engstrand so. One would think you were actually afraid—

MRS. ALVING *(More calmly)*: That's not the point. I am looking

after Regine now and she will stay here with me. *(Listens)*
Sh! Dear Mr. Manders, let's not discuss this any further.
(Her face lights up with joy) Here comes Osvald. We'll
think about *him* now.

*(OSVALD ALVING enters left. He has on a light overcoat and is
carrying his hat. He is smoking a large meerschaum pipe.)*

OSVALD *(Standing in the doorway)*: Oh, I'm sorry—I thought you
were in the library—I didn't mean to disturb you. *(Comes
in)* How do you do, Mr. Manders!

MANDERS *(Stares at him)*: Well, what an amazing—!

MRS. ALVING: What do you think of him, Mr. Manders?

MANDERS: Can it really be—?

OSVALD: Yes—it's the Prodigal Son, Mr. Manders!

MANDERS: My dear boy—!

OSVALD: Or the wandering son returned to the fold—if you
prefer.

MRS. ALVING: He's only joking, Mr. Manders—He's referring to
your disapproval of an artist's career.

MANDERS: We are not infallible in our judgments; certain steps
may seem to us dangerous that turn out in the end to
be—*(Shakes hands with him)* so, welcome! Welcome home,
my dear Osvald! I may still call you Osvald, I trust?

OSVALD: What else should you call me, Mr. Manders?

MANDERS: Splendid!—I was just going to say—you must not
imagine, my dear Osvald, that I unconditionally condemn the artist's life. I dare say there are many who
succeed, in spite of everything, in preserving their integrity of character.

OSVALD: Let us hope so!

MRS. ALVING *(Beaming with pleasure)*: Well—this one's managed
to do so, Mr. Manders—you've only to look at him to see
that!

OSVALD *(Pacing the room)*: There, there—Mother dear—never
mind—!

MANDERS: Yes, fortunately, that's undeniable! And you've begun to make quite a name for yourself. I've often seen you mentioned in the papers, and always most favorably. Though recently I haven't seen so much about your work.

OSVALD *(Going to the conservatory)*: No—I haven't done much painting lately.

MRS. ALVING: Even an artist needs to rest now and then.

MANDERS: Most understandable—At such times you gather new strength, for even finer work.

OSVALD: Quite so—Will dinner be ready soon, Mother?

MRS. ALVING: In half an hour, dear. There's nothing wrong with his appetite, thank God!

MANDERS: And I see he's partial to tobacco too.

OSVALD: I found this old pipe of Father's up in his study—

MANDERS: Oh—so that accounts for it!

MRS. ALVING: How do you mean?

MANDERS: When Osvald came in just now—with that pipe in his mouth—I thought for a moment it was his father come to life again.

OSVALD: Really?

MRS. ALVING: How can you say that! Osvald takes after me.

MANDERS: Yes—perhaps; but, still, there's something about his mouth—something in the expression—that reminds me very strongly of Alving—especially when he smokes.

MRS. ALVING: I don't see it at all—Osvald's mouth is much more sensitive. There's something almost ascetic about it.

MANDERS: It's true—some of my colleagues have a similar expression.

MRS. ALVING: But put down your pipe now, Osvald dear. I don't allow smoking in this room.

OSVALD *(Puts down the pipe)*: Very well, Mother. I only wanted to try it; I smoked it once before you see—when I was a child.

MRS. ALVING: *You* did?

OSVALD: Yes—I was very little at the time—I remember I went up to Father's study one evening; he was in a very gay, jolly mood.

MRS. ALVING: How could you possibly remember? It's so long ago!

OSVALD: Oh, but I do! I remember it very distinctly; he sat me on his knee and told me to smoke his pipe. "Smoke, son," he said—"go on, son—have a good smoke"; so I smoked away with all my might, until I felt deathly ill and great beads of perspiration stood out on my forehead. He thought it was very funny. I remember he roared with laughter at me.

MANDERS: What a very odd thing to do!

MRS. ALVING: It's a lot of nonsense. Osvald must have dreamed it.

OSVALD: No, Mother, I assure you I didn't! Don't you remember, you came in and rushed me off to the nursery. And then I was sick—and I noticed you'd been crying—I suppose it *was* rather odd—did Father often play tricks like that?

MANDERS: He was a great joker in his young days.

OSVALD: Yet think of all the good he did. The fine and useful things he was able to accomplish—though he died comparatively young.

MANDERS: Yes—you have a fine heritage, Osvald Alving. It should be a great incentive to you!

OSVALD: Yes, you're right! Indeed it should.

MANDERS: And it was good of you to come home for the ceremony tomorrow.

OSVALD: That's the least I could do for Father's memory.

MRS. ALVING: And he plans to stay here for a while—that's the nicest thing of all!

MANDERS: Yes, I understand you intend to spend the winter here.

OSVALD: I plan to stay here indefinitely, Mr. Manders. It's so good to be home again!

MRS. ALVING *(Beaming)*: Yes, it is, isn't it, dear?

MANDERS *(Looks at him sympathetically)*: You were very young when you left home, my dear Osvald.

OSVALD: A little too young, perhaps.

MRS. ALVING: What nonsense! It's good for a strong healthy boy—especially an only child—to get away from home. Much better than being petted and spoiled by doting parents!

MANDERS: I think that is open to debate, Mrs. Alving. A home and parents are still a child's best refuge.

OSVALD: I'm inclined to agree with Mr. Manders there.

MANDERS: Take your own son here as an example—there's no harm in discussing it before him—what has been the result in his case? Here he is, twenty-three or twenty-four years old, and he has never yet known what a normal, well-regulated home can be.

OSVALD: I beg your pardon, Mr. Manders—you're quite wrong in that.

MANDERS: Really? But I thought you'd been living exclusively in artistic circles.

OSVALD: So I have.

MANDERS: And mostly among the younger artists, I believe.

OSVALD: Quite right.

MANDERS: But surely the majority of such people are in no position to found a home and family.

OSVALD: Most of them are in no position to get married—that's true enough—

MANDERS: That's just what I say—

OSVALD: But that doesn't necessarily mean that they can't have homes of their *own*—and many of them have—very comfortable and well run homes too.

(MRS. ALVING, *who has been listening attentively, nods in agreement but says nothing.*)

MANDERS: I'm not thinking of bachelor-establishments; when I use the word "home," I mean a family—a home where a man lives with his wife and children.

OSVALD: Or with his children—and their mother.

MANDERS *(With a start, clasping his hands)*: Good heavens!

OSVALD: Well?

MANDERS: Lives with—with—his children's mother!

OSVALD: Would you rather he abandoned her?

MANDERS: Then you're speaking of illegal unions—dissolute relationships—!

OSVALD: I've never noticed anything especially dissolute in the lives these people lead.

MANDERS: How can any decent young man or woman possibly degrade themselves by living openly in such shameful circumstances!

OSVALD: Well—what do you expect them to do? A poor young artist—a poor young girl—marriage is an expensive business—what do you expect them to do?

MANDERS: I would expect them to resist temptation, Mr. Alving—to part before it is too late.

OSVALD: That's a lot to expect of young people in love, Mr. Manders.

MRS. ALVING: Indeed it is!

MANDERS *(Persistently)*: And to think that the authorities put up with such behavior—that it should be openly tolerated. *(To MRS. ALVING)* You see how right I was to be concerned about your son. Living in circles where such rampant immorality prevails, where it's taken for granted, one might say—

OSVALD: Let me tell you something, Mr. Manders—I've spent many a Sunday at some of these "illegal homes"—as you call them—

MANDERS: On a Sunday too—!

OSVALD: Sunday happens to be a holiday—I've never once heard a single vulgar or indecent word—nor have I ever witnessed any behavior that could possibly be called immoral. But do you know when and where I *have* met with such behavior?

MANDERS: No! God forbid!

OSVALD: Then permit me to tell you: When some of your highly respected citizens—your model fathers and husbands from back home here—when they take a trip abroad to "see a bit of life"—when *they* condescend to honor us poor artists with their presence—then you would see "rampant immorality" if you like! These respectable gentlemen could tell us about things that we had never even dreamed of!

MANDERS: You dare imply that honorable men here from home—?

OSVALD: You must have heard these same "honorable men," when they get safely home again, hold forth on the outrageous immorality that prevails abroad?

MANDERS: Of course I have.

MRS. ALVING: I've heard them too—

OSVALD: Well, you may take their word for it! They speak with true authority! *(Clutches his head in his hands)* It's an outrage that that free and beautiful life should be distorted by their filth!

MRS. ALVING: Don't get so excited, Osvald. It's bad for you.

OSVALD: You're right, Mother. It's bad for me I know—it's just that I'm so tired. I think I'll take a little walk before dinner. Forgive me, Mr. Manders—I shouldn't have let go like that. I know you can't possibly understand my feelings. *(He goes out by the upstage door right.)*

MRS. ALVING: Poor boy!

MANDERS: You may well say so!—That he should have sunk to this! *(*MRS. ALVING *looks at him in silence.* MANDERS *paces up and down)* He called himself the Prodigal Son—Tragic!—Tragic! *(*MRS. ALVING *continues to look at him silently)* And what do you say to all this?

MRS. ALVING: I say Osvald was right in every word he said.

MANDERS: *(Stops pacing)*: Right?—You mean you agree to such principles?

MRS. ALVING: Living here alone all these years, I've come to the same conclusions—but I've never put my thoughts into words—Well—now my boy can speak for me.

MANDERS: You are greatly to be pitied, Mrs. Alving!—I have always had your best interests at heart. For many years I have advised you in business matters, and for many years I have been your friend and your late husband's friend. As your spiritual adviser I once saved you from a reckless and foolhardy action; and it is as your spiritual adviser that I now feel it my duty to talk to you with the utmost solemnity.

MRS. ALVING: And what have you to say to me, as my "spiritual adviser," Mr. Manders?

MANDERS: Look back over the years—it's appropriate that you should do so today, for tomorrow is the tenth anniversary of your husband's death and his memorial will be unveiled; tomorrow I shall speak to the crowd assembled in his honor—but today I must speak to you alone.

MRS. ALVING: I'm listening.

MANDERS: You had been married scarcely a year when you took the step that might have wrecked your life: You left house and home and ran away from your husband—yes,

Mrs. Alving, ran away—and refused to go back to him in spite of all his entreaties.

MRS. ALVING: I was miserably unhappy that first year—don't forget that.

MANDERS: What right have we to expect happiness in this life? It is the sign of a rebellious spirit—No! Mrs. Alving, we are here to do our duty, and it was your duty to stay with the man you had chosen and to whom you were bound in holy matrimony.

MRS. ALVING: You know the kind of life Alving led in those days; his dissipation—his excesses—

MANDERS: It's true, I heard many rumors about him—and had those rumors been true, I should have been the first to condemn his conduct at that time; but it is not a wife's place to judge her husband; your duty was to resign yourself and bear your cross with true humility. But you rebelled against it and, instead of giving your husband the help and support he needed, you deserted him, and by so doing jeopardized your own good name and reputation—and that of others too.

MRS. ALVING: Of "others"? Of *one*, you mean.

MANDERS: It was highly imprudent to come to me, of all people, for help.

MRS. ALVING: But why? Weren't you our "spiritual adviser" as well as our friend?

MANDERS: All the more reason. You should go down on your knees and thank God that I found the necessary strength of mind to dissuade you from your reckless purpose, to guide you back to the path of duty, and home to your husband.

MRS. ALVING: Yes, Mr. Manders—that was certainly your doing.

MANDERS: I was merely an instrument in God's hand. And, as I had foreseen—once you had returned to your duties, and humbled your spirit in obedience—you were repaid a hundredfold. Alving reformed entirely, and remained a good and loving husband to the end of his days. He became a real benefactor to this whole community, and he allowed you to share, as his fellow-worker, in all his enterprises—and a very able fellow-worker too—I am aware of that, Mrs. Alving—I must pay you that tribute; but now I come to the second great error of your life.

MRS. ALVING: What do you mean by that?

MANDERS: You first betrayed your duty as a wife—you later betrayed your duty as a mother.

MRS. ALVING: Ah—!

MANDERS: All your life you have been possessed by a willful, rebellious spirit. Your natural inclinations always led you toward the undisciplined and lawless. You could never tolerate the slightest restraint; you have always disregarded any responsibility—carelessly and unscrupulously—as though it were a burden you had a right to cast aside. It no longer suited you to be a wife—so you left your husband. The cares of motherhood were too much for you—so you sent your child away to be brought up by strangers.

MRS. ALVING: That's true—I did do that.

MANDERS: And for that reason you are now a stranger to him.

MRS. ALVING: No! No! I'm not!

MANDERS: Of course you are! How could you be otherwise? And now you see the result of your conduct. You have much to atone for; you were guilty as a wife, Mrs. Alving, you failed your husband miserably—you are seeking to atone for that by raising this memorial in his honor; how are you going to atone for your failure toward your son? It may not be too late to save him: by redeeming yourself—you may still help him to redemption! I warn you! *(With raised forefinger)* You are guilty as a mother, Mrs. Alving. I felt it my duty to tell you this. *(Pause.)*

MRS. ALVING *(Slowly, with great control)*: I have listened to you talk, Mr. Manders. Tomorrow you will be making speeches in my husband's honor; I shall not make any speeches tomorrow; but now I intend to talk to you—just as frankly—just as brutally—as you have talked to me!

MANDERS: Of course—it's natural that you should try and justify your conduct.

MRS. ALVING: No—I only want to make a few things clear to you.

MANDERS: Well?

MRS. ALVING: You've just talked a great deal about my married life after you—as you put it—"led me back to the path of duty." What do you really know about it? From that day on you never set foot inside our house—you who had been our closest friend—

MANDERS: But you and your husband left town, immediately afterwards—

MRS. ALVING: And you never once came out here to see us during my husband's lifetime. It wasn't until this orphanage business that you felt compelled to visit me.

MANDERS *(In a low uncertain tone)*: If that is meant as a reproach, my dear Helene, I beg you to consider—

MRS. ALVING: That in your position you had to protect your reputation! After all—I was a wife who had tried to leave her husband! One can't be too careful with such disreputable women!

MANDERS: My dear!—Mrs. Alving—what a gross exaggeration!

MRS. ALVING: Well—never mind about that—the point is this: your opinions of my married life are based on nothing but hearsay.

MANDERS: That may be so—what then?

MRS. ALVING: Just this: that now, Manders, I am going to tell you the truth! I swore to myself that one day I would tell it to you—to you alone!

MANDERS: Well? And what is the truth?

MRS. ALVING: The truth is this: My husband continued to be a depraved profligate to the day of his death.

MANDERS *(Feeling for a chair)*: What did you say?

MRS. ALVING: After nineteen years of marriage—just as depraved, just as dissolute—as he was the day you married us!

MANDERS: How can you use such words—!

MRS. ALVING: They are the words our doctor used.

MANDERS: I don't understand you.

MRS. ALVING: It's not necessary that you should.

MANDERS: I can't take it in. You mean—that this seemingly happy marriage—those long years of comradeship—all that was only a pretense—to cover up this hideous abyss?

MRS. ALVING: That is just exactly what it was—nothing else.

MANDERS: But—it's inconceivable—I can't grasp it! How was it possible to—? How could the truth remain concealed?

MRS. ALVING: My life became one long fight to that end: After Osvald was born, Alving seemed to me a little better—but it didn't last long! And then I had to fight for my son as well. I was determined that no living soul should ever know the kind of father my boy had—As a matter of fact, you know how charming Alving could be—it was hard for people to think ill of him. He was one of those fortunate men whose private lives never seem to damage their public reputation. But then, Manders—I want you to know the whole story—then the most horrible thing of all happened.

MANDERS: How could anything be worse than—?

MRS. ALVING: I knew well enough all that was going on—and I

put up with it as long as I didn't have to see it—but, when I was faced with it here—in my own home—!

MANDERS: Here?

MRS. ALVING: Yes—in this very house. The first time I became aware of it, I was in there—*(Points to the downstage door right)* in the dining room—I was busy with something, and the door was ajar—then I heard the maid come up from the garden with water for the plants—

MANDERS: Yes?

MRS. ALVING: In a few moments, I heard Alving come in after her—he said something to her in a low voice—and then I heard—*(With a short laugh)* it still rings in my ears—it was so horrible, and yet somehow so ludicrous—I heard my own servant-girl whisper: "Let me go, Mr. Alving!— Leave me alone!"

MANDERS: But he couldn't have meant anything by it, Mrs. Alving—believe me—I'm sure he didn't—!

MRS. ALVING: I soon found out what to believe: My husband had his way with the girl, and there were—consequences, Mr. Manders.

MANDERS *(As though turned to stone)*: To think—that in this house—!

MRS. ALVING: I had been through a lot in this house! Night after night—in order to keep him home—I sat up in his study with him—pretending to join him in his private drinking bouts. I sat there alone with him for hours on end listening to his obscene, senseless talk—I had to struggle with him—fight with sheer brute force—in order to drag him to his bed.

MANDERS *(Shaken)*: How were you able to endure all this?

MRS. ALVING: I had to endure it—I had my little boy to think of. But when I discovered this final outrage—with a servant—in our own house—! That was the end. From that day on I became master here. I took full control—over him and over everything. Alving didn't dare say a word—he knew he was in my power. It was then I decided to send Osvald away. He was nearly seven and was beginning to notice things and ask questions, as children do. This I could not endure, Manders. I felt the child would be poisoned in this sordid, degraded home. That's why I sent him away. Now perhaps you understand why I never let him set foot in this house as long as his father was alive. What you could never understand—is what agony it was to have to do it!

MANDERS: To think of all you have been through—!

MRS. ALVING: I could never have stood it if I hadn't had my work. For I can honestly say I have worked! Alving received all the praise—all the credit—but don't imagine he had anything to do with it! The increase in the value of our property—the improvements—all those fine enterprises you spoke of—all that was *my* work. All he did was to sprawl on the sofa in his study reading old newspapers. In his few lucid moments I did try to spur him to some effort—but it was no use. He sank back again into his old habits and then spent days in a maudlin state of penitence and self-pity.

MANDERS: And you're building a memorial to such a man—?

MRS. ALVING: That's what comes of having a bad conscience.

MANDERS: A bad—? What do you mean?

MRS. ALVING: It seemed to me inevitable that the truth must come out, and that people would believe it; so I decided to dedicate this orphanage to Alving—in order to dispel once and for all any possible rumors—any possible doubts.

MANDERS: You've fully succeeded in that.

MRS. ALVING: But I had another reason: I didn't want my son to inherit anything whatsoever from his father.

MANDERS: I see—so you used Alving's money to—?

MRS. ALVING: Precisely. The money that has gone into the orphanage amounts to the exact sum—I've calculated it very carefully—to the exact sum of the fortune that once made people consider Lt. Alving a good match.

MANDERS: I understand you.

MRS. ALVING: I sold myself for that sum. I don't want Osvald to touch a penny of it. Everything he has will come from me—everything!

(OSVALD enters from the door upstage right. He has left his hat and coat outside.)

MRS. ALVING *(Goes toward him)*: Back already, dear?

OSVALD: Yes—what can one do—out in this everlasting rain! But I hear dinner's nearly ready—splendid!

(REGINE enters from the dining room carrying a small parcel.)

REGINE: This parcel just came for you, Mrs. Alving. *(Hands her the parcel.)*

MRS. ALVING *(With a glance at MANDERS)*: Ah! The songs for tomorrow's ceremony, I expect.

MANDERS: Hm—

REGINE: And dinner is served, Mrs. Alving.

MRS. ALVING: Good, we'll be there in a moment. I just want to see—

REGINE *(To OSVALD)*: Would you like red or white wine, Mr. Alving?

OSVALD: Both, by all means, Miss Engstrand.

REGINE: *Bien*—Very good, Mr. Alving. *(Exits into dining room.)*

OSVALD: Let me help you uncork it—*(Follows her into the dining room, half closing the door.)*

MRS. ALVING *(Who has opened the parcel)*: Yes—just as I thought—the songs for tomorrow, Mr. Manders.

MANDERS *(Clasping his hands)*: How I shall ever have the courage to make my speech tomorrow—!

MRS. ALVING: You'll manage—somehow.

MANDERS *(Softly, so as not to be heard in the dining room)*: It would never do to arouse suspicion—

MRS. ALVING *(Quietly but firmly)*: No—And from tomorrow on, I shall be free at last—the long, hideous farce will be over—I shall forget that such a person as Alving ever lived in this house—there'll be no one here but my son and me.

(The noise of a chair being overturned is heard from the dining room—at the same time REGINE'S *voice.)*

REGINE'S *voice (In a sharp whisper)*: Osvald!—Are you mad?—Let me go!

MRS. ALVING *(Stiffens with horror)*: Ah—!

(She gazes distractedly at the half-open door. OSVALD *is heard coughing and humming a tune—then the sound of a bottle being uncorked.)*

MANDERS *(In agitation)*: But what *is* all this? What's the *matter,* Mrs. Alving?

MRS. ALVING *(Hoarsely)*: Ghosts—Those two in the conservatory—Ghosts—They've come to life again!

MANDERS: What do you mean? Regine—? Is *she*—?

MRS. ALVING: Yes—Come—Not a word!

(She takes MANDERS' *arm and goes falteringly toward the dining room.)*

CURTAIN

Act Two

SCENE: *The same room. The landscape is still shrouded in rain and mist.* MANDERS *and* MRS. ALVING *enter from the dining room.*

MRS. ALVING *(In the doorway, calls back into the dining room)*: Aren't you coming too, Osvald?

OSVALD *(Off stage)*: No, thanks; I think I'll go out for a bit.

MRS. ALVING: Yes, do, dear; I think it's cleared up a little. *(She closes the dining room door, crosses to the hall door and calls:)* Regine!

REGINE *(Off stage)*: Yes, Mrs. Alving?

MRS. ALVING: Go down to the laundry and help them with the wreaths.

REGINE: Very well, Mrs. Alving.

*(*MRS. ALVING *makes sure that* REGINE *has gone and then closes the door.)*

MANDERS: You're sure he can't hear us in there?

MRS. ALVING: Not with the door shut—besides, he's going out.

MANDERS: I'm still so overcome. I don't know how I managed to eat a morsel of that delicious food.

MRS. ALVING *(In suppressed anguish, pacing up and down)*: No— Well—What's to be done?

MANDERS: What's to be done indeed? I wish I knew what to suggest—I don't feel competent to deal with a crisis of this sort.

MRS. ALVING: One thing I'm convinced of—that, so far, nothing serious has happened.

MANDERS: God forbid!—But it's a shameful business all the same.

MRS. ALVING: It's just a foolish whim on Osvald's part; I'm sure of that.

MANDERS: As I said before—I have no experience in such things—but I can't help thinking—

MRS. ALVING: One thing's clear: she must leave this house at once—before it's too late.

MANDERS: That goes without saying.

MRS. ALVING: But where can she go? We certainly wouldn't be justified in—

MANDERS: She must go home to her father, of course.

MRS. ALVING: To whom—did you say?

MANDERS: To her—But of course. Engstrand isn't her—Good heavens, Mrs. Alving—all this is impossible—there must be some mistake!

MRS. ALVING: I'm afraid there is no mistake, Manders. The girl confessed to me herself. And Alving didn't deny it; so the only thing we could do was to try and hush the matter up.

MANDERS: Yes—I suppose so.

MRS. ALVING: The girl left my service at once and was given a handsome sum to keep her mouth shut. She then took matters into her own hands—went back to town and renewed an old friendship with the carpenter, Engstrand. She hinted that she had money—told him some cock-and-bull story about a foreigner with a yacht—the outcome of all this was, that they were married in great haste. You married them yourself, I believe.

MANDERS: But—I can't understand it! I remember distinctly Engstrand coming to arrange about the wedding: He was overcome with confusion—and kept reproaching himself bitterly for his and his fiancée's shameless behavior.

MRS. ALVING: Well, I suppose he had to take the blame on himself.

MANDERS: I certainly never would have believed Jakob

Engstrand capable of such duplicity—and to me of all people! I shall have to teach him a good lesson, I can see that—The immorality of such a marriage—and for money too! How much did the girl receive?

MRS. ALVING: Three hundred dollars.

MANDERS: It's almost unbelievable—for a paltry three hundred dollars—consenting to marry a loose woman.

MRS. ALVING: What about me? Didn't I marry a "loose" man?

MANDERS: What on earth are you talking about!

MRS. ALVING: Was Alving any better when he married me, than the girl Johanna was when she married Engstrand?

MANDERS: But—good heavens—the two cases are utterly different—

MRS. ALVING: Perhaps not so very different, after all. There was a colossal difference in the price—that's true enough! A paltry three hundred dollars as against a large fortune.

MANDERS: But there *can* be no comparison in this instance! Your decision was based on the advice of relatives and friends—as well as the promptings of your heart.

MRS. ALVING *(Without looking at him)*: My heart, as you call it, was involved elsewhere at the time—as I thought you knew.

MANDERS *(In a reserved tone)*: Had I known any such thing, I should not have been a constant visitor in your husband's house.

MRS. ALVING: One thing is certain; I never really consulted my own feelings in the matter.

MANDERS: Perhaps not—but you consulted your mother—your two aunts—all those nearest to you—as was only right.

MRS. ALVING: Yes—those three! They were the ones that settled the whole business for me. As I look back on it, it seems incredible. They pointed out, in the most forceful terms, that it would be nothing short of folly to refuse an offer of such magnificence! Poor Mother. If she only knew what that "magnificence" has led to.

MANDERS: No one can be held responsible for the outcome— The fact remains, that your marriage in every way conformed to the strictest rules of law and order.

MRS. ALVING *(At the window)*: All this talk about law and order!—I often think all the suffering in the world is due to that.

MANDERS: That is a very wicked thing to say, Mrs. Alving.

MRS. ALVING: That may be; but I will not be bound by these responsibilities, these hypocritical conventions any longer—I simply cannot! I must work my way through to freedom.

MANDERS: What do you mean by that?

MRS. ALVING *(Drumming on the windowpane)*: I should never have lied about Alving—but I didn't dare do anything else at the time—and it wasn't only for Osvald's sake—it was for my own sake too. What a coward I've been!

MANDERS: A coward?

MRS. ALVING: A coward, yes—I could just hear what people would say if they found out the truth: Poor man! One can hardly blame him with a wife like that! She tried to leave him, you know!

MANDERS: They would have been justified to some extent.

MRS. ALVING *(Looking at him steadily)*: If I'd had the strength I should have taken Osvald into my confidence; I should have said, "Listen, my son, your father was a corrupt, contaminated man—"

MANDERS: Good God—!

MRS. ALVING: And then I should have told him the whole story—word for word—just as I told it to you.

MANDERS: You horrify me, Mrs. Alving!

MRS. ALVING: I know—God, yes!—I know!—I'm horrified myself at the thought of it! That's how much of a coward I am.

MANDERS: How can you call yourself a coward for doing what was merely your duty? Have you forgotten that a child should love and honor his father and mother?

MRS. ALVING: Don't let us talk in generalities! Let us ask: Should Osvald love and honor Captain Alving?

MANDERS: You're his mother—how could you find it in your heart to shatter his ideals?

MRS. ALVING: Oh—ideals, ideals! What about the truth?—If only I weren't such a coward!

MANDERS: You shouldn't scoff at ideals, Mrs. Alving—they have a way of avenging themselves. God knows—Osvald doesn't seem to have many—unfortunately. But his father seems to be somewhat of an ideal to him.

MRS. ALVING: Yes, that's quite true.

MANDERS: Your letters must be responsible for that feeling in him—you must have fostered it.

MRS. ALVING: Yes. I was treading the path of duty and obedience, Mr. Manders—I therefore lied to my son, religiously, year after year. What a coward—what a coward I was!

MANDERS: You have fostered a happy illusion in your son's mind, Mrs. Alving—you shouldn't underestimate its value.

MRS. ALVING: Its value may turn out to be dubious, who knows? But I won't tolerate any nonsense with Regine—he mustn't be allowed to get her into trouble.

MANDERS: Good heavens, no—that would be unthinkable!

MRS. ALVING: If I thought she would really make him happy—if he were really serious about it—

MANDERS: What do you mean?

MRS. ALVING: Oh, but he couldn't be—Regine could never be enough for him—

MANDERS: What are you talking about?

MRS. ALVING: If I weren't such a miserable coward I'd say to him, "Marry her—come to any arrangement you like with her—only be honest about it!"

MANDERS: A marriage between them—? How could you condone anything so abominable—so unheard of!

MRS. ALVING: Unheard of, you say? Why not face the truth, Manders? You know there are dozens of married couples out here in the country who are related in the same way.

MANDERS: I refuse to understand you.

MRS. ALVING: But you *do* understand me all the same!

MANDERS: There may be a few instances—family life is not always as blameless as it should be, unfortunately. But in nine cases out of ten the relationship is unsuspected—or at worst, unconfirmed. Here—on the other hand—That you, a mother, should be willing to allow your son—!

MRS. ALVING: But I'm *not* willing to allow it—that's just what I'm saying—I wouldn't allow it for anything in the world.

MANDERS: Only because you're a coward—as you express it. But if you weren't a coward! Such a revolting marriage—God forgive you!

MRS. ALVING: We're all of us descended from that kind of marriage—so they say. And who was responsible for that arrangement, Mr. Manders?

MANDERS: I refuse to discuss these matters with you, Mrs. Alving—you are in no fit state to touch on such things—How you can have the effrontery to call yourself a coward for not—!

MRS. ALVING: I'll tell you what I mean by that; I live in constant fear and terror, because I can't rid myself of all these ghosts that haunt me.

MANDERS: Ghosts, you say?

MRS. ALVING: Yes—Just now, when I heard Regine and Osvald in there—I felt hemmed in by ghosts—You know, Manders, the longer I live the more convinced I am that we're all haunted in this world—not only by the things we inherit from our parents—but by the ghosts of innumerable old prejudices and beliefs—half-forgotten cruelties and betrayals—we may not even be aware of them—but they're there just the same—and we can't get rid of them. The whole world is haunted by these ghosts of the dead past; you have only to pick up a newspaper to see them weaving in and out between the lines—Ah! if we only had the courage to sweep them all out and let in the light!

MANDERS: So this is the result of all this reading of yours—this detestable, pernicious, free-thinking literature!

MRS. ALVING: You're mistaken, my dear Manders. It was you who first goaded me into thinking—I shall always be grateful to you for that.

MANDERS: I?

MRS. ALVING: Yes. When you forced me to obey what you called my conscience and my duty; when you hailed as right and noble what my whole soul rebelled against as false and ugly—that's when I started to analyze your teachings; that's when I first started to *think*. And one day I saw quite clearly that all that you stand for—all that you preach—is artificial and dead—there's no life or truth in it.

MANDERS *(Softly, with emotion)*: So that's all I achieved by the hardest struggle of my life.

MRS. ALVING: I'd call it your most ignominious defeat.

MANDERS: It was a victory over myself, Helene; my greatest victory.

MRS. ALVING: It was a crime against us both.

MANDERS: The fact that by my entreaties I persuaded you to return to your lawful husband, when you came to me distracted and overwrought crying: "Here I am. Take me!" You consider that a crime?

MRS. ALVING: Yes; I think it was.

MANDERS: There is no possible understanding between us.

MRS. ALVING: Not any more, at any rate.

MANDERS: You have always been to me—even in my most secret thoughts—another man's wife.

MRS. ALVING: You really believe that, Manders?

MANDERS: Helene—!

MRS. ALVING: It's so easy to forget one's feelings!

MANDERS: I don't forget. I am exactly the same as I always was.

MRS. ALVING *(With a change of tone)*: Oh, don't let's talk any more about the old days! Now you're up to your eyes in committee meetings and advisory boards—and I sit out here and battle with ghosts—the ghosts within myself and those all around me.

MANDERS: Those around you, I can at least help you to conquer. After the dreadful things you've said to me today, I couldn't dream of leaving a young, unprotected girl alone in your house.

MRS. ALVING: I think the best thing would be to arrange a good match for her—don't you agree?

MANDERS: Unquestionably. It would be best for her in every respect. Regine has reached the age when—of course, I know very little about these things—

MRS. ALVING: Yes—she developed early.

MANDERS: So it seemed to me. I remember thinking when I prepared her for Confirmation, that she was remarkably well-developed for a child of her age. For the present she had better go home, under her father's care—but, of course, Engstrand isn't—How could he—*he* of all people—conceal the truth from me!
(There is a knock at the hall door.)

MRS. ALVING: Who can *that* be? Come in!

(ENGSTRAND *appears in the doorway; he is in his Sunday clothes.*)

ENGSTRAND: I most humbly beg pardon—but—

MRS. ALVING: Oh, it's you, Engstrand.

ENGSTRAND: None of the maids seemed to be about—so I took the liberty of knocking, ma'am—

MRS. ALVING: Oh, very well—come in. Do you wish to speak to me?

ENGSTRAND *(Coming in)*: No—thank you all the same, Mrs. Alving. But—if I might have a word with the Reverend—

MANDERS *(Pacing up and down)*: With me—eh? So you want to talk to me, do you?

ENGSTRAND: I'd be most grateful—

MANDERS *(Stopping in front of him)*: Well—what is it?

ENGSTRAND: It's just this, sir; we're being paid off down there—and many thanks to you, ma'am—our work's all finished; and, I thought how nice and helpful it would be to all of us who've worked together so hard and faithfully—if we could have a few prayers this evening.

MANDERS: Prayers?—Down at the orphanage?

ENGSTRAND: Yes, sir; of course if it isn't convenient to you, sir—

MANDERS: Oh, it's convenient enough—but—hm—

ENGSTRAND: I've taken to saying a few prayers myself down there of an evening—

MRS. ALVING: *You* have?

ENGSTRAND: Yes—now and then; we can all do with a little edification, I thought; but I'm just a simple, humble fellow—I'm not much good at it, God help me! But as long as the Reverend happened to be here—I thought—

MANDERS: Look here, Engstrand; I must first ask you a question: Are you in a proper state of mind for prayer? Have you a clear, untroubled conscience?

ENGSTRAND: God help me! Perhaps we'd better not talk about my conscience, Mr. Manders.

MANDERS: That is exactly what we must talk about. Well—answer me!

ENGSTRAND: Well, sir—of course, now and then, it does trouble me a bit—

MANDERS: I'm glad you admit that at least. Now—will you be so kind as to tell me honestly—what is the truth about Regine?

MRS. ALVING *(Rapidly)*: Mr. Manders!

MANDERS *(Calming her)*: I'll handle this—

ENGSTRAND: Regine!—Lord, how you frightened me! *(Gives* MRS. ALVING *a look)* There's nothing wrong with Regine, is there?

MANDERS: It is to be hoped not. But what I mean is this: What is your true relationship to Regine? You pretend to be her father, do you not?

ENGSTRAND *(Uncertain)*: Yes—hm—well, sir—you know all about me and poor Johanna—

MANDERS: No more prevarication, please! Your late wife confessed the whole truth to Mrs. Alving before she left her service.

ENGSTRAND: Do you mean to say she—? Oh, she did, did she?

MANDERS: Yes; so it's no use lying any longer, Engstrand.

ENGSTRAND: Well! And after her swearing up and down—

MANDERS: Swearing, you say—?

ENGSTRAND: I mean, she gave me her solemn word, sir.

MANDERS: And all these years you've kept the truth from me—from *me*, who have always had the utmost faith in you!

ENGSTRAND: Yes, sir—I'm afraid I have.

MANDERS: Have I deserved that, Engstrand? Haven't I always

done everything in my power to help you? Answer me—haven't I?

ENGSTRAND: Yes, sir. Things would often have looked pretty black for me, if it hadn't been for you.

MANDERS: And this is how you repay me! You cause me to enter erroneous statements in the Church Register, and withhold from me for years the truth which it was your duty to impart to me. Your conduct has been inexcusable, Engstrand; from now on, I shall have nothing more to do with you.

ENGSTRAND *(With a sigh)*: Yes, sir; I suppose that's how it has to be!

MANDERS: I don't see how you can possibly justify your conduct.

ENGSTRAND: We felt it better not to add to her shame by talking about it. Supposing you'd been in poor Johanna's place, Mr. Manders—

MANDERS: I!

ENGSTRAND: Lord bless me! I don't mean that the way it sounds! What I mean is: suppose you had done something you were ashamed of in the eyes of the world, as they say; we men oughtn't to judge a poor woman too hard, Mr. Manders.

MANDERS: But I don't judge her—it's *you* I'm accusing.

ENGSTRAND: Mr. Manders, would you allow me to ask you just one little question?

MANDERS: Very well—what is it?

ENGSTRAND: Shouldn't a decent, honorable man help those who've gone astray?

MANDERS: Well—naturally—

ENGSTRAND: And isn't a man bound to keep his word of honor?

MANDERS: Yes, of course, but—

ENGSTRAND: Well—you see, after Johanna got into trouble with that Englishman—or maybe he was American—or one of those Russians even—anyway, she came back to town. Poor thing—she'd already refused me twice; she only had eyes for the handsome fellows—and, of course, I had this deformed leg of mine. You remember, sir, I was once rash enough to enter one of those dance-halls—one of those dives where sailors spend their time drinking and carousing, as they say—I was just trying to persuade them to try another kind of life—

MRS. ALVING *(By the window)*: Hm—

MANDERS: Yes, I know, Engstrand; those dreadful men threw you downstairs; I remember your telling me of that tragic experience; you bear your deformity with honor.

ENGSTRAND: I don't mean to brag about it, sir. Well—anyway, she came to me, and confided her whole trouble to me, with tears and lamentations—it broke my heart to listen to her—

MANDERS: Did it, indeed, Engstrand! Well—and then—?

ENGSTRAND: Well, then I said to her, I said, "That American is wandering on the seas of the world; and you, Johanna, are a sinful fallen creature," I said. "But Jakob Engstrand," I said, "stands here on two solid legs," I said; of course I only meant that in a manner of speaking, you know, sir—

MANDERS: Yes, yes—I understand—go on—

ENGSTRAND: Well, then, sir, I married her—I made her an honest woman—so no one would know of her reckless behavior with that foreigner—

MANDERS: All of that was very right and good of you, Engstrand; but I cannot condone your consenting to accept money—

ENGSTRAND: Money? Me? Not a penny—

MANDERS *(In a questioning tone, to MRS. ALVING)*: But—?

ENGSTRAND: Oh, yes—wait a bit—now I remember. Johanna did say something about some money she had—but I refused to hear anything about it! "Get thee behind me, Satan," I said. "It's Mammon's gold" (or bank notes or whatever it was). "We'll throw it back in the American's face," I said; but, of course, he had disappeared, sir—disappeared over the vast ocean, you see—

MANDERS: Yes—I see—my dear Engstrand—

ENGSTRAND: Yes, sir; and then Johanna and I agreed that every penny of that money should go to the child's upbringing; and that's where it went, sir; and I can account for every cent of it.

MANDERS: But this puts things in an entirely different light—

ENGSTRAND: That's the way it was, Mr. Manders. And though I say it myself, I've tried to be a good father to Regine—to the best of my ability, that is—you know what a weak man I am, sir—unfortunately—

MANDERS: Yes, yes—I know, dear Engstrand—

ENGSTRAND: I can truly say I gave the child a decent upbringing and made poor Johanna a good and loving husband; but it never would have occurred to me to go to you, Mr. Manders, and brag about it and pat myself on the back for doing a good action; I'm not made like that. And most of the time, unfortunately, I've little enough to brag about. When I go and talk to you, sir, it's mostly to confess my sins and weaknesses. For, as I said just now, my conscience troubles me quite a bit.

MANDERS: Give me your hand, Jakob Engstrand.

ENGSTRAND: Oh—Lord, sir!—

MANDERS: Come now—no nonsense! *(Grasps his hand)* There!

ENGSTRAND: I most humbly ask you to forgive me, sir—

MANDERS: On the contrary—it's I who must ask your forgiveness—

ENGSTRAND: Oh, no, sir!

MANDERS: Most certainly—and I do so with all my heart. Forgive me, dear Engstrand, for so misjudging you. I wish I might give you some proof of my sincere regret and of the esteem in which I hold you—

ENGSTRAND: You'd really like to do that, sir?

MANDERS: It would give me the greatest of pleasure.

ENGSTRAND: Well—it just happens—there is something you could do for me, sir; I've managed to put by a bit of money from my earnings here, and I'm thinking of opening a kind of seamen's home when I get back to town, sir—

MRS. ALVING: You—*what?*

ENGSTRAND: It'd be like a kind of refuge for them, you see, ma'am. These poor sailors have so many temptations when they get to port—I thought in my house, they'd find a father's care—

MANDERS: What do you say to that, Mrs. Alving?

ENGSTRAND: Of course, I haven't much capital to go on—and I thought if I could just find a helping hand—

MANDERS: I shall give it some thought. I find your scheme most interesting. But now, go and get everything ready—light the lights—and prepare for our little celebration. Now I feel sure you are in a fit state for prayer, my dear Engstrand—

ENGSTRAND: Yes—I really believe I am. Well, good-bye, Mrs. Alving, and thank you for everything; be sure and take good care of Regine for me. *(Wipes away a tear)* Poor Johanna's child—it's strange how she's managed to creep into my heart—but, she has—there's no denying it! *(He bows and goes out by the hall door.)*

MANDERS: Well—what do you think of him now, Mrs. Alving? It certainly puts things in an entirely different light.

MRS. ALVING: It does indeed!

MANDERS: It just shows you how careful one must be in judging one's fellow-men. And what a satisfaction to find oneself mistaken! What do you say now?

MRS. ALVING: I say you're a great big baby, Manders, and always will be!

MANDERS: *I!*

MRS. ALVING *(Puts her hands on his shoulders)*: Yes; and I say I should like very much to give you a big hug!

MANDERS *(Hastily drawing back)*: Good heavens—What ideas you have!

MRS. ALVING *(With a smile)*: Oh, you needn't be afraid of me!

MANDERS *(By the table)*: You have such an extravagant way of expressing yourself! I'll just gather up all these documents and put them in my bag. *(He does so)* There! Keep an eye on Osvald when he returns; I'll leave you for the present—but I'll come back and see you later. *(He takes his hat and goes out through the hall door.)*

MRS. ALVING *(Gives a sigh, glances out of the window, straightens up one or two things in the room and is about to go into the dining room but stops in the doorway and gives a low exclamation)*: Osvald—are you still there?

OSVALD *(From the dining room)*: I'm just finishing my cigar.

MRS. ALVING: I thought you'd gone out for a walk.

OSVALD: In this kind of weather?
(Noise of a glass clinking. MRS. ALVING *leaves the door open and sits down on the sofa with some knitting.)*

OSVALD *(Off stage)*: Was that Mr. Manders who went out just now?

MRS. ALVING: Yes, he went down to the orphanage.

OSVALD: Hm—
(The clinking of a bottle on a glass is heard again.)

MRS. ALVING *(With an uneasy glance)*: Osvald dear—be careful with that liqueur—it's quite strong, you know.

OSVALD: It'll do me good, Mother! I feel so chilly.

MRS. ALVING: Wouldn't you rather come in here with me?

OSVALD: You don't allow smoking in there, you said.

MRS. ALVING: I don't mind a cigar, dear.

OSVALD: Very well, then I'll come in—I'll just have another little drop—there! *(He comes in smoking a cigar. Closes the door after him. A short silence)* Where did Mr. Manders go?

MRS. ALVING: I just told you; he went down to the orphanage.

OSVALD: Oh, yes—so you did.

MRS. ALVING: It's not good for you to sit so long at table, Osvald dear.

OSVALD *(Holding his cigar behind his back)*: But it's so cozy, Mother. *(He pats her face and caresses her)* You don't know what it means. To be home! To sit at my mother's table—in my mother's own room—to eat my mother's delicious food—!

MRS. ALVING: My dear, dear boy!

OSVALD *(Walks up and down impatiently)*: And what on earth is there to do here? I can't seem to settle to anything—

MRS. ALVING: Can't you?

OSVALD: In this gloomy weather—never a ray of sunshine. *(Paces up and down)* God! Not to be able to work—!

MRS. ALVING: Perhaps you shouldn't have come home, Osvald.

OSVALD: I had to come, Mother.

MRS. ALVING: But if you're unhappy, Osvald. You know I'd ten times rather give up the joy of having you here than—

OSVALD *(Stopping by the table)*: Tell me honestly, Mother—is it really such a joy to you to have me home again?

MRS. ALVING: How can you ask such a thing!

OSVALD *(Crumpling up a newspaper)*: I should have thought you didn't much care one way or the other.

MRS. ALVING: How have you the heart to say that to me, Osvald?

OSVALD: After all—you managed to live without me all these years.

MRS. ALVING: That's true—I've managed to live without you— (*A pause. Twilight is falling gradually.* OSVALD *paces up and down. He has put out his cigar. He suddenly stops in front of* MRS. ALVING.)

OSVALD: May I sit beside you on the sofa, Mother?

MRS. ALVING (*Making room for him*): Of course, dear.

OSVALD (*Sits beside her*): There's something I must tell you.

MRS. ALVING (*Anxiously*): Well?

OSVALD (*Staring in front of him*): I don't think I can bear it any longer.

MRS. ALVING: Bear what? What is it?

OSVALD (*As before*): I somehow couldn't bring myself to write to you about it—and, since I've been home—

MRS. ALVING (*Grips his arm*): Osvald—what is it?

OSVALD: All day yesterday and again today, I've tried to get rid of the thought—free myself of it—but I can't—

MRS. ALVING (*Rising*): You must be honest with me, Osvald—

OSVALD (*Pulls her down on the sofa again*): No, don't get up! Sit still! I'll try and tell you. I've complained a lot about being tired after my journey—

MRS. ALVING: Yes—well, what of that—?

OSVALD: But that isn't really what's the matter with me; this is no ordinary fatigue—

MRS. ALVING (*Tries to get up*): You're not ill, are you, Osvald?

OSVALD (*Pulling her down again*): No, don't get up, Mother. Try and be calm. I'm not really ill either—not in the usual sort of way—(*Clasping his head in his hands*) It's a kind of mental breakdown, Mother—I'm destroyed—I'll never be able to work again. (*He hides his face in his hands, and lets his head fall into her lap—shaking with sobs.*)

151

MRS. ALVING *(Pale and trembling)*: Osvald! It's not true! Look at me!

OSVALD *(Looking up in despair)*: I'll never be able to work again! Never—never! I'll be like a living corpse! Mother—can you imagine anything more frightful—?

MRS. ALVING: But, my darling! How could such a dreadful thing happen to you?

OSVALD *(Sitting up again)*: That's just it—I don't know! I can't possibly imagine! I've never lived a dissipated life—not in any kind of way—you must believe that, Mother—I haven't!

MRS. ALVING: I believe that, Osvald.

OSVALD: And yet, in spite of that—this ghastly thing has taken hold of me!

MRS. ALVING: It'll come out all right, my darling. It's just overwork—believe me!

OSVALD *(Dully)*: Yes—I thought that too at first—but it's not so.

MRS. ALVING: Tell me all about it.

OSVALD: Yes, I will.

MRS. ALVING: When did you first notice anything?

OSVALD: It was just after I went back to Paris—after my last visit here. I started to get terrible headaches—all up the back of my head—it was as if an iron band was screwed round my head—from the neck up—

MRS. ALVING: And then—?

OSVALD: At first I thought it was just the usual kind of headache I'd always had—since I was a child—

MRS. ALVING: Yes—?

OSVALD: But it wasn't that—I soon found that out. I was no longer able to work. I'd start on a new picture and all my strength would suddenly fail me—it was as though I were paralyzed; I couldn't concentrate—and I felt sick and dizzy; it was the most ghastly sensation; at last I went to see a doctor—and then I found out the truth.

MRS. ALVING: What do you mean?

OSVALD: He was one of the best doctors there. I described to him just how I felt—and then he started asking me all sorts of questions—questions about things that seemed to have no bearing on the case—I couldn't make out what he was driving at—

MRS. ALVING: Well—?

OSVALD: At last he said: "Your constitution has been undermined from birth"; he used the word "vermoulu."

MRS. ALVING *(Anxiously)*: What did he mean by that?

OSVALD: I didn't know what he meant either; I asked him to explain. And do you know what he said—that cynical old man—? *(Clenching his fist)* Oh!

MRS. ALVING: No—what?

OSVALD: He said: "The sins of the fathers are visited upon the children."

MRS. ALVING *(Rises slowly)*: The sins of the fathers—!

OSVALD: I almost hit him in the face.

MRS. ALVING *(Pacing the floor)*: The sins of the fathers—

OSVALD *(With a sad smile)*: Can you believe it? Of course I assured him that such a thing was out of the question—but he paid no attention—he repeated what he'd said. I had some of your letters with me—and I had to translate to him the parts that referred to Father—

MRS. ALVING: Yes—?

OSVALD: Then he had to admit he must be on the wrong tack. And then I learned the truth—the incredible truth! The sort of life I'd been leading—gay and carefree, but innocent enough I thought—had been too much for my strength; I should have been more careful. So, you see, I've brought it on myself—

MRS. ALVING: No! You mustn't believe that, Osvald!

OSVALD: He said that was the only possible explanation. My

whole life ruined—thrown away—through my own carelessness. All that I dreamed of achieving, of accomplish-
ing—I dare not think of it—I mustn't think of it! If I could
only live my life over again—if I could wipe it all out and
start afresh! *(He flings himself face downward on the sofa.
After a pause looks up, leaning on his elbows)* It wouldn't be
so bad if it was something I'd inherited—if it were
something I couldn't help. But, deliberately—out of
carelessness—out of shameful stupidity to throw away
happiness, health—everything that's worthwhile in this
world—my future—my whole life!

MRS. ALVING: No—no! It's impossible, Osvald—my darling—my
boy! *(Bending over him)* It's not true—it's not as desperate
as that—!

OSVALD *(Jumping up)*: Oh, Mother, you don't know! And to
think I should bring you such unhappiness! I've often
hoped and prayed that you didn't care much about me,
after all—

MRS. ALVING: Not care about you, Osvald? You're all I have in
the world—you're the only thing on earth that matters to
me—

OSVALD *(Takes both her hands and kisses them)*: Yes, Mother, I
know; when I'm home I realize that—and it makes it
doubly hard for me. Well—now you know all about it;
don't let's discuss it any more today; I can't bear to
dwell on it too long. *(Paces about the room)* Give me something to drink, Mother.

MRS. ALVING: To drink? What do you want, Osvald?

OSVALD: Oh, it doesn't matter—anything! You must have
something in the house—

MRS. ALVING: Yes, but Osvald—don't you think—?

OSVALD: Don't refuse me, Mother—be a dear! I must have
something to help me drown these agonizing thoughts!
(He goes up to the conservatory and looks out) Oh, it's so
dark—so terribly dark! (MRS. ALVING *goes to the bell-pull and*

rings) This incessant rain! It may go on for weeks—for months! Never a ray of sunshine! I never remember seeing any sunshine here!

MRS. ALVING: You're not thinking of leaving me, Osvald?

OSVALD *(With a deep sigh)*: I'm not thinking of anything, Mother; I'm not capable of thinking—*(In a low voice)* I've had to give that up!

(REGINE comes in from the dining room.)

REGINE: Did you ring, Mrs. Alving?

MRS. ALVING: Yes; bring in the lamp.

REGINE: At once, Mrs. Alving—I have it ready. *(She goes out.)*

MRS. ALVING *(Goes to OSVALD)*: Don't keep anything from me, Osvald.

OSVALD: I won't, Mother. *(Goes to the table)* It seems to me I've been very frank with you.

(REGINE brings in the lamp and puts it on the table.)

MRS. ALVING: Oh, and Regine—you might bring us a half bottle of champagne.

REGINE: Very good, Mrs. Alving. *(She goes out.)*

OSVALD *(Takes her face in his hands)*: That's right, Mother! I knew you wouldn't let me go thirsty!

MRS. ALVING: My own poor boy! As if I could refuse you anything!

OSVALD *(Eagerly)*: You really mean that, Mother?

MRS. ALVING: What?

OSVALD: That you couldn't refuse me anything?

MRS. ALVING: But, my dear Osvald—

OSVALD: Sh!

(REGINE enters with a small tray on which are a bottle of champagne and two glasses; she sets it down on the table.)

REGINE: Shall I open it, Mrs. Alving?

OSVALD: No thanks—I'll do it myself.

(REGINE goes out.)

MRS. ALVING *(Sits down at the table)*: Osvald—be honest with me—what is it you don't want me to refuse you—?

OSVALD *(Busy opening the bottle)*: First, let's have a glass of wine—*(He opens the bottle and pours out one glass and is about to pour another.)*

MRS. ALVING *(Puts her hand over the glass)*: Thanks—not for me.

OSVALD: For me, then! *(He empties his glass, refills it and empties it again; he sits down at the table.)*

MRS. ALVING *(Expectantly)*: Well—

OSVALD: Mother, tell me—what was the matter with you and Mr. Manders at dinner just now? Why were you so quiet and solemn?

MRS. ALVING: Oh—did you notice that?

OSVALD: Yes. Hm—*(A pause)* Mother, what do you think of Regine?

MRS. ALVING: What do I think of her?

OSVALD: Don't you think she's wonderful?

MRS. ALVING: You don't know her as well as I do, Osvald—

OSVALD: Well—what of that?

MRS. ALVING: I should have taken charge of her sooner—I'm afraid she spent too many years at home—

OSVALD: But she's so wonderful to look at, Mother! *(Fills up his glass.)*

MRS. ALVING: She has many grave faults, Osvald—

OSVALD: As if that mattered! *(He drinks.)*

MRS. ALVING: But I'm fond of her all the same; I feel responsible for her. I wouldn't have anything happen to her for all the world.

OSVALD *(Jumps up)*: Mother! The one thing that could save me is Regine!

MRS. ALVING *(Rising)*: What do you mean?

OSVALD: I mean I can't endure this agony alone!

MRS. ALVING: But I'm here to help you, Osvald—

OSVALD: Yes, I know; I thought that would be enough—that's why I came home to you; but it's no use; I see that now. My life here would be intolerable.

MRS. ALVING: Osvald—!

OSVALD: I must live a different sort of life; that's why I must go away again. I don't want you to see it happening to me—

MRS. ALVING: But you can't go away when you're so ill, Osvald.

OSVALD: If it were just an ordinary illness, of course I'd stay home, Mother; I know you're the best friend I have in the world—

MRS. ALVING: You do know that—don't you?

OSVALD *(Moves about the room restlessly)*: But it's the anguish, the remorse, the deadly fear—oh—that terrible fear!

MRS. ALVING *(Follows after him)*: Fear? Fear of what?

OSVALD: Don't ask me any more about it! I don't know—I can't describe it to you—(MRS. ALVING *goes to the bell-pull and rings)* What do you want?

MRS. ALVING: I want my boy to be happy, that's what I want—I won't let you suffer here! *(To* REGINE*)* More champagne, Regine! A whole bottle!

*(*REGINE *goes.)*

OSVALD: Mother!

MRS. ALVING: We country people know how to live too—you'll see.

OSVALD: Isn't she wonderful to look at? So beautifully built! So radiant with health.

MRS. ALVING *(Sitting down at the table)*: Sit down, Osvald; let's talk quietly for a moment—

OSVALD *(Sits down)*: You don't know about it, Mother—but I haven't been quite fair to Regine—

MRS. ALVING: Not fair—?

OSVALD: No—it was just thoughtlessness on my part—nothing serious; but last time I was home—

MRS. ALVING: Yes—?

OSVALD: She kept on asking questions about Paris—I told her a bit about my life there—and one day I said to her, quite casually: "Perhaps you'd like to go there and see it all for yourself, Regine—"

MRS. ALVING: Well—?

OSVALD: Then she blushed and got quite excited and said she'd give anything to go; then I said, perhaps some day it might be arranged—or something of that sort—

MRS. ALVING: I see.

OSVALD: Of course I'd forgotten all about it; but the other day, when I arrived, I asked her if she was glad I intended to spend such a long time here—

MRS. ALVING: Yes—?

OSVALD: And then she looked at me so strangely and said, "Then what about my trip to Paris?"

MRS. ALVING: Her trip—?

OSVALD: Yes—it seems she'd taken me quite seriously; she'd been thinking about it all this time—thinking about *me*. She'd even tried to teach herself some French—

MRS. ALVING: So that was why—

OSVALD: I'd never noticed her much before, Mother—but suddenly I saw her there—so beautiful—so vital—she stood there as though waiting to come into my arms—

MRS. ALVING: Osvald—!

OSVALD: I suddenly realized that she could save me; she was so full of the joy of life!

MRS. ALVING *(Startled)*: Joy of life—? Is there salvation in that? *(REGINE comes in with the champagne.)*

REGINE: Excuse me for being so long, Mrs. Alving. I had to go down to the cellar—*(Puts the bottle on the table.)*

OSVALD: Fetch another glass.

REGINE *(Looks at him surprised)*: Mrs. Alving has a glass, sir.

OSVALD: Yes—but fetch one for yourself, Regine. *(REGINE starts and gives a quick frightened glance at* MRS. ALVING*)* Well?

REGINE *(Softly, with hesitation)*: Do you wish me to, Mrs. Alving?

MRS. ALVING: Fetch the glass, Regine.

*(*REGINE *goes into the dining room.)*

OSVALD *(Looking after her)*: Have you noticed her walk, Mother—so strong—so sure.

MRS. ALVING: This can't be allowed to happen, Osvald.

OSVALD: But it's all settled—you must see that—there's no use forbidding it. *(*REGINE *comes in with an empty glass and keeps it in her hand)* Sit down, Regine. *(*REGINE *looks questioningly at* MRS. ALVING.*)*

MRS. ALVING: Sit down. *(*REGINE *sits on a chair by the dining room door, with the empty glass in her hand)* Osvald—What were you saying about the joy of life?

OSVALD: Yes—the joy of life, Mother—you don't know much about that here at home. I could never find it here.

MRS. ALVING: Not here with me?

OSVALD: No. Never at home. But you don't understand that.

MRS. ALVING: Yes—I believe I'm beginning to understand it—now.

OSVALD: That—and the joy of work. They're really the same thing you know. But of course, you don't know anything about that here either.

MRS. ALVING: No; you may be right. Tell me more about it.

OSVALD: Well—I simply mean that here people look on work as a curse—as a kind of punishment. They look on *life* as a wretched, miserable business—to be got through as soon as possible—

MRS. ALVING: I know—a "vale of tears"—we do our best to make it so—

OSVALD: But, you see, abroad, people don't look at it like that. They don't believe in that old-fashioned preaching any longer. The mere fact of being alive in this world seems to them joyous and marvelous. You must have noticed, Mother, everything I paint is filled with this joy of life; always and forever the joy of life! My paintings are full of light, of sunshine, of glowing happy faces. That's why I'm afraid to stay here, Mother.

MRS. ALVING: Afraid? What are you afraid of—here with me?

OSVALD: I'm afraid that all the strongest traits in my nature would become warped here—would degenerate into ugliness.

MRS. ALVING *(Looks at him intently)*: You really believe that is what would happen?

OSVALD: Yes—I'm convinced of it! Even if I lived the same life here as I live abroad—it still wouldn't *be* the same life.

MRS. ALVING *(Who has listened intently, rises; a thoughtful look in her eyes.)*: Now I see it! It's all becoming clear to me—

OSVALD: What do you see?

MRS. ALVING: The whole pattern—for the first time, I see it—and now I can speak.

OSVALD *(Rising)*: I don't understand you, Mother.

REGINE *(Who has risen too)*: Perhaps I'd better go—

MRS. ALVING: No, no—stay where you are. Now I can speak. Now you must know everything, Osvald—and then you can choose. Osvald! Regine!

OSVALD: Sh! Here comes Manders.

MANDERS *(Enters from hall door)*: Well—I must say—we've had a most edifying time—

OSVALD: So have we.

MANDERS: There can be no doubt about it—We must make it possible for Engstrand to start that seamen's home of his. Regine must go back with him; she can be most helpful—

REGINE: No thank you, Mr. Manders!

MANDERS *(Notices her for the first time)*: What—? You in here? And with a glass in your hand?

REGINE *(Hastily puts down her glass)*: Pardon!

OSVALD: Regine is going with me, Mr. Manders.

MANDERS: Going with you—?

OSVALD: Yes; as my wife—if she insists on that.

MANDERS: But—good heavens—!

REGINE: It's no fault of mine, Mr. Manders—

OSVALD: Or if I decide to stay here—she'll stay too.

REGINE *(Involuntarily)*: Stay here—!

MANDERS: I am amazed at you, Mrs. Alving.

MRS. ALVING: None of this will happen—for now I can tell the truth at last.

MANDERS: But you won't—you can't!

MRS. ALVING: I can and I will—and nobody's ideals will be the worse for it.

OSVALD: Mother, what is all this—what are you hiding from me?

REGINE *(Listening)*: Mrs. Alving—Listen!—I hear people shouting out there. *(She goes to the conservatory.)*

OSVALD *(Going to the window stage left)*: What's happening? What's that glare in the sky?

REGINE *(Calls out)*: It's the orphanage—the orphanage is on fire!

MRS. ALVING *(Going to the window)*: On fire—?

MANDERS: On fire—? Impossible! I've just come from there.

OSVALD: Give me my hat!—Oh, never mind—Father's orphanage! *(He runs out into the garden.)*

MRS. ALVING: My shawl, Regine! The whole place is in flames!

MANDERS: How horrible! It's a judgment, Mrs. Alving—a judgment on this house.

MRS. ALVING: Yes—undoubtedly, Manders. Come, Regine.
*(*MRS. ALVING *and* REGINE *hurry out through the hall door.)*

MANDERS *(Clasping his hands)*: And to think it's not insured!
(He follows them as the curtain falls.)

Act Three

SCENE: *The room as before. All the doors stand open. The lamp is still burning on the table. It is dark outside; there is only a faint glow from the fire in the background to the left.*

As the curtain rises MRS. ALVING, *with a shawl over her head, stands in the conservatory looking out.* REGINE, *also with a shawl on, stands a little behind her.*

MRS. ALVING: Nothing left—burned to the ground!

REGINE: The cellar is still in flames.

MRS. ALVING: Why doesn't Osvald come?—There's no hope of saving anything.

REGINE: Shall I take his hat down to him?

MRS. ALVING: Is he out there without it?

REGINE *(Pointing to the hall)*: Yes—it's hanging in the hall—

MRS. ALVING: No—leave it—he'll be back in a moment—I think I'll go and look for him. *(Exits to the garden.)*

MANDERS *(Enters from hall)*: Isn't Mrs. Alving here?

REGINE: She just went down to the garden.

MANDERS: What a night—I've never gone through anything as dreadful!

REGINE: It's a terrible thing, Mr. Manders!

MANDERS: Don't speak of it!—I can't bear the thought of it.

REGINE: But how could it possibly have happened?

MANDERS: Oh, don't ask me, Miss Engstrand—how should I know! You're not implying—? Isn't it enough that your father should—?

REGINE: What's he been up to—?

MANDERS: He's driven me half mad—

ENGSTRAND *(Enters through hall)*: Oh, there you are, Mr. Manders—

MANDERS *(Turning around with a start)*: Must you follow me in here too!

ENGSTRAND: Oh, Mr. Manders!—Such a terrible thing, sir—!

MANDERS *(Pacing up and down)*: Yes, yes! We know! We know!—

REGINE: What's the meaning of this?

ENGSTRAND: It was all due to the prayer meeting, you see! *(Aside to* REGINE*)* We've hooked the old fool now, my girl! *(Aloud)* That poor Mr. Manders should be the cause of such a calamity—and through my fault too!

MANDERS: But I tell you, Engstrand—

ENGSTRAND: No one touched the lights but you, sir!

MANDERS *(Standing still)*: That's what *you* claim—but I could swear I never went *near* the lights!

ENGSTRAND: But I saw you with my own eyes, sir!—I saw you snuff one of the candles and throw the bit of wick right into a pile of shavings!

MANDERS: You say you *saw* this?

ENGSTRAND: So help me God, sir!

MANDERS: Incredible!—I'm not in the habit of snuffing candles with my fingers.

ENGSTRAND: No, sir—I thought at the time it didn't look quite like you. It'll be quite a serious thing, won't it, sir?

MANDERS *(Walks restlessly back and forth)*: Don't ask me about it!

ENGSTRAND *(Follows him about)*: You hadn't insured the place, had you, sir?

MANDERS *(Still pacing)*: I told you I hadn't!

ENGSTRAND *(Following him)*: Hadn't insured it! And then to go and set the whole place on fire like that! Lord! What a bit of bad luck, sir!

MANDERS *(Wipes the perspiration from his brow)*: You may well say so, Engstrand.

ENGSTRAND: A charitable institution too! A place dedicated, you might say, to the good of the community!—It's likely the papers won't treat you any too kindly, Mr. Manders.

MANDERS: That's just it! That's what I'm thinking about—all the spiteful attacks and accusations! That's the worst part of the whole business—I can't bear the thought of it!

MRS. ALVING *(Enters from the garden)*: He won't come—he can't seem to tear himself away.

MANDERS: Oh, it's you, Mrs. Alving.

MRS. ALVING: Well, Manders! You got out of making your speech after all!

MANDERS: I'd be only too glad to make it!

MRS. ALVING *(In a subdued tone)*: It's all for the best; that poor orphanage could never have brought good to anyone!

MANDERS: You really feel that?

MRS. ALVING: Well—don't you?

MANDERS: All the same—it's a great tragedy.

MRS. ALVING: Nonsense! Now—let's discuss it from a business point of view—Are you waiting for Mr. Manders, Engstrand?

ENGSTRAND *(By the hall door)*: Yes, ma'am, I am.

MRS. ALVING: Well then—sit down.

ENGSTRAND: I'd rather stand, thank you, ma'am.

MRS. ALVING *(To MANDERS)*: I suppose you'll be leaving by the next boat?

MANDERS: Yes—there's one in an hour.

MRS. ALVING: Please take all the documents with you—I don't want to hear another word about it! I've other things to think about now.

MANDERS: Mrs. Alving—

MRS. ALVING: I'll arrange to send you power of attorney and you can wind things up as you think best.

MANDERS: I'll be glad to look after it for you. Of course now the original terms of the bequest will have to be radically altered.

MRS. ALVING: Naturally—

MANDERS: I would suggest making the actual land over to the parish under the circumstances; it's not without value, and could be used for many purposes. As to the interest on the capital—I feel sure I can find some worthy project in need of support—something that would prove beneficial to the life of the community.

MRS. ALVING: Do anything you like with it—it makes no difference to me.

ENGSTRAND: You might give a thought to my seamen's home, Mr. Manders.

MANDERS: To be sure. A good suggestion. Well worth looking into.

ENGSTRAND *(Aside)*: Looking into! That's a good one!

MANDERS *(With a sigh)*: Of course I may not be long in charge of these affairs; public opinion may compel me to withdraw; there will naturally be an investigation to determine the cause of the fire; it all depends on the outcome of that.

MRS. ALVING: What *are* you talking about, Manders?

MANDERS: It's impossible to tell what that outcome will be.

ENGSTRAND *(Coming closer)*: Oh, no it's not, Mr. Manders! Don't forget *me*—don't forget Jakob Engstrand!

MANDERS: But—I don't see—

ENGSTRAND *(In a low voice)*: And Jakob Engstrand is not one to desert a benefactor in his hour of need—as they say!

MANDERS: But, my dear man—how could you possibly—?

ENGSTRAND: Jakob Engstrand won't desert you, sir! He'll be like a guardian angel to you, sir!

MANDERS: But I could never consent—!

ENGSTRAND: You'll have nothing to do with it, sir. It wouldn't be the first time I'd taken the blame for others.

MANDERS: Jakob! *(Wringing his hands)* You're one in a million! I'll see that you get funds for your seamen's home—You can count on that. *(ENGSTRAND tries to thank him but is overcome with emotion;* MANDERS *slings his traveling-bag over his shoulder)* And now—let's be off. We'll travel together, of course.

ENGSTRAND *(At the hall door, aside to* REGINE*)*: You'd better come with me, hussy! You'll live like a queen!

REGINE *(Tosses her head)*: Merci! *(She fetches* MANDERS' *things from the hall.)*

MANDERS: Good-bye, Mrs. Alving. May the spirit of truth and righteousness soon enter into this house.

MRS. ALVING: Good-bye, Manders. *(She goes to meet* OSVALD *who enters from the garden.)*

ENGSTRAND *(As he and* REGINE *help* MANDERS *with his coat)*: Good-bye, my dear child. And if anything should happen to you, remember Jakob Engstrand's always there—you know where to find him. Harbor Street—you know! *(To* MRS. ALVING *and* OSVALD*)* My home for poor seamen shall be called "Captain Alving's Haven," and if it turns out the way I want it, ma'am—I humbly hope it may prove worthy of Captain Alving's memory!

MANDERS *(In the doorway)*: Hm—yes. Come along, my dear Engstrand. Good-bye again—good-bye! *(They exit through the hall.)*

OSVALD *(Goes toward the table)*: What does he mean? What "home" is he talking about?

MRS. ALVING: It's some sort of a hostel he and Manders are thinking of starting.

OSVALD: It'll only burn down—just like this one.

MRS. ALVING: Why do you say that?

OSVALD: Everything will be burned. Father's memory will be wiped out. I shall soon be burned up too.

(REGINE *looks at him in amazement.*)

MRS. ALVING: Osvald! You poor boy! You shouldn't have stayed down there so long.

OSVALD (*Sits down at the table*): I expect you're right about that.

MRS. ALVING: Your face is wet, Osvald; let me dry it for you. (*Wipes his face with her handkerchief.*)

OSVALD (*Indifferently*): Thanks, Mother.

MRS. ALVING: You must be tired, Osvald. You'd better get some sleep.

OSVALD (*Apprehensively*): No! No! I don't want to sleep! I never sleep—I only pretend to . . . (*Dully*) I'll sleep soon enough!

MRS. ALVING (*Looking at him anxiously*): I'm afraid you're really ill, my darling!

REGINE (*Intently*): Is Mr. Alving ill?

OSVALD (*Impatiently*): And close the doors!—I want all the doors closed!—this terrible fear—

MRS. ALVING: Close the doors, Regine.

(REGINE *closes the doors and remains standing by the one to the hall.* MRS. ALVING *takes off her shawl, and* REGINE *does likewise.*)

MRS. ALVING (*Draws up a chair and sits next to* OSVALD): There!— I'll sit here beside you.

OSVALD: Yes—do, Mother. And Regine must stay here too— she must never leave me. You'll be there to help me, won't you, Regine?

REGINE: I don't understand—

MRS. ALVING: There to help you?

OSVALD: Yes—when the time comes.

MRS. ALVING: Can't you trust your mother to do that?

OSVALD: You? (*Smiles*) You'd never do it. (*With a melancholy laugh)* You! *(Looks at her gravely)* And yet you're the only one who has the right to do it. Why are you always so formal with me, Regine? Why don't you call me Osvald?

REGINE *(In a low voice)*: Mrs. Alving might not like it.

MRS. ALVING: You may soon have a right to—so sit down with us, Regine. *(REGINE hesitates, then sits down quietly at the far side of the table)* And now, my darling, I'm going to free you from this torment; you won't have to bear this dreadful burden any longer.

OSVALD: You're going to free me, Mother?

MRS. ALVING: Yes—from this remorse, this sense of guilt, this self-reproach . . .

OSVALD: Do you think you can do that?

MRS. ALVING: Yes, I believe I can now. Earlier this evening you were talking about the joy of life—and suddenly everything became clear to me; I saw my whole life in a new light.

OSVALD *(Shaking his head)*: I don't understand this.

MRS. ALVING: You should have known your father when he was a young lieutenant. He was filled with that joy of life, I can tell you!

OSVALD: Yes—so I've heard.

MRS. ALVING: He seemed to radiate light and warmth—he was filled with a turbulent, joyous vitality.

OSVALD: Well—?

MRS. ALVING: And this boy, so full of the joy of life—he was like a boy then—was cooped up in this drab little provincial town—which could offer him no real joy—only dissipation. He had no real aim in life—no work that could stimulate his mind or feed his spirit—nothing but a dull, petty, routine job. He found no one here who understood that pure joy of life that was in him; what friends he had were bent on idling their time away or drinking themselves into a stupor—

OSVALD: Mother!

MRS. ALVING: And so, the inevitable happened.

OSVALD: The inevitable?

MRS. ALVING: You told me a little while ago, what would happen to you if you stayed here.

OSVALD: Do you mean by that—that Father—?

MRS. ALVING: Your poor father could find no outlet for that overpowering joy of life that was in him—and I'm afraid I brought him no happiness either.

OSVALD: Why, Mother?

MRS. ALVING: All my life I'd been taught a great deal about duty—that seemed the all-important thing. Everything was reduced to a question of duty—*my* duty—*his* duty—your poor father—I'm afraid I must have made home intolerable for him, Osvald.

OSVALD: Why did you never write me about all this?

MRS. ALVING: You were his son—I felt it would be wrong to talk to you about it; you see, I didn't see things clearly then.

OSVALD: How did you see them?

MRS. ALVING *(Slowly)*: I was aware of one thing only; that your father was a broken, dissolute man, long before you were born.

OSVALD *(A smothered cry)*: Ah! *(He rises and goes to the window.)*

MRS. ALVING: And day in and day out I was tormented by the thought that Regine actually had the same rights in this house that you have.

OSVALD *(Turns quickly)*: Regine!

REGINE *(Jumps up and says in a choking voice)*: I?

MRS. ALVING: Yes. Now you know everything—both of you.

OSVALD: Regine!

REGINE *(To herself)*: So Mother was—*that* sort of woman.

MRS. ALVING: Your mother had many fine qualities, Regine.

REGINE: She was that sort all the same. There've been times when I guessed she might be—but—Mrs. Alving! Please allow me to leave at once.

MRS. ALVING: You really want to go, Regine?

REGINE: I certainly do, Mrs. Alving.

MRS. ALVING: Of course you must do as you wish, but—

OSVALD *(Goes to* REGINE*)*: Leave now? But you belong here.

REGINE: *Merci,* Mr. Alving—I suppose I can call you Osvald now—though this wasn't the way I wanted it to happen.

MRS. ALVING: Regine—I haven't been honest with you—

REGINE: No! You certainly haven't, Mrs. Alving! If I'd known that Osvald was a sick man—And now that there can never be anything serious between us—No! I can't waste my time out here in the country looking after invalids.

OSVALD: Not when it's your own brother, Regine?

REGINE: I should say not! I'm poor—all I have is my youth—I can't afford to waste it. I don't want to be left stranded. I have some of that "joy of life" in me too, Mrs. Alving!

MRS. ALVING: No doubt. But don't throw yourself away, Regine.

REGINE: If I do—I *do*—that's all! If Osvald takes after his father, I take after my mother, I suppose.—May I ask, Mrs. Alving, if Mr. Manders knows about all this?

MRS. ALVING: Mr. Manders knows everything.

REGINE *(Rapidly putting on her shawl)*: Then I'd better try and catch that boat. Mr. Manders is such a kind man, he's sure to help me. It seems to me I have a right to some of that money too—a better right than that filthy old carpenter.

MRS. ALVING: You're welcome to it, Regine.

REGINE *(With a hard look)*: And I must say, Mrs. Alving—it seems to me I also had a right to a decent upbringing—one suited to a gentleman's daughter. *(Tosses her head)*

Well—what do I care! *(Casts a bitter glance at the unopened bottle)* Some day I may be drinking champagne with the best of them—who knows?

MRS. ALVING: If you should ever need a home, Regine—come to me.

REGINE: No thank you, Mrs. Alving! Mr. Manders'll look after me I'm sure. And if the worse comes to the worst, I know of a place where I'd be quite at home.

MRS. ALVING: Where do you mean?

REGINE: In Captain Alving's Hostel, of course!

MRS. ALVING: Be careful, Regine! Don't destroy yourself!

REGINE: What do I care!—Well—good-bye! *(She bows to them and goes out through the hall.)*

OSVALD *(Stands at the window gazing out)*: Has she gone?

MRS. ALVING: Yes.

OSVALD *(Mutters to himself)*: How stupid it all is!

MRS. ALVING *(Stands behind him and puts her hands on his shoulders)*: Osvald—my dear, has it been a very great shock to you?

OSVALD *(Turns his face toward her)*: All that about Father, you mean?

MRS. ALVING: Yes, your poor father!—I'm afraid it's been too much for you.

OSVALD: Why do you say that? It was a great surprise to me, I admit; but after all, it doesn't really matter.

MRS. ALVING *(Withdraws her hands)*: Not matter? That your father was so unspeakably unhappy?

OSVALD: I feel sorry for him of course—as I would for anyone who suffered.

MRS. ALVING: No more than that?—But he was your *father*, Osvald.

OSVALD *(Impatiently)*: Father! Father! I never *knew* my father.

The only thing I remember about him is that he once made me sick!

MRS. ALVING: What a dreadful thought! But surely a child must have some love for his father, in spite of everything.

OSVALD: Even if he owes his father nothing? Even if he never knew him? Come now, Mother! You're too broadminded to believe in that superstitious nonsense!

MRS. ALVING: Superstitious nonsense—you think that's all it is?

OSVALD: Of course, Mother—you must see that. It's one of those old-fashioned illusions people go on clinging to—

MRS. ALVING *(Shaken)*: Ghosts—

OSVALD *(Paces up and down)*: Yes—call them ghosts if you like.

MRS. ALVING *(In a burst of emotion)*: Osvald—then you don't love me either!

OSVALD: Well, at least I know *you*—

MRS. ALVING: You know me—yes; but is that all?

OSVALD: I know how much you care for me; I should be grateful to you for that. And now that I'm ill, you can be of great help to me.

MRS. ALVING: I can—can't I, Osvald? I'm almost glad you're ill—since it's brought you home to me. I understand—you don't belong to me yet—I'll have to win you.

OSVALD *(Impatiently)*: Oh, don't let's have a lot of phrases, Mother! You must remember I'm ill. I can't be bothered with other people; I've got to think about myself.

MRS. ALVING *(Gently)*: I'll be very quiet and patient, Osvald.

OSVALD: And, for God's sake, *happy*, Mother!

MRS. ALVING: Yes, my darling—you're right. *(Goes to him)* And you've no more doubts, no more remorse? I've freed you of all that?

OSVALD: Yes, Mother, you have. But who's to free me of the terror—?

MRS. ALVING: Terror!

OSVALD *(Pacing up and down)*: Regine would have done it, if I'd asked her.

MRS. ALVING: I don't understand. What is this terror—and what has Regine to do with it?

OSVALD: Mother—is it very late?

MRS. ALVING: It's early morning. *(She goes to the conservatory and looks out)* The dawn is just breaking. It's going to be a lovely day, Osvald! In a little while you'll see the sun!

OSVALD: I'll be glad of that. Perhaps after all there are lots of things I could be glad about, Mother—lots of things I'd like to live for—

MRS. ALVING: Of course there are!

OSVALD: And even if I'm not able to work—

MRS. ALVING: You'll soon be able to work again, you'll see. Now that you're rid of all those depressing, gloomy thoughts.

OSVALD: Yes—it's good that you were able to wipe out that obsession. Now, if I can just get over this other—*(Sits down on the sofa)* Come here, Mother. I want to talk to you—

MRS. ALVING: Yes, Osvald. *(She pushes an armchair over near the sofa and sits close to him.)*

OSVALD: Meanwhile the sun is rising. And now that you know—I don't feel—so afraid anymore.

MRS. ALVING: Now that I know—what?

OSVALD *(Without listening to her)*: Mother—didn't you say a little while ago that there was nothing in this world you wouldn't do for me, if I asked you?

MRS. ALVING: Yes—of course I did.

OSVALD: And you stand by that, Mother?

MRS. ALVING: You can depend on me, my darling. You're the only thing on earth I have to live for.

OSVALD: Well, then—listen, Mother; you have a strong, gallant spirit—I know that; I want you to sit quite still while I tell you something.

MRS. ALVING: What dreadful thing are you going to—?

OSVALD: Don't scream or get excited, do you hear? Promise me! We'll sit here and talk it over quietly. Promise!

MRS. ALVING: Yes, yes—I promise! Tell me what it is!

OSVALD: Well, then—listen: this fatigue of mine—my inability to work—all of that is not the *essence* of my illness—

MRS. ALVING: How do you mean?

OSVALD: You see—my illness *is* hereditary—it—(*Touches his forehead and speaks very quietly*) It is centered—here.

MRS. ALVING (*Almost speechless*): Osvald! No—no!

OSVALD: Don't scream, Mother—I can't stand it! It's lurking here—lying in wait—ready to spring at any moment.

MRS. ALVING: How horrible!

OSVALD: Quiet, Mother! Now you understand the state I'm in.

MRS. ALVING (*Springing up*): It's not true, Osvald—it's impossible!

OSVALD: I had one attack while I was abroad—it didn't last long. But when I realized the condition I'd been in, I was filled with unspeakable terror—and I could think of nothing but getting home to you.

MRS. ALVING: So that's what you mean by "the terror"!

OSVALD: Yes—unspeakable, sickening terror! If it had only been an ordinary illness—even a fatal one—I wouldn't have minded so much—I'm not afraid of death—though I should like to live as long as possible—

MRS. ALVING: You will, Osvald—you must!

OSVALD: But there's something so utterly revolting about this! To become a child again—a helpless child—to have to be fed—to have to be—oh! It's too ghastly to think of!

MRS. ALVING: I'll be here to look after you, Osvald.

OSVALD *(Jumping up)*: No, never; I won't stand it! I can't endure the thought of lingering on like that—of growing old like that—old and gray-haired like that! And you might die and I should be left alone. *(Sits down in* MRS. ALVING'S *chair)* For the doctor said I might live for years, you see. He called it "softening of the brain" or something of the sort. *(With a sad smile)* Charming expression! It makes one think of cherry-colored velvet curtains—soft and delicate to stroke—

MRS. ALVING *(Screams)*: Osvald!

OSVALD *(Springs up and paces up and down)*: And now you've taken Regine away from me—if only I had her. She'd have been willing to help me, I know.

MRS. ALVING *(Goes to him)*: What do you mean by that, my darling?—You know I'd give my life to help you—

OSVALD: I recovered from that attack abroad—but the doctor said that the next time—and there's bound to be a "next time"—it would be hopeless.

MRS. ALVING: How could he be so brutal!

OSVALD: I insisted on the truth—I made him tell me. I explained that I had certain arrangements to make *(With a cunning smile)* and so I had. *(Takes a small box from his breast pocket)* Do you see this, Mother?

MRS. ALVING: What is it?

OSVALD: Morphine tablets—

MRS. ALVING *(Looks at him in terror)*: Osvald—

OSVALD: I managed to save up twelve of them—

MRS. ALVING *(Snatching at it)*: Give me the box, Osvald!

OSVALD: Not yet, Mother. *(Puts the box back in his pocket.)*

MRS. ALVING: I can't endure this!

OSVALD: You must endure it, Mother. If only Regine were here—I'd have explained to her how matters stood; I'd have asked her to help me put an end to it; she'd have done it, I know.

MRS. ALVING: Never!

OSVALD: Oh, yes, she would! If she'd seen that ghastly thing take hold of me—if she'd seen me lying there like an imbecile child—beyond help—hopelessly, irrevocably lost—

MRS. ALVING: Regine would never have done it!

OSVALD: Oh, yes! She'd have done it! Regine has such a magnificently light and buoyant nature. She wouldn't have put up long with an invalid like me!

MRS. ALVING: Then I can only thank God Regine is not here!

OSVALD: Yes, but then you'll have to help me, Mother.

MRS. ALVING *(With a loud scream)*: I!

OSVALD: Who has a better right?

MRS. ALVING: I—your mother.

OSVALD: For that very reason.

MRS. ALVING: I, who gave you life!

OSVALD: I didn't ask you for life—and what kind of a life did you give me! I don't want it—take it back again!

MRS. ALVING: Help—help! *(She runs out into the hall.)*

OSVALD *(Following her)*: Don't leave me! Where are you going?

MRS. ALVING *(In the hall)*: I must fetch a doctor, Osvald—let me out!

OSVALD *(In the hall)*: You shall not go out—and no one shall come in.

(Sound of a key turning in the lock.)

MRS. ALVING *(Reentering the room)*: Osvald—Osvald! My little one!

OSVALD *(Follows her in)*: Mother—if you love me—how can you bear to see me suffer this agony of fear!

MRS. ALVING *(After a moment's silence, in a firm voice)*: I give you my word, Osvald.

OSVALD: Then, you will—?

MRS. ALVING: Yes—If it becomes necessary—but it won't become necessary! That's impossible!

OSVALD: Let us hope so—Meanwhile we'll live together as long as we can. Thank you, Mother. *(He sits in the armchair that MRS. ALVING had moved to the sofa.)*
(Day breaks; the lamp is still burning on the table.)

MRS. ALVING *(Approaching him cautiously)*: Do you feel calmer now?

OSVALD: Yes.

MRS. ALVING *(Bends over him)*: This has all been a nightmare, Osvald—just something you've imagined. It's been a dreadful strain, but now you're home with me and you'll be able to get some rest. I'll spoil you as I did when you were a tiny little boy—you shall have everything you want. There! The attack's over now—You see how easily it passed. It's not so serious—I was sure it couldn't be! And it's going to be such a lovely day, Osvald. Bright sunshine! Now you'll really be able to see your home. *(She goes to the table and puts out the lamp. The sun rises. The glaciers and peaks in the background are bathed in the bright morning light.)*

OSVALD *(Immovable in his armchair with his back to the view outside, suddenly speaks)*: Mother—give me the sun.

MRS. ALVING *(By the table, looks at him in amazement)*: What did you say?

OSVALD *(Repeats in a dull toneless voice)*: The sun—the sun.

MRS. ALVING *(Goes to him)*: Osvald—what's the matter with you?
(OSVALD seems to crumple up in the chair; all his muscles relax; his face is expressionless—his eyes vacant and staring.)

MRS. ALVING *(Trembling with terror)*: What is it? *(Screams)* Osvald! What's the matter with you? *(Throws herself on her knees beside him and shakes him)* Osvald! Osvald! Look at me! Don't you know me?

OSVALD *(Tonelessly as before)*: The sun—the sun.

MRS. ALVING *(Springs up in despair, tears at her hair with both hands and screams):* I can't bear it! *(Whispers, paralyzed with fear)* I can't bear it! Never! *(Suddenly)* Where did he put them? *(Passes her hand rapidly over his breast)* Here! *(Draws back a couple of steps and cries)* No! no! no!—Yes! No! no! *(She stands a few steps away from him, her hands clutching her hair, and stares at him in speechless terror.)*

OSVALD *(Immovable as before):* The sun—the sun.

CURTAIN

The
Wild Duck

A Play in Five Acts

Characters

WERLE,
a wholesale merchant and manufacturer

GREGERS WERLE,
his son

OLD EKDAL

HJALMAR EKDAL,
his son, a photographer

GINA EKDAL,
Hjalmar's wife

HEDVIG,
their daughter, a girl of fourteen

MRS. SÖRBY,
Werle's housekeeper

RELLING,
a doctor

MOLVIK,
a former student of theology

GRAABERG,
Werle's bookkeeper

PETTERSEN,
Werle's servant

JENSEN,
a hired waiter

NINE GENTLEMEN,
guests at Werle's party

SEVERAL HIRED WAITERS

The first act takes place in WERLE'S *house,*
the four following acts at HJALMAR EKDAL'S.

Act One

SCENE: *In* WERLE'S *house. A study richly and comfortably furnished; bookcases and upholstered furniture; a desk covered with papers and documents stands in the center of the room; several lamps with green shades give a subdued light. In the back wall double doors stand open, with portières drawn back. Beyond them is seen a large elegantly furnished room, brightly lighted with lamps and branched candlesticks. A small baize door down right leads to* WERLE'S *office. Down left a fireplace with a brightly burning coal fire, and above this a double door to the dining room.*

WERLE'S *servant* PETTERSEN, *in livery, and* JENSEN, *a hired waiter in black, are straightening up the room. In the large room beyond, two or three other waiters move about tidying up and lighting more candles. From the dining room comes the hum of conversation, laughter, the sound of many voices; a glass is tapped with a knife; silence follows, then a toast is proposed. Shouts of "Bravo!" and then again the buzz of conversation.*

PETTERSEN *(As he lights a lamp on the mantelpiece and replaces the shade)*: Hear that, Jensen? The old boy's on his feet again toasting Mrs. Sörby. Listen to him holding forth!

JENSEN *(Pushing forward an armchair)*: Is it true what people say? That he's sweet on her, I mean?

PETTERSEN: Hell! How should I know!

JENSEN: I'll bet he was quite a chaser in his day!

PETTERSEN: I shouldn't wonder.

JENSEN: He's giving this party for his son, I hear.

PETTERSEN: Yes; he got home yesterday.

JENSEN: I never even knew Werle had a son.

PETTERSEN: He has a son all right. But he spends most of his time up at the works, in Höjdal; he hasn't been back once; not in all the years I've worked here.

A WAITER *(In the doorway of the inner room)*: Pettersen! There's an old fellow out here—says he wants—

PETTERSEN *(Muttering)*: What is it now!

(OLD EKDAL *appears from the right in the inner room. He wears a threadbare overcoat with a turned-up collar; has on woollen mittens and carries a stick and an old fur cap. There is a brown paper parcel under his arm. He wears a dirty reddish-brown wig and has a small gray mustache.)*

PETTERSEN *(Going toward him)*: What the devil are *you* doing here?

EKDAL *(In the doorway)*: Got to get into the office, Pettersen.

PETTERSEN: The office was closed an hour ago—

EKDAL: I know—the porter told me. But Graaberg's still there, isn't he? Let me slip in this way, Pettersen—there's a good fellow! *(Points to the baize door)* Not the first time I've used this door, eh?

PETTERSEN: All right. *(Opens the door)* But when you leave, go out the other way—don't come back through here. We have company, you know.

EKDAL: Oh, yes—I know; I know. Hm! Thanks, Pettersen. Thanks, old man. You're a good friend. *(Mutters under his breath)* Ass! *(He goes into the office;* PETTERSEN *closes the door after him.)*

JENSEN: Does *he* belong to the office?

PETTERSEN: No! He just does a bit of copying now and then— when they're extra busy. Takes it home with him. Poor old Ekdal! Quite a swell in his day, he was.

JENSEN: He still has a way with him—

PETTERSEN: Yes, indeed! A military man he was. A lieutenant, no less.

JENSEN: A lieutenant! *Him?*

PETTERSEN: It's a fact. Then he went into business—something to do with timber, I believe. They say he once played

Mr. Werle a very dirty trick. They were running the
Höjdal Works together—they were partners then, you
see. Oh, I know old Ekdal well. Many's the time we've
drunk a bottle of ale at Mrs. Eriksen's; we've downed
many a glass of bitters there together he and I.

JENSEN: Shouldn't think there was much chance of a treat
from him!

PETTERSEN: Don't be a fool, Jensen! I'm the one who does the
treating. It's as well to be kind to a gent like that who's
come down in the world.

JENSEN: What happened? Did he go bankrupt?

PETTERSEN: Worse than that; he went to jail.

JENSEN: To jail!

PETTERSEN: Some kind of penitentiary, at any rate. *(Listens)* Sh!
They're getting up from table.
*(The dining room door is flung open from within by a couple of
waiters.* MRS. SÖRBY *comes out talking to two gentlemen.* WERLE
and the other guests follow gradually. Finally HJALMAR EKDAL
and GREGERS WERLE *appear.)*

MRS. SÖRBY *(In passing)*: You can serve the coffee in the music
room, Pettersen.

PETTERSEN: Very well, madam. *(She and the two gentlemen go into
the inner room and off right.* PETTERSEN *and* JENSEN *go out the
same way.)*

FAT GENTLEMAN *(To* BALD GENTLEMAN*)*: Phew! That was hard
work! Quite a meal!

BALD GENTLEMAN: With a little good will it's quite amazing
what one can put away in three hours!

FAT GENTLEMAN: Oh, my dear fellow—I'm thinking of the
aftermath!

A THIRD GENTLEMAN: They say coffee and liqueurs are being
served in the music room.

FAT GENTLEMAN: Splendid! Perhaps Mrs. Sörby will play a tune
for us.

BALD GENTLEMAN: If we aren't careful she may play us the wrong kind of tune someday!

FAT GENTLEMAN: Don't worry about Bertha! She's not the kind to go back on old friends!

WERLE *(In a low tone, dejectedly)*: I don't think anyone noticed— did they, Gregers?

GREGERS *(Looks at him)*: Noticed what?

WERLE: Then you didn't notice either?

GREGERS: No. What do you mean?

WERLE: We were thirteen at table.

GREGERS: Really? Were we?

WERLE *(With a glance toward* HJALMAR EKDAL*)*: As a rule we're never more than twelve. *(To the others)* This way, gentlemen! *(*WERLE *and the others go out through the inner room to the right. Only* HJALMAR *and* GREGERS *remain.)*

HJALMAR *(Who has overheard)*: Gregers—you shouldn't have invited me.

GREGERS: Don't be absurd! Not invite my best and only friend—? The party was given for me, wasn't it?

HJALMAR: Your father didn't approve, I'm afraid. I'm never asked to the house, you know.

GREGERS: So I gather. But I had to see you and have a talk. I'll be going away again soon—We've drifted so far apart since the old days at school. Do you realize it's sixteen or seventeen years since we last met?

HJALMAR: Is it really as long as that?

GREGERS: It is indeed! Well—how have you been? You're looking well. You've put on weight, I think; you've grown quite stout.

HJALMAR: I wouldn't exactly call it stout. I'm no longer a boy—if that's what you mean. I've filled out a bit—that's only natural.

GREGERS: Yes, of course. Well—outwardly you seem in splendid shape.

HJALMAR *(In a gloomy tone)*: But inwardly—that's another story! I don't have to tell you all that I've been through. You know all about *that* catastrophe!

GREGERS: Yes. What's happened to your father? What's he doing now?

HJALMAR: Don't speak of it! The poor, miserable old man! I look after him, of course; he lives with me. He has no one else to turn to. But it's too painful to talk about—Tell me about yourself. Have you been getting on well—up at the works?

GREGERS: I've been living in splendid isolation. I've had plenty of time for contemplation, I can tell you. Let's sit here and be comfortable. *(He sits down in an armchair by the fire, and pulls* HJALMAR *down to another one beside him.)*

HJALMAR *(Sentimentally)*: As a matter of fact, Gregers, I'm very grateful that you asked me here today. It proves that you no longer have anything against me.

GREGERS *(Surprised)*: Why on earth should you think I had anything against you?

HJALMAR: You had at first, you know.

GREGERS: At first? How do you mean?

HJALMAR: Directly after the—catastrophe. It was understandable enough. It was only by a miracle that your father escaped being dragged into all that ghastly business.

GREGERS: But that's no reason why I should have had anything against *you*. What put that into your head?

HJALMAR: I happen to know you did, Gregers. Your father told me so himself.

GREGERS: *Father* did? Well! Hm—was that why I never heard from you? Why you never wrote to me?

HJALMAR: Of course.

GREGERS: You never even told me you'd decided to take up photography.

HJALMAR: I know. Your father advised me not to write to you at all.

GREGERS *(Gazes straight before him)*: Well—well! Perhaps he was wise in that—But, tell me—are you happy in your work? Does it appeal to you, I mean?

HJALMAR *(With a sigh)*: Yes—more or less; I really can't complain. It all seemed very strange to me at first. I found myself in such totally different circumstances, you see. Father had lost absolutely everything—he was completely ruined. And then there was all the scandal—the disgrace—

GREGERS *(Moved)*: Yes, yes. I understand.

HJALMAR: I naturally had to give up my studies—I was forced to leave the university. We hadn't a penny left—nothing but debts—mostly to your father, I believe.

GREGERS: Hm.

HJALMAR: I thought it best to break off all my former friendships—sever all my old connections. In fact it was your father who advised me to do so; and since he seemed to want to help me—

GREGERS: Father did?

HJALMAR: You must be aware of that. Where was *I* to get the money to learn photography, furnish a studio, and buy all the necessary equipment? It takes quite a bit of capital to make a start, you know.

GREGERS: You mean—*Father* provided that?

HJALMAR: Of course; didn't you know? I understood him to say he'd written you about it.

GREGERS: No—he never mentioned it. He must have forgotten, I suppose. Actually we've never exchanged anything but business letters. So it was *Father* who—!

HJALMAR: Yes, it was. He didn't want it generally known, he said—but it was he. He also made it possible for me to marry. Didn't you know that either?

GREGERS: No—I didn't. *(Shakes him by the arm)* My dear Hjalmar—I can't tell you how glad I am about all this.

But I feel guilty, too. I've misjudged Father all these years—in some ways, anyhow. I thought he had no heart—no feelings. This proves me wrong. It's funny— one would almost think he was trying to atone for something—

HJALMAR: Atone?

GREGERS: Yes—it's as though he were suffering from a sense of guilt; I don't know *what* to call it. But I'm certainly delighted to hear all this about him. So you're married, are you? You're a braver man than I am! How does it feel? Are you content?

HJALMAR: Yes—I'm very happy, thank you. She's a thoroughly good wife—and very capable, as well. And, after all— she's not *entirely* without education.

GREGERS *(Rather surprised)*: No—I don't suppose she is—

HJALMAR: Life's the best education, when you come right down to it. And, being so much with me, she—And I've a couple of very brilliant friends who drop in almost every day. She's learning—Gina's learning! You'd never recognize her.

GREGERS: Gina?

HJALMAR: Yes; Gina's her name—don't you remember?

GREGERS: *Whose* name is Gina? I don't know what you're—

HJALMAR: You must remember Gina! She worked here for a while.

GREGERS *(Looks at him)*: You don't mean Gina Hansen?

HJALMAR: Gina Hansen, yes—of course.

GREGERS: —who kept house for us those last few years—when Mother was so ill?

HJALMAR: Yes, that's the one. But—my dear fellow—your father wrote you all about it; I'm *positive* he did!

GREGERS *(Who has risen)*: He wrote and told me you were married, but not that—*(Walks about the room)* Wait, though! On second thought—I think he may have—His letters were always so very brief. *(Sinks down on the arm of the chair)* Tell me, Hjalmar—this is most interesting—how did you happen to meet this Gina—your wife, I mean?

HJALMAR: It was all quite simple. Gina didn't stay here long, you know. Things were very upset here at the time— what with your mother's illness; it was all too much for Gina, so she left. It was the year before your mother died, I think; or the same year, perhaps—I'm not quite sure.

GREGERS: It was the same year; I was away—up at the works. And then what happened?

HJALMAR: Gina went home to her mother—Mrs. Hansen; an honest, hard-working woman who ran a little restaurant. They had a room to rent—a nice, comfortable room—

GREGERS: And I suppose you were lucky enough to acquire it?

HJALMAR: Yes. It was your father who recommended it. And, of course, there I got to know Gina very well.

GREGERS: And then you got engaged?

HJALMAR: Yes. It doesn't take young people long to fall in love—hm—

GREGERS *(Rises and paces about)*: Tell me—was it *after* you became engaged that Father—I mean—was it after that, that you took up photography?

HJALMAR: Yes; I had to work at something; I was anxious to have a home of my own, you see. Your father and I agreed that a photographer's career would be practical and easy. And Gina thought so too—especially as she'd done a bit of retouching herself and knew quite a lot about it.

GREGERS: So it worked out very neatly, didn't it?

HJALMAR *(Rises, pleased)*: Yes—wasn't it amazing? It really worked out very neatly!

GREGERS: No doubt of that! My father seems to have played the part of Divine Providence where you're concerned!

HJALMAR: He came to the rescue of his old friend's son. That shows what a kind heart he has!

(MRS. SÖRBY *enters arm in arm with* WERLE.)

MRS. SÖRBY: It's no use arguing, dear Mr. Werle! You mustn't stay in those bright lights another moment. It's bad for you!

WERLE *(Lets go of her arm and passes his hand over his eyes)*: You know—I believe you're right.

(PETTERSEN *and* JENSEN *carry around trays of refreshments.*)

MRS. SÖRBY *(To the guests in the inner room)*: Do come in here, gentlemen, and have some punch.

FAT GENTLEMAN *(Comes up to* MRS. SÖRBY*)*: It can't be true! No smoking? You surely don't mean to deprive us of that precious prerogative!

MRS. SÖRBY: I'm afraid it can't be helped, Your Excellency! Smoking is not allowed in Mr. Werle's sanctum.

BALD GENTLEMAN: My dear lady! And when did you inaugurate this harsh decree?

MRS. SÖRBY: After our last dinner party, Mr. Balle. Several of our guests quite overstepped the mark.

BALD GENTLEMAN: Isn't it ever permitted to overstep the mark, dear Madam Bertha! Not even by an inch or two?

MRS. SÖRBY: Never! Under any circumstances, Mr. Balle.

(Most of the guests are now gathered in the study; servants hand around glasses of punch.)

WERLE *(To* HJALMAR, *who is standing apart beside a table)*: What are you so engrossed in, Ekdal?

HJALMAR: I was just looking at this album, Mr. Werle.

BALD GENTLEMAN *(Who is wandering about)*: Ah, photographs! Of course—that's your line, isn't it?

FAT GENTLEMAN *(In an armchair)*: I do hope you've brought some of your own!

HJALMAR: No, I'm afraid I haven't.

FAT GENTLEMAN: Too bad! It's good for the digestion to look at pictures after dinner.

BALD GENTLEMAN: And it provides entertainment, too.

NEARSIGHTED GENTLEMAN: All such contributions thankfully received!

MRS. SÖRBY: In other words, gentlemen, you mean a guest should sing for his supper!

FAT GENTLEMAN: Certainly, Mrs. Sörby—especially when the supper is so excellent!

BALD GENTLEMAN: Still—when it involves one's livelihood—

MRS. SÖRBY: Of course! I quite agree! *(They go on laughing and joking.)*

GREGERS *(Softly)*: You ought to join in the conversation, Hjalmar.

HJALMAR *(Squirming)*: What have I got to talk about?

FAT GENTLEMAN: Werle—I claim that Tokay is a comparatively mild wine; don't you agree?

WERLE *(By the mantelpiece)*: Yes, I suppose so. I'll vouch for that Tokay you had today, at any rate. It's quite an exceptional vintage; an unusually good year—but I needn't tell *you* that!

FAT GENTLEMAN: I admit it had a most delicate bouquet.

HJALMAR *(Diffidently)*: Is there a difference in the years, then?

FAT GENTLEMAN *(Laughing)*: Come now! What a question!

WERLE *(Smiles, to HJALMAR)*: Fine wines are lost on you it seems!

BALD GENTLEMAN: Wines are like photographs, Mr. Ekdal—they both need sunshine. Or am I mistaken?

HJALMAR: No—light is certainly important.

MRS. SÖRBY: What about court chamberlains? I hear they thrive on sunshine too!

BALD GENTLEMAN: Such sarcasm! Is that kind?

NEARSIGHTED GENTLEMAN: Mrs. Sörby will have her joke, you know!

FAT GENTLEMAN: Yes! And at our expense! *(Wags his finger at her)* Oh, Madam Bertha! Madam Bertha!

MRS. SÖRBY: Joking apart, however, Mr. Ekdal—wines differ greatly according to the year. Old vintages are nearly always best.

NEARSIGHTED GENTLEMAN: Am *I* an old vintage, Mrs. Sörby?

MRS. SÖRBY: Far from it, Excellency!

BALD GENTLEMAN: There! You see? How about me, dear Mrs. Sörby—?

FAT GENTLEMAN: And me! What would *my* vintage be?

MRS. SÖRBY: A most sweet vintage, Excellency! *(She sips her glass of punch. The men all laugh and flirt with her.)*

WERLE: Trust Mrs. Sörby to find a way out—when she wants to! Fill up your glasses, gentlemen! See to it, Pettersen—! Drink with me, Gregers, won't you? *(GREGERS doesn't move)* And you, Ekdal—won't you join us? There was no opportunity to drink with you at dinner.

(GRAABERG, the bookkeeper, sticks his head in at the baize door.)

GRAABERG: Excuse me, sir. I'm afraid I can't get out—

WERLE: Have they locked you in again?

GRAABERG: I'm afraid so, sir—Flakstad went off with the keys.

WERLE: Never mind—come through this way.

GRAABERG: But—I'm not alone, sir; there are two of us, sir.

WERLE: It doesn't matter; come along! The two of you!

(GRAABERG and OLD EKDAL come out of the office.)

WERLE *(Involuntarily)*: Ugh!

(The laughter and talk among the guests breaks off suddenly. HJALMAR starts at the sight of his father, puts down his glass and turns toward the fireplace.)

EKDAL *(Without looking up, makes little bows to right and left as he passes through, murmuring)*: Excuse me. Came in the wrong way. Door was locked. Door locked. Excuse me. *(He and GRAABERG go into the inner room and off right.)*

WERLE *(Between his teeth)*: That blasted Graaberg!

GREGERS *(Stares open-mouthed; to* HJALMAR*)*: Surely—that couldn't have been—!

FAT GENTLEMAN: What's going on? Who *was* that?

GREGERS: Nobody; just the bookkeeper, and someone with him.

NEARSIGHTED GENTLEMAN *(To* HJALMAR*)*: Who *was* that man? Did you know him?

HJALMAR: No—I don't know—I didn't notice—

FAT GENTLEMAN *(Rising)*: What the devil's happening? *(He joins another group, who are talking under their breath.)*

MRS. SÖRBY *(To* PETTERSEN *in a whisper)*: Give him something to take home with him; something nice—you understand?

PETTERSEN *(Nods)*: I'll see to it. *(Goes out.)*

GREGERS *(Softly, with emotion, to* HJALMAR*)*: It really was he, then!

HJALMAR: Yes.

GREGERS: And you actually stood there and said you didn't know him!

HJALMAR *(In a vehement whisper)*: But how could I—!

GREGERS: —acknowledge your own father?

HJALMAR *(Miserably)*: If you were in *my* place, you—
(The conversation among the guests, which has been carried on in a low tone, now swells into forced joviality.)

BALD GENTLEMAN *(In a friendly manner approaches* HJALMAR *and* GREGERS*)*: Aha! Reminiscing about old days at college, eh? Don't you smoke, Mr. Ekdal? May I give you a light? Oh—but of course!—it's not allowed!

HJALMAR: Thank you—I don't think I—

FAT GENTLEMAN: How about reciting a poem for us, Mr. Ekdal? You used to be so good at it.

HJALMAR: I'm afraid I don't remember any.

FAT GENTLEMAN: What a pity! Well—what can we find to do, Balle? *(They move away and go into the other room.)*

HJALMAR *(Gloomily)*: I'm going, Gregers. When a man's been through what I've been through, you see—Say good-bye to your father for me.

GREGERS: Yes—of course. Do you think you'll go straight home?

HJALMAR: Yes—why do you ask?

GREGERS: I thought I might drop in a little later.

HJALMAR: No, don't do that—don't come to my place, Gregers; it's too sad and depressing there. Especially on top of all this splendor! We'll arrange to meet somewhere in town.

MRS. SÖRBY *(Comes over to them and speaks in a low voice)*: Are you going, Ekdal?

HJALMAR: Yes.

MRS. SÖRBY: Remember me to Gina.

HJALMAR: Thanks.

MRS. SÖRBY: Tell her I'll drop in one of these days.

HJALMAR: Thanks—I will. *(To* GREGERS*)* Don't come with me. I'll slip out without being seen. *(He strolls across the room, into the inner room, and out to the right.)*

MRS. SÖRBY *(In a low voice to* PETTERSEN, *who has returned)*: Did you give the old man something?

PETTERSEN: A nice bottle of brandy, Madam.

MRS. SÖRBY: You might have thought of something better than that!

PETTERSEN: Oh, no, Mrs. Sörby! He'd rather have that than anything!

FAT GENTLEMAN *(In the doorway, with a sheet of music in his hand)*: How about playing a duet, Mrs. Sörby?

MRS. SÖRBY: Yes! That would be delightful!

GUESTS: Bravo! Bravo! *(She joins the guests in the inner room and they all go out to the right.* GREGERS *remains standing by the fireplace.* WERLE *pretends to be looking for something on the desk and seems to want* GREGERS *to go;* GREGERS *doesn't move,* WERLE *goes toward the door.)*

GREGERS: Can you spare a moment, Father?

WERLE: Yes; what is it?

GREGERS: I'd like to talk to you.

WERLE: Can't it wait till we're alone?

GREGERS: No, it can't; we may never be alone again, you see.

WERLE *(Comes toward him)*: And what does *that* mean?
(During the following the sound of a piano is heard in the distance, from the music room.)

GREGERS: Why has that family been allowed to go downhill like that?

WERLE: You're referring to the Ekdals, I presume.

GREGERS: Yes; I'm referring to the Ekdals. There was a time when you and Lt. Ekdal were close friends.

WERLE: Yes; too close for comfort—I've suffered for it for years. That friendship almost cost me my good name.

GREGERS: Was he the only guilty one? You're sure of that?

WERLE: What do you mean?

GREGERS: You were in that big timber deal together, weren't you?

WERLE: Ekdal was in charge of the entire transaction. He surveyed the land—he drew up the maps. How was I to know that they were fraudulent! He deliberately encroached on property belonging to the government; he felled all that timber—acres of it!—belonging to the state. Lt. Ekdal acted entirely on his own responsibility. I never for a moment realized what he was up to.

GREGERS: Perhaps he didn't quite realize it himself.

WERLE: That may be. The fact remains that he was found guilty, and I was acquitted.

GREGERS: Yes; I know nothing was ever proved against you.

WERLE: An acquittal is an acquittal. But what makes you bring up that distressing business? God knows it turned my hair gray long before its time. Is that the kind of thing you've spent all these years brooding about up there? I assure you here in town it's been forgotten long ago—at least as far as *I'm* concerned.

GREGERS: But what about the Ekdals?

WERLE: What do you expect me to do for them? Ekdal came out of prison a broken man; he was beyond all help. There are certain people in this world who, given the slightest blow, dive straight to the bottom and never come up again. Believe me, Gregers, I did everything I could—short of exposing myself to suspicion and endless gossip—

GREGERS: Suspicion? Yes—I see.

WERLE: I've arranged for Ekdal to do some odd jobs for the office—copying and so forth—and I pay him ten times what the work is worth—

GREGERS *(Without looking at him)*: I don't doubt *that* for a moment.

WERLE: Why do you laugh? Do you think I'm not telling you the truth? I admit there's no record of it on the books; I never enter payments of that sort.

GREGERS *(With a cold smile)*: You're very wise.

WERLE *(Taken aback)*: What do you mean?

GREGERS *(Summoning up his courage)*: How about the money you gave Hjalmar Ekdal to learn photography? Is *that* entered on the books?

WERLE: Entered—how? I don't—

GREGERS: I know now it was you who paid for his tuition; I also know that it was you who set him up in business.

WERLE: And you call that doing nothing for the Ekdals! Those people have cost me plenty, I assure you!

GREGERS: And are *those* expenses entered on the books?

WERLE: Why do you ask me that?

GREGERS: I have my reasons. Now, tell me: when you evinced

this sudden interest in your old friend's son—it was just before his marriage, wasn't it?

WERLE: Good heavens! You don't expect me—after all, it's years ago—!

GREGERS: You wrote me a letter at that time—a business letter, naturally—and you mentioned briefly, in a postscript, that Hjalmar Ekdal had married a Miss Hansen.

WERLE: Quite right. That was her name.

GREGERS: But you omitted the fact that this Miss Hansen was *Gina* Hansen—our former housekeeper.

WERLE *(With a slightly forced laugh of derision)*: It never occurred to me you were so interested in our former housekeeper.

GREGERS: You're right; I wasn't. But—*(Lowers his voice)* I happen to know there were others in this house who were; *extremely* interested.

WERLE: What do you mean by that? *(Flaring up)* You're not referring to *me*, by any chance?

GREGERS *(Softly but firmly)*: But I *am* referring to you.

WERLE: How *dare* you! How dare you presume to—! I'll teach that photographer fellow—ungrateful wretch! Spreading lies about me—!

GREGERS: Hjalmar hasn't said a single word about it. I'm certain he hasn't the faintest suspicion of such a thing.

WERLE: Then where did you get it from? Who put such ideas into your head?

GREGERS: It was poor Mother; it was she who told me about it; the very last time I ever saw her.

WERLE: Your mother! Yes—of course. I might have known. You and she—! You always held together. She turned you against me from the start.

GREGERS: That's not true; it was because of all she suffered—all she had to bear; till she broke down and went utterly to pieces.

WERLE: Nonsense! She had no more to bear, and she suffered no more than the majority of women. But it's impossible to deal with sickly, hysterical people—I've learned that to my cost!—How could you harbor these suspicions— how could you bring yourself to rake up all these malicious rumors against your own father, Gregers? I don't understand it. I should think at your age you could apply yourself to something more constructive.

GREGERS: It's about time, isn't it?

WERLE: It would do you good; I'm sure you'd feel much happier. What do you expect to accomplish up there at the works, slaving away year after year at a routine office job? Refusing to accept a penny above the regular wages? It's sheer madness!

GREGERS: Yes; well—I'm not so sure of that.

WERLE: I understand your reasons well enough; you don't want to owe me anything; you want to be completely independent—Now, it so happens, an excellent opportunity has opened up; one that would give you complete independence—full authority.

GREGERS: Indeed? What kind of opportunity?

WERLE: In my last letter—when I said it was essential for you to come back home at once—

GREGERS: Yes; what had you in mind? I've been waiting all day for you to tell me.

WERLE: What I had in mind was this: I propose to offer you a partnership.

GREGERS: In *your* firm? A partnership with *you?*

WERLE: It needn't be too *close* a partnership; we wouldn't necessarily have to work *together.* You could handle the business here, and I would move up to the works.

GREGERS: To the works? *You?*

WERLE: Yes; I no longer have the strength I used to have. It's time I started to let down a bit, you see. And I have to be careful of my eyes—they've been bad lately; I've had a lot of trouble with them.

GREGERS: That's nothing new; they've always troubled you.

WERLE: But not as they do now. There are other circumstances, too, that make it advisable for me to move up there—for a while, at any rate.

GREGERS: I certainly never expected anything like this.

WERLE: We've never been close—I know that, Gregers; but, after all, we *are* father and son. There must be some way we can come to an understanding.

GREGERS: In the eyes of the world, I suppose you mean.

WERLE: Well—at least that would be something, wouldn't it? Think it over, Gregers. I'm sure we can manage it. Don't you agree?

GREGERS *(Looks at him coldly)*: What's your real motive in all this?

WERLE: My motive?

GREGERS: You're depending on me for something. You plan to make use of me somehow.

WERLE: It's only natural for a father to depend upon his son.

GREGERS: Yes—so they say.

WERLE: I'm most anxious that you should stay home with me a little while. I'm very lonely, Gregers. All my life I've been a lonely man—and one feels it more as one gets older. I need someone near me—someone who—

GREGERS: You have Mrs. Sörby, haven't you?

WERLE: That's true—I have; and I don't know what I'd do without her. She's good-natured and intelligent; and she's so cheerful too—that means a lot to me.

GREGERS: Then what more do you want?

WERLE: But it's an awkward situation—for her, I mean. I'm afraid it can't go on much longer. It puts her in a false position—there might be talk. And that kind of thing doesn't do a man any good either.

GREGERS: I think you can afford to risk it! As long as you go on giving the dinner parties you can give.

WERLE: But what about *her*, Gregers? I'm afraid she may find it impossible to accept the situation any longer. And even if her affection for me prompted her to stay—at the risk of talk and scandal and all the rest of it—would I be justified in—? You, with your high sense of integrity, tell me—?

GREGERS: You're thinking of marrying her, aren't you? Why not say so?

WERLE: And supposing I were? What then?

GREGERS: What then? Exactly!

WERLE: Would you be unalterably opposed to it?

GREGERS: By no means. Not at all.

WERLE: I wasn't sure. I thought perhaps—devotion to your mother's memory—

GREGERS: I'm not hysterical, you know.

WERLE: Well—whatever you may or may not be—you've taken a great weight off my mind. I'm delighted to know I can depend on your support.

GREGERS *(Looks at him intently)*: Of course! *That's* how you plan to use me!

WERLE: Use you, indeed! What an expression!

GREGERS: Don't let's be fussy in our choice of words—not when we're alone, at any rate. *(With a short laugh)* Yes! Now I see! That's why it was so absolutely essential for me to come back here. We are to play the "Happy Family" in Mrs. Sörby's honor! The devoted father and the loving son! A touching picture! A new experience, indeed!

WERLE: Don't take that tone with me!

GREGERS: When was there ever a "Happy Family" in this

house I'd like to know? Never—so far as I remember! But your plans require something of the sort. It'll make such a good impression—won't it? The beloved son rushing home to attend his dear old father's wedding! And what of all those ugly rumors about the miseries and torments the first wife had to bear? It'd be the end of them, wouldn't it? They'd be wiped out once and for all—and by her own son too!

WERLE: I don't think there's a man living you hate as much as you hate me.

GREGERS *(Softly)*: I've seen you at close range.

WERLE: You've seen me through your mother's eyes. *(Lowers his voice a little)* You should remember that those eyes were—shall we say "clouded," now and then?

GREGERS *(Trembling)*: I know what you're implying. But who was responsible for Mother's tragic weakness? It was you, and all your—! The last of them being that woman you palmed off on Hjalmar Ekdal when you no longer—! Pah!

WERLE *(Shrugs his shoulders)*: I hear your mother in every word you say.

GREGERS *(Takes no notice of him)*: Yes! And he's there now—with that noble, trusting, childlike mind of his—living under the same roof with that degraded creature—quite unaware that what he calls his home is built on nothing but a lie! *(Comes a step nearer)* When I look back on all the wicked things you've done, I feel as though I were gazing at some ghastly battlefield—strewn with shattered corpses!

WERLE: I'm afraid the gulf between us is too wide to bridge.

GREGERS *(Bowing stiffly)*: I share that opinion; so I shall take my hat and go.

WERLE: Go? Leave the house, you mean?

GREGERS: Yes. My purpose in life is clear to me at last.

WERLE: What purpose, may I ask?

GREGERS: You'd only laugh if I told you.

WERLE: I don't know, Gregers; a lonely man doesn't laugh so easily.

GREGERS *(Points toward the inner room)*: Look, Father! Your distinguished guests are playing blindman's buff with Mrs. Sörby—Good night and good-bye.

(He goes out by the back to the right. Sounds of laughter and gay conversation from the guests, who are now seen in the inner room.)

WERLE *(Mutters contemptuously)*: Ha—! He's not hysterical, eh? Poor fellow!

CURTAIN

Act Two

SCENE: HJALMAR EKDAL'S *studio. It is a good-sized room evidently on the top floor of the building. On the right a large studio window is let into the sloping roof; it is half covered by a blue curtain. In the right-hand corner at the back is the hall door. Farther downstage on the same side is a door leading to the sitting room. Two doors on the opposite side and between them an iron stove. At the back a wide double door with sliding panels. The studio is plainly but comfortably fitted out and furnished. Between the doors on the right, standing out a little from the wall, a sofa with a table and some chairs; on the table a lighted lamp with a shade; beside the stove an old armchair. Photographic instruments and equipment of different kinds lying about the room. Against the back wall, to the left of the double door, stands a bookcase containing a few books, boxes and bottles of chemicals, instruments, tools and other objects. Photographs and small articles such as camel's hair brushes, paper and so forth, lie on the table.*

GINA EKDAL *sits on a chair by the table sewing.* HEDVIG *is sitting on the sofa, with her hands shading her eyes and her thumbs in her ears, reading a book.*

GINA *(Glances at her a couple of times as if in secret anxiety)*: Hedvig!

HEDVIG *(Doesn't hear her.)*

GINA *(Louder)*: Hedvig!

HEDVIG *(Takes away her hands and looks up)*: Yes, Mother?

GINA: You mustn't go on reading any longer, Hedvig dear.

HEDVIG: Oh, just a *little* longer, Mother! A *tiny* bit longer—please!

GINA: No; put your book down now—there's a good girl. Your father'd be angry. *He* never reads of an evening, you know.

HEDVIG *(Closes the book)*: But Father doesn't care much for reading.

208

GINA *(Lays aside her sewing and takes up a pencil and a little account book from the table)*: How much was the butter today—do you remember?

HEDVIG: One sixty-five.

GINA: That's right. *(Marks it down)* We certainly use enough butter in the house! Then there was the sausage, and the cheese—let's see—*(Puts it down)*—and then the ham— *(Adding up)* that comes to nearly—

HEDVIG: And don't forget the beer—

GINA: Oh, yes—of course. *(Puts it down)* It mounts up all right! Well—it can't be helped!

HEDVIG: But since Father was out to dinner, we saved a bit on that.

GINA: Yes, that's true. And I took in eight fifty for those photographs.

HEDVIG: Did you? As much as that!

GINA: Yes; eight fifty exactly.

(A pause. GINA *picks up her sewing again.* HEDVIG *takes a pencil and a piece of paper and starts to draw, shading her eyes with her left hand.)*

HEDVIG: It's fun to think of Father at Mr. Werle's; at that grand dinner party—isn't it?

GINA: But it wasn't really Mr. Werle who invited him—it was his son. *(After a pause)* We have nothing to do with Mr. Werle.

HEDVIG: I do hope Father'll come home soon; I'm looking forward to it. He promised he'd ask Mrs. Sörby to give him something nice for me.

GINA: They've plenty of good things to spare in *that* house!

HEDVIG *(Goes on drawing)*: I'm beginning to be a bit hungry, too.

*(*OLD EKDAL *comes in by the hall door. He has a paper parcel under his arm, and another parcel in his coat pocket.)*

GINA: Why Grandfather! How late you are today!

EKDAL: They'd locked the office. Had to wait in Graaberg's room. Then had to go through—hm.

HEDVIG: Grandfather—did they give you some more copying to do?

EKDAL: All of this—look!

GINA: Good!

HEDVIG: And you've got a parcel in your pocket, too.

EKDAL: Never mind that! That's nothing. *(Puts his stick away in a corner)* This'll keep me busy quite a while, Gina—eh? *(Opens one of the sliding panels in the back wall a little)* Hush! *(Peeps inside the opening for a moment and slides the panel closed again)* He! he! They've all gone to sleep together. And she's gone into her basket of her own accord. He! he!

HEDVIG: You're sure she's not cold in that basket, Grandfather?

EKDAL: What nonsense! Cold? In all that straw? *(He goes toward the farthest door on the left)* Are there any matches in there?

GINA: On the chest of drawers.

(EKDAL goes into his room.)

HEDVIG: I'm glad Grandfather got all that copying to do.

GINA: Yes, poor old Grandfather. At least it'll mean a little pocket money for him.

HEDVIG: And it'll keep him from hanging round that horrid bar at Mrs. Eriksen's.

GINA: That's true, too.

HEDVIG: Do you suppose they're still sitting at the dinner table, Mother?

GINA: Lord knows; I shouldn't wonder.

HEDVIG: I expect Father's having some lovely things to eat! He'll be in an awfully jolly mood when he gets home. Don't you think so, Mother?

GINA: Yes. But I wish we could tell him that room was rented.

HEDVIG: Oh, we shan't need that this evening.

GINA: It'd be a real help, you know. And we don't use it.

HEDVIG: No—I meant we won't need it this evening, because he'll be in a good mood anyway. The news about the room'll come in handy another time.

GINA *(Looks up at her)*: You like having a bit of good news to tell your father, don't you?

HEDVIG: It makes things pleasanter.

GINA *(Thinks this over)*: There's something in that.
(OLD EKDAL comes in again and starts toward the door down left.)

GINA *(Half turning in her chair)*: Do you want anything in the kitchen, Grandfather?

EKDAL: I just want—No! Don't get up! *(Goes out.)*

GINA: I hope he won't go messing about the stove. *(Waits a moment)* Better go and see what he's up to, Hedvig.
(EKDAL comes in again carrying a small jug of steaming hot water.)

HEDVIG: Did you go to get hot water, Grandfather?

EKDAL: I did—yes. Need it for something. Got to do some writing; ink's as thick as porridge—hm.

GINA: But you'll eat your supper first, won't you, Grandfather? It's in there ready for you.

EKDAL: Can't be bothered with supper, Gina. Busy, I tell you. Don't want anyone coming in my room—not anyone—hm.
(He goes into his room. GINA and HEDVIG look at each other.)

GINA *(Softly)*: Wonder where he got the money.

HEDVIG: From Graaberg, I suppose.

GINA: No! Graaberg always sends *me* his money.

HEDVIG: Then he got it on credit, I expect.

GINA: Poor Grandfather, who'd give *him* credit?

(HJALMAR EKDAL, *wearing an overcoat and a gray felt hat, comes in from the hall door.*)

GINA (*Throws down her sewing and rises*): Why, Hjalmar! Are you back so soon?

HEDVIG (*Jumps up at the same time*): Fancy your being back already, Father!

HJALMAR (*Taking off his hat*): Most of the guests were leaving.

HEDVIG: So early?

HJALMAR: Well—it was an early dinner, after all. (*Starts to take off his overcoat.*)

GINA: Let me help you.

HEDVIG: Me too! (*They help him off with his coat;* GINA *hangs it up on a hook on the back wall.*)

HEDVIG: Were there a lot of people, Father?

HJALMAR: No, not many; about twelve or fourteen, I should think.

GINA: I suppose you had a chance to talk to all of them?

HJALMAR: Yes, of course. Though I must say Gregers took up most of my time.

GINA: Is he just as plain as ever?

HJALMAR: I can't say he's particularly handsome—Isn't the old man home yet?

HEDVIG: Yes; Grandfather's in his room. He's busy writing.

HJALMAR: Did he say anything?

GINA: What about?

HJALMAR: Then he didn't mention—? I heard something about his being with Graaberg, you see. I'll just look in on him a minute.

GINA: No—I don't think I'd do that—

HJALMAR: Why not? Did he say he didn't want to see me?

GINA: He doesn't want to see *anyone* this evening—

HEDVIG *(Signaling)*: Hm—hm!

GINA *(Not noticing)*: He fetched himself some hot water from the kitchen.

HJALMAR: You mean he's—?

GINA: Yes—I suppose so.

HJALMAR: Ah, well! Poor old man! My poor old father! Let him be—If it makes him a little happier—!
(OLD EKDAL, in a dressing gown and smoking a pipe, comes in from his room.)

EKDAL: Home, are you? Thought I heard your voice.

HJALMAR: I just got back.

EKDAL: You didn't see me, did you?

HJALMAR: No; but someone told me you'd passed through, so I thought I'd come on after you.

EKDAL: Hm. Nice of you, Hjalmar—Who were all those people?

HJALMAR: Oh, I don't know—just people. There was Court Chamberlain Balle; and then there was Flor—and Kaspersen—they're court chamberlains too—honorary, of course. I don't remember all the others—but I know most of them had titles of some sort.

EKDAL: Titled people, eh? D'you hear that, Gina?

GINA: Yes. They're very grand over there these days.

HEDVIG: What did all these titled people do, Father? Did they sing—or give recitations?

HJALMAR: No; they just talked a lot of rubbish. They tried to persuade me to recite something—but, of course, I wouldn't hear of that.

EKDAL: Wouldn't hear of that, eh?

GINA: Oh—perhaps you should have, Hjalmar.

HJALMAR: Certainly not. One shouldn't cater to every Tom, Dick and Harry. *(Paces about the room)* I don't intend to, anyhow.

EKDAL: No; Hjalmar's not that kind.

HJALMAR: I see no reason why *I* should be expected to entertain the guests, on the rare occasions when I go into Society. That's up to those other fellows; they spend their lives going from one dinner table to another, gorging and guzzling day in and day out. It's only right they should do something to earn all that good food they eat.

GINA: I hope you didn't tell them that!

HJALMAR *(Humming)*: Hm-hm-hm—I think I made my position clear.

EKDAL: To all those titled people, eh?

HJALMAR: Why not? *(Casually)* We also had a slight argument about Tokay.

EKDAL: Tokay! There's a fine wine!

HJALMAR: Yes—it *can* be. It's all according to the year, of course; vintages differ. It depends on the amount of sunshine the grapes have.

GINA: Hjalmar—I believe there's nothing you don't know!

EKDAL: They surely didn't dispute that?

HJALMAR: Oh—they tried to; but they were reminded that there was a difference in the vintage of court chamberlains too; their quality also varies according to the year—so they were told.

GINA: The things you think up, Hjalmar!

EKDAL: He! he! You really gave it to them, eh?

HJALMAR: Straight in their silly faces!

EKDAL: Hear that, Gina? All those titled people! Straight in their silly faces!

GINA: Straight in their silly faces! Fancy!

HJALMAR: I wouldn't want this to go any further, mind you. It's not right to repeat things like that; and it was all perfectly amicable, of course. They're nice friendly fellows; I wouldn't want to hurt their feelings.

EKDAL: But—straight in their silly faces, eh?

HEDVIG *(Ingratiatingly)*: It's nice to see you in a dinner jacket, Father. It's so becoming to you!

HJALMAR: It is, isn't it? This one fits beautifully—almost as if it had been made for me—A little tight in the armholes, perhaps. Here—help me, Hedvig. *(Takes off the dinner jacket)* I'll put on my old house coat. Where is it, Gina?

GINA: Here it is. *(Brings him the coat and helps him on with it.)*

HJALMAR: There we are! See that Molvik gets his jacket back first thing in the morning.

GINA *(Laying it away)*: I'll see to it.

HJALMAR *(Stretching himself)*: Ah! That feels more comfortable! And you know—I really think a loose, casual coat like this suits my figure even better. What do *you* think, Hedvig?

HEDVIG: Yes, Father—I believe you're right!

HJALMAR: Now—I'll tie my necktie in a loose knot, with flowing ends—There! See?

HEDVIG: That looks lovely with your mustache, and your long curly hair!

HJALMAR: I don't think I'd call it *curly;* wavy, perhaps.

HEDVIG: Yes. They're too big for curls.

HJALMAR: *Wavy*—definitely.

HEDVIG *(After a pause, tugs at his coat)*: Father!

HJALMAR: Well—what is it?

HEDVIG: Oh! *You* know what it is!

HJALMAR: No, I don't—

HEDVIG *(Half laughing, half whimpering)*: Father—please don't tease me any longer!

HJALMAR: I don't know what you mean.

HEDVIG *(Shaking him)*: Of course you do! Oh, please, Father! Aren't you going to give them to me? All those nice things you promised to bring home?

HJALMAR: Good Lord!—I forgot about them!

HEDVIG: You're only teasing me! It's mean of you! Where are they?

HJALMAR: No, honestly—I really *did* forget. But, wait! I've brought you something else. *(He goes and looks in the pockets of the dinner jacket.)*

HEDVIG *(Jumps up and down, clapping her hands)*: Oh, Mother, Mother!

GINA: You see; if you're just patient—

HJALMAR *(With a piece of paper)*: Look—here it is.

HEDVIG: This? But it's just a piece of paper.

HJALMAR: It's the bill of fare, that's what it is—the entire bill of fare. Do you see—it says here: menu? That means bill of fare.

HEDVIG: Is that really all you brought?

HJALMAR: I told you—I forgot. But you just take it from me—all these fancy dishes are greatly overrated. Now you sit at the table and study the bill of fare, and I'll tell you what all the dishes taste like. Won't that be fun?

HEDVIG *(Gulping down her tears)*: Thanks.
(She sits down, but doesn't read the menu. GINA *signals to her;* HJALMAR *sees her.)*

HJALMAR *(Pacing up and down the room)*: The head of the family is expected to think of everything—it's quite amazing! If by chance he forgets the slightest thing, he's immediately surrounded by glum faces. Well—one has to get used to it, I suppose. *(Stops by the stove near the old man)* Have you taken a look in there this evening, Father?

EKDAL: You bet I have! She's in her basket!

HJALMAR: No! Is she really? Then she's beginning to get used to it.

EKDAL: Told you she would, didn't I? But there are still a couple of little things—

HJALMAR: A few improvements—yes.

EKDAL: They *must* be done, you know.

216

HJALMAR: Yes—let's just go over them. We'll sit here on the sofa.

EKDAL: All right. Hm. First I'll fill my pipe. Got to clean it, too. Hm. *(Goes into his room.)*

GINA *(Smiles, to HJALMAR)*: His pipe, indeed!

HJALMAR: Leave him alone, Gina—never mind! Poor wretched old man!—About those improvements—yes. I think I'll have a go at them tomorrow.

GINA: You won't have time tomorrow, Hjalmar.

HEDVIG: Oh, yes he will, Mother!

GINA: Those prints have got to be retouched; they've sent for them several times, you know.

HJALMAR: Oh, do stop nagging me about those prints! I'll get them done. Anything happen today? Any new orders?

GINA: No; I'm afraid not. I have those two sittings for tomorrow, though.

HJALMAR: And that's all, eh? Of course—if no one makes the smallest effort—

GINA: But what more can I do? I've advertised in several papers—all we could afford.

HJALMAR: Advertising! A lot of good *that* does! And what about the room? I suppose nothing's happened about that either?

GINA: Not yet, no.

HJALMAR: What else can one expect? Rooms don't rent themselves! Everything requires a little effort, Gina!

HEDVIG *(Going toward him)*: Would you like me to fetch your flute, Father?

HJALMAR: No thanks. No flute for me; no pleasures of any sort for *me*. *(Pacing about)* All I have to look forward to is *work*. As long as my strength holds out, I suppose I'll have to keep on working—!

GINA: Hjalmar dear—I didn't mean—

HEDVIG: Let me get you a nice bottle of beer, Father.

HJALMAR: No; not for me. I require nothing—*(Stops)* Beer?—Beer did you say?

HEDVIG *(Cheerfully)*: Yes, Father. Nice, cool beer.

HJALMAR: Oh, very well—if you insist; you might bring in a bottle.

GINA: Yes, do. That would be very nice.

(HEDVIG runs toward the kitchen door.)

HJALMAR *(By the stove, stops her, puts his arm around her and draws her to him)*: Hedvig! Hedvig!

HEDVIG *(With tears of joy)*: Dear, *darling* Father!

HJALMAR: No—don't call me that. I sat there at the rich man's table—stuffing myself at that festive board—and I couldn't even—!

GINA *(Sitting at the table)*: Oh, don't talk nonsense, Hjalmar!

HJALMAR: No—it's not nonsense! But don't be too hard on me. You know how much I love you—

HEDVIG *(Throws her arms around him)*: And we love you too, Father! More than we can ever say!

HJALMAR: And remember—if I'm difficult at times—it's because I have so many problems—so many cares. There, there! *(Dries his eyes)* No! No beer at a time like this—give me my flute. *(HEDVIG runs to the bookshelf and fetches it.)* Thanks! There! That's right—my flute in my hand, and you two at my side—!

(HEDVIG sits at the table near GINA; HJALMAR walks up and down and starts to play with gusto; it is a Bohemian peasant dance; his tempo is slow and plaintive and his attack highly sentimental. He breaks off in the middle of the tune, gives his left hand to GINA and says emotionally) Our rooms may be poor and humble, Gina—but they're home all the same. And I can say from the bottom of my heart: it's good to be here!

(He starts to play again; soon after there is a knock at the hall door.)

GINA *(Rises)*: Just a minute, Hjalmar. I think there's someone at the door.

HJALMAR *(Puts the flute back on the shelf)*: Who can it be? How tiresome!

(GINA goes and opens the door.)

GREGERS: Excuse me—

GINA *(Takes a step back)*: Oh!

GREGERS: Does Mr. Ekdal, the photographer, live here?

GINA: Yes, he does.

HJALMAR *(Going toward the door)*: Gregers! So you came after all. Well—come in then.

GREGERS *(Coming in)*: I said I'd come to see you.

HJALMAR: Yes, but this evening—? Did you leave the party?

GREGERS: Both the party and my father's house—Good evening; do you recognize me, Mrs. Ekdal?

GINA: It's not hard to recognize young Mr. Werle.

GREGERS: That's true—I'm very like my mother; you remember her, I expect?

HJALMAR: Left your father's house you say?

GREGERS: Yes; I've gone to a hotel.

HJALMAR: Have you really? Well—since you're here, sit down; take off your things.

GREGERS: Thanks. *(He takes off his overcoat. He has changed his clothes and now wears a plain tweed suit.)*

HJALMAR: Here—sit on the sofa. Make yourself at home.

(GREGERS sits on the sofa, HJALMAR on a chair by the table.)

GREGERS *(Looking around)*: So this is your home, Hjalmar. This is where you live.

HJALMAR: Yes; this is the studio, of course—

GINA: But it's such a nice large room—we nearly always sit here.

HJALMAR: We had a better place before; but this has great advantages; there's a lot of extra space—

GINA: And there's another room we can rent out—just down the passage.

GREGERS: Oh—you have lodgers then?

HJALMAR: Well—not just now. They're not so easy to find, you know; you have to keep your wits about you. *(To* HEDVIG*)* We might have that beer now. *(*HEDVIG *nods and goes out to the kitchen.)*

GREGERS: Is that your daughter?

HJALMAR: That's Hedvig, yes.

GREGERS: Is she your only child?

HJALMAR: Yes; she's the only one. She's our greatest joy, and—*(Lowers his voice)* our greatest sorrow too.

GREGERS: How do you mean?

HJALMAR: She's in danger of losing her eyesight, you see.

GREGERS: Of going blind!

HJALMAR: Yes; so far her eyes are not too seriously affected, and they may continue to be all right for a while; but eventually, the doctor says, it's bound to come.

GREGERS: What a dreadful thing! Has he any idea what caused it?

HJALMAR *(Sighs)*: It may be hereditary, he thinks.

GREGERS *(With a slight start)*: Hereditary?

GINA: Hjalmar's mother's eyes were bad, you see.

HJALMAR: So Father says. I don't remember her.

GREGERS: Poor child!—How does she take it?

HJALMAR: We naturally haven't told her anything about it; she suspects nothing. She's like a gay, carefree little bird, twittering away as it flutters toward the inevitable darkness. *(Overcome)* It's a terrible grief for me; it's heartbreaking to think of, Gregers.
*(*HEDVIG *brings in a tray with beer and glasses and puts it on the table.)*

HJALMAR *(Stroking her hair)*: Thank you, Hedvig, thank you!
*(*HEDVIG *puts her arm around his neck and whispers in his ear.)*

HJALMAR: No—no sandwiches now. *(Looks at* GREGERS*)* Unless you'd like one, Gregers?

GREGERS *(With a gesture of refusal)*: No—no thank you.

HJALMAR *(Still melancholy)*: You might bring a few anyway—especially if there's a nice crusty piece of bread. And don't spare the butter, will you?

*(*HEDVIG *nods gaily and goes out to the kitchen.)*

GREGERS *(Who has been following her with his eyes)*: She seems so strong and healthy otherwise.

GINA: There's nothing wrong with her apart from that, thank goodness.

GREGERS: She'll grow up to look like you—don't you think so, Mrs. Ekdal? How old is she now?

GINA: Nearly fourteen; her birthday's the day after tomorrow.

GREGERS: Tall for her age, isn't she?

GINA: She's shot up very fast in the past year.

GREGERS: It makes one feel old to see the youngsters growing up. How long is it now since you were married?

GINA: Let's see—we've been married nearly fifteen years.

GREGERS: Really! Is it as long as that?

GINA *(Becoming attentive; looks at him)*: It is indeed.

HJALMAR: That's right. Fifteen years—all but a few months. *(Changing the subject)* They must have been long years for you, Gregers—up there at the works.

GREGERS: They seemed long at the time; yet in looking back at them, they went by very quickly.

*(*OLD EKDAL *comes in from his room, without his pipe, but wearing his old military cap; his walk is a bit unsteady.)*

EKDAL: All right, Hjalmar my boy—I'm ready now to talk about those—hm. What was it we were supposed to talk about?

HJALMAR *(Goes to him)*: Father—we have a visitor; Gregers Werle—I don't know if you remember him—

EKDAL *(Looks at* GREGERS, *who has risen)*: Werle? The son is it? What does he want with me?

221

HJALMAR: Nothing; he came to see me, Father.

EKDAL: Oh. Then there's nothing wrong?

HJALMAR: Of course not.

EKDAL *(Waves his arms)*: Not that I'm afraid, you know—but—

GREGERS *(Goes over to him)*: I bring you greetings from your old hunting grounds, Lt. Ekdal.

EKDAL: Hunting grounds?

GREGERS: Yes—up by the Höjdal Works; remember?

EKDAL: Oh, up there. I was well known in those parts once.

GREGERS: You were a mighty hunter in those days.

EKDAL: I was; that's true enough! You're looking at my cap, I see. I ask no one's permission to wear it in the house. As long as I don't walk about the streets in it—

(HEDVIG brings in a plate of sandwiches and sets it on the table.)

HJALMAR: Sit down, Father; have a glass of beer. Help yourself, Gregers.

(EKDAL mutters something and stumbles over to the sofa, GREGERS sits on the chair nearest to him, and HJALMAR on the other side of GREGERS. GINA sits slightly away from the table with her sewing; HEDVIG stands by her father.)

GREGERS: Do you remember, Lt. Ekdal, how Hjalmar and I used to come up and visit you—in the summer, and at Christmas?

EKDAL: Did you? No—I don't remember that. Yes—I was a mighty hunter in my day. Shot bears too. Nine of them.

GREGERS *(Looks at him sympathetically)*: I suppose you don't go hunting any more.

EKDAL: I wouldn't say that, my friend. I still get a bit of hunting now and then. Not *that* kind, of course. For the forest, you see—the forest—! *(Drinks)* Is the forest up there just as fine as ever?

GREGERS: Not as fine as it was in your time. It's been thinned out quite a bit.

EKDAL: Thinned out, eh? *(Softly, as though afraid)* That's a dangerous business. That brings trouble. The forest takes revenge, you see.

HJALMAR *(Filling his glass)*: Have a little more, Father.

GREGERS: It must be hard on a man like you—a man used to the open—to live in a stuffy town, cooped up in a little room—

EKDAL *(Laughs and glances at* HJALMAR*)*: Oh, it's really not so bad here. No. Not bad at all.

GREGERS: But don't you miss the open spaces—the cool sweep of the wind through the trees—and all the animals and birds—?

EKDAL *(Smiles)*: Let's show it to him, Hjalmar.

HJALMAR *(Hastily, with some embarrassment)*: No—not this evening, Father.

GREGERS: What is it he wants to show me?

HJALMAR: Oh, nothing—you can see it some other time.

GREGERS *(Goes on talking to the old man)*: Do you know what I was thinking, Lt. Ekdal? Why don't you come up to the works with me? I expect to be going back there soon. They'll have plenty of copying for you to do up there, I'm sure. This is no place for you. You've nothing here to cheer you up—or keep you interested.

EKDAL *(Looks at him in amazement)*: Nothing here to keep me—!

GREGERS: You have Hjalmar here I know; but he has his own work to attend to. And a man like you—accustomed to an active outdoor life—

EKDAL *(Thumps the table)*: Hjalmar—he's *got* to see it!

HJALMAR: This is a bad time, Father. It's dark, remember—

EKDAL: Nonsense! There's the moonlight, isn't there? *(Rises)* I tell you he *must* see it! Let me get by. Hjalmar—come and help me!

HEDVIG: Yes—*do*, Father!

HJALMAR *(Rising)*: Oh! very well.

GREGERS *(To* GINA*)*: What can it be?

GINA: It's nothing very wonderful—!

*(*EKDAL *and* HJALMAR *have gone to the back wall and each opens his side of the sliding door.* HEDVIG *helps the old man;* GREGERS *remains standing by the sofa;* GINA *continues sewing undisturbed. Through the opening one sees a large, deep, irregularly shaped attic, filled with nooks and corners; a couple of stovepipes run through it from the rooms below. There are skylights through which the moon shines brightly on parts of the big room—while other parts are in deep shadow.)*

EKDAL *(To* GREGERS*)*: Come closer, if you like.

GREGERS *(Going over to them)*: What is it I'm supposed to see?

EKDAL: Take a good look now! Hm.

HJALMAR *(Somewhat embarrassed)*: All this belongs to Father— you realize that, of course.

GREGERS *(At the opening peers into the attic)*: Oh! I *see*, Lt. Ekdal— you keep poultry!

EKDAL: I should say we *do* keep poultry! They've gone to roost now—but you should see our hens by daylight!

HEDVIG: And then there's—

EKDAL: Sh! Not a word about that yet!

GREGERS: And I see doves there, too.

EKDAL: Yes! There are doves there right enough! Their nesting boxes are up under the eaves. Doves like to roost high, you know.

HJALMAR: They're not a common variety, by any means; at least not all of them.

EKDAL: Common! No indeed! We have tumblers—and a pair of pouters too. And now—look here! You see that hutch over by the wall?

GREGERS: What's that used for?

EKDAL: That, sir, is where the rabbits sleep at night.

GREGERS: Then you have rabbits, too?

EKDAL: I should damn well say we *do* have rabbits! He wants to know if we have rabbits, Hjalmar! Hm. But just you wait! We're coming to the *real* thing now! Out of the way, Hedvig! Now you stand here—that's it. And look down there—Do you see a basket there with straw in it?

GREGERS: Yes—and isn't there a bird there, too?

EKDAL: Hm. "A bird," he says—!

GREGERS: It's a duck, isn't it?

EKDAL *(Annoyed)*: Yes—it's a duck; that's clear!

HJALMAR: But what *kind* of a duck do you think?

HEDVIG: It's not just an *ordinary* duck, you know—

EKDAL: Sh!

GREGERS: And it doesn't look like a Muscovy duck, either.

EKDAL: No—it's no Muscovy duck, dear Mr. Werle. It happens to be a *wild* duck, you see.

GREGERS: A wild duck! Is it really?

EKDAL: That's what it is! That "bird," as you called it, that is the wild duck. It's our wild duck, sir.

HEDVIG: *My* wild duck. It belongs to me.

GREGERS: How does it manage in there? Is it all right?

EKDAL: It has its own trough of water, of course, to splash about in.

HJALMAR: And we change the water every other day.

GINA *(Turning toward* HJALMAR*)*: It's getting to be freezing in here, Hjalmar dear.

HJALMAR: Let's close her up, then. Anyway—they don't like to be disturbed at night. Go on, Hedvig—close her up! *(*HJALMAR *and* HEDVIG *close the sliding doors.)*

EKDAL: You'll be able to see her better some other time. *(Sits in the armchair by the stove)* Remarkable creatures those wild ducks, I can tell you!

GREGERS: How did you manage to catch it, Lt. Ekdal?

225

EKDAL: I didn't catch it myself. There's a certain man here in town, you see—we have him to thank for that.

GREGERS *(With a slight start)*: That man wasn't my father, by any chance?

EKDAL: Your father—that's it; he's the man. Hm.

HJALMAR: Strange that you should guess that, Gregers!

GREGERS: You were telling me how much you owed to Father—in many different ways, you said; so I thought, perhaps—

GINA: But Mr. Werle didn't actually give us the duck himself—

EKDAL: Still, Gina—Haakon Werle is the man we have to thank for her. *(To GREGERS)* He was out shooting in a boat. He fired at her and brought her down. But his sight isn't too good now, you see—and so he only winged her. Hm.

GREGERS: But she was wounded, I suppose?

HJALMAR: Oh, yes—she had some shot in her.

HEDVIG: Her wing was broken, poor thing; she couldn't fly.

GREGERS: Did she dive to the bottom then?

EKDAL *(Sleepily, with thickened speech)*: Course she did! Always do that—wild ducks do. Make straight for the bottom—as far as they can go. Then they get trapped down there among the slimy roots and tangled reeds—and they never come up again.

GREGERS: But *your* wild duck came up again, Lt. Ekdal.

EKDAL: Had an amazingly clever dog, your father had. That dog—he dived down after her and brought her back.

GREGERS *(Turning to HJALMAR)*: And then they gave her to you?

HJALMAR: No; not at once. First they took her to your father's house; but she started to pine away—so Pettersen was told to put an end to her—

EKDAL *(Half asleep)*: That ass Pettersen—hm—

HJALMAR *(Lowers his voice)*: And that's how we happened to get hold of her. Father knows Pettersen quite well, so when he heard about the wild duck he persuaded him to let *us* have her.

GREGERS: And the attic seems to agree with her, does it? She's doing well in there?

HJALMAR: Remarkably well—amazing, isn't it? She's grown quite plump, and she doesn't seem to miss her freedom. She's been there some time now, and I suppose she's forgotten all about it; that's what counts, you know.

GREGERS: I expect you're right; as long as she's kept away from the sky and the water—and has nothing to remind her— But I must be going now. Your father's gone to sleep, I think.

HJALMAR: Don't go on that account—

GREGERS: Oh, by the way—did you say you had an extra room? A room to rent, I mean?

HJALMAR: Yes, we have. Do you know anyone who—?

GREGERS: Would you let me have it?

HJALMAR: You?

GINA: Oh no, Mr. Werle, you—

GREGERS: If so, I'll move in first thing tomorrow morning.

HJALMAR: We'd be delighted!

GINA: But, Mr. Werle—it's not *your* kind of room—*really* it's not!

HJALMAR: What are you talking about, Gina?

GINA: I mean—it wouldn't be big enough, or light enough—

GREGERS: That doesn't matter, Mrs. Ekdal.

HJALMAR: It seems like a very nice room to me! And not badly furnished either.

GINA: How about those two fellows underneath?

GREGERS: What fellows?

GINA: There's one that says he's been a tutor—

HJALMAR: That's Molvik—Mr. Molvik—a B.A.

GINA: And the other one calls himself a doctor; his name's Relling.

GREGERS: Relling? I think I know him slightly. He had a practice up at Höjdal for a while.

GINA: Well—they're a no good, rowdy lot! Out till all hours every night—drinking themselves silly—

GREGERS: I shan't mind them; I'll soon get used to it. I'll try to be as adaptable as the wild duck—

GINA: All the same—you'd better sleep on it.

GREGERS: You don't seem very anxious to have me as a lodger, Mrs. Ekdal.

GINA: Who, *me?* Why do you say that?

HJALMAR: I must say, Gina—you're being very odd about it. *(To GREGERS)* You plan to stay in town then—for the present?

GREGERS: That's what I've decided, yes.

HJALMAR: Not at your father's house, though? What do you plan to do?

GREGERS: I only wish I knew. When one has the misfortune to bear the name of "Gregers," followed by the name of "Werle"—a pretty hideous combination, don't you think?

HJALMAR: I don't think so at all.

GREGERS: Pah! I'd feel like spitting on a man with a name like that! But since I'm doomed to go on being Gregers Werle in this world—

HJALMAR *(Laughs)*: Ha! Ha! Well—if you weren't Gregers Werle, what would you choose to be?

GREGERS: I think I'd choose to be a clever dog.

GINA: A dog!

HEDVIG *(Involuntarily)*: Oh, no!

GREGERS: Yes, a very clever dog; the kind that plunges after wild ducks when they dive to the bottom, and get trapped down in the mud.

HJALMAR: That's beyond me, Gregers! What *are* you driving at?

GREGERS: Just nonsense; never mind. I'll move in early tomorrow morning then. *(To* GINA*)* I won't be any trouble; I'm used to doing things myself. *(To* HJALMAR*)* We'll discuss details tomorrow—Good night, Mrs. Ekdal. *(Nods to* HEDVIG*)* Good night!

GINA: Good night, Mr. Werle.

HEDVIG: Good night.

HJALMAR *(Who has lighted a candle)*: Wait; I'll see you out. The stairs are rather dark.

*(*GREGERS *and* HJALMAR *go out by the hall door.)*

GINA *(Sits with her sewing in her lap gazing before her)*: What a queer thing to say—that he'd like to be a dog.

HEDVIG: You know, Mother—I think he really meant something quite different.

GINA: What else *could* he have meant?

HEDVIG: I don't know; but it's almost as though everything he said *really* meant something different.

GINA: Do you think so? Well—it seems very queer to me.

HJALMAR *(Comes back)*: The lamp down in the hall was still alight. *(Blows out the candle and puts it down)* Ah! Now, perhaps we can have a bite to eat! *(Starts to eat the sandwiches)* You see, Gina, what happens when you keep your wits about you—?

GINA: What do you mean—"wits about you"?

HJALMAR: We rented the room, didn't we? And to an old friend like Gregers, too.

GINA: I don't know what to think of that.

HEDVIG: It'll be fun, Mother—you'll see!

HJALMAR: You really are amazing! I thought you were so hipped on renting it—and now you behave as if you didn't want to.

GINA: If it had only been to someone else—What will Mr. Werle say I wonder.

HJALMAR: Old Werle? It's no business of his.

GINA: I expect they've been quarreling again; otherwise young Werle would never have left home. You know they've never been able to get on together.

HJALMAR: That may be, but still—

GINA: You never know; Mr. Werle may think it's all your doing.

HJALMAR: Well—let him! Mr. Werle's done a lot for me—God knows I'm the first one to admit it—but he can't expect me to go on kowtowing to him forever!

GINA: But—Hjalmar dear—he might take it out on Grandfather; he might tell Graaberg not to give him any more copying to do.

HJALMAR: I could almost say: I wish he would! You don't seem to understand how humiliating it is for a man like me to see his old father treated like a servant. But some day the pendulum will swing the other way; it won't be long now—I feel it! *(Takes another sandwich)* I have a sacred duty in life, and I intend to perform it to the full!

HEDVIG: You will, Father! I know you will!

GINA: Hush! Don't wake him!

HJALMAR *(Lowers his voice)*: To the *full*, I say! There'll come a day when—That's another reason why I'm glad we've rented the room, you see. It'll make me a bit more independent. A man needs independence if he's to face the task *I* have to face. *(By the armchair; with emotion)* Poor white-haired old man!—Don't you be afraid—lean on your Hjalmar; his shoulders are broad. They're strong,

230

at any rate. One of these fine days you'll wake up to see—*(To* GINA*)* Don't you believe me?

GINA *(Rising)*: Yes, of course I do. But let's get him to bed.

HJALMAR: Yes—very well.

(They lift up the old man carefully.)

CURTAIN

Act Three

SCENE: HJALMAR EKDAL'S *studio. It is morning; daylight streams through the large window in the slanting roof, and the curtain is drawn back.* HJALMAR *sits at the table busy retouching a photograph; several others lie before him. After a few moments* GINA *comes in through the hall door, wearing a hat and coat and with a basket on her arm.*

HJALMAR: Back already, Gina?

GINA: Yes; I've no time for dawdling.

HJALMAR: Did you look in at Gregers?

GINA: I certainly did! You should just see the mess in there! He's made a good start, he has!

HJALMAR: Why? What's he done?

GINA: Used to doing things for himself, says he! So he lights the stove, but leaves the damper shut; the whole room's filled with smoke. The smell in there's enough to—

HJALMAR: Oh, dear!

GINA: But that isn't the worst of it: he decides to put the fire *out* again; so what does he do but take the pitcher from his washstand and empty every blessed drop of water right into the stove! The floor's a mess!

HJALMAR: What a nuisance.

GINA: I got the porter's wife to come and clean it up for him—the pig! But it'll be afternoon before the place is fit to live in.

HJALMAR: What's Gregers doing now?

GINA: He went out for a bit.

HJALMAR: While you were gone, I stopped in to see him too.

GINA: I know; you've asked him to lunch, I hear.

HJALMAR: Not *lunch* exactly—more of a snack, you know. After all, it's his first day here—I didn't know what else to do. You must have something in the house.

GINA: I'll have to try and find something, I suppose.

HJALMAR: Don't be *too* skimpy, though. Relling and Molvik are coming too, I think. I ran into Relling on the stairs, and I couldn't very well—

GINA: Oh, dear! Do we have to have *them* too?

HJALMAR: Good heavens—one more or less—what difference does it make?

EKDAL *(Opens his door and looks in)*: Look here, Hjalmar—*(Sees* GINA*)* Oh!

GINA: Anything you want, Grandfather?

EKDAL: No, no. It doesn't matter. Hm! *(Goes into his room again.)*

GINA *(Picking up her basket)*: Don't let him go out will you? Keep an eye on him.

HJALMAR: All right, all right—I will. Oh, Gina; some herring salad might be just the thing: Relling and Molvik were on a bit of a spree last night.

GINA: Just so long as they don't get here before I'm ready.

HJALMAR: Of course they won't. Just take your time.

GINA: Very well. Meanwhile you can get a bit of work done.

HJALMAR: Work! I *am* working, aren't I? What more can I do?

GINA: I just meant—the sooner you get it done, the sooner it'll be over with. *(She takes the basket and goes out to the kitchen.* HJALMAR *sits for a few moments working reluctantly on the photograph.)*

EKDAL *(Peeps in, looks around the studio, and says softly)*: Are you busy, Hjalmar?

HJALMAR: Slaving away at these blasted pictures—!

EKDAL: Well—never mind; as long as you're busy—Hm! *(He goes into his room again but leaves the door open.)*

HJALMAR *(Goes on working for some time in silence, then lays down*

233

his brush and goes over to the open door): Are you busy, Father?

EKDAL *(In a low growl, from his room):* If you're busy then I'm busy too. Hm.

HJALMAR: Yes; very well. *(Goes back to his work.)*

EKDAL *(Presently, coming to the door again):* Hm. Hjalmar, I'm not as busy as all *that,* you know.

HJALMAR: I thought you were writing.

EKDAL: To hell with it! It's not a matter of life and death, after all. It won't hurt Graaberg to wait a day or two.

HJALMAR: No, and you're not his slave, either.

EKDAL: There's that job in there, you see—

HJALMAR: Just what *I* was thinking of. Would you like to go in? I'll open up for you.

EKDAL: It mightn't be a bad idea.

HJALMAR *(Rises):* Then we'd have it all done, wouldn't we?

EKDAL: And we've got to finish it before tomorrow morning. It *is* tomorrow, isn't it? Hm?

HJALMAR: Of course it's tomorrow.

(HJALMAR *and* EKDAL *each pull open a side of the sliding door. Inside the attic the morning sun pours through the skylights; some doves are flying about, others sit cooing on their perches; the clucking of hens can be heard farther back in the attic.)*

HJALMAR: There! Now you can get to work, Father.

EKDAL *(Goes into the attic):* Aren't you coming too?

HJALMAR: Well, you know—Yes! I believe I—*(Sees* GINA *at the kitchen door)* No, no! I can't—haven't time! Too much work to do! How about our new invention, though?
(He pulls a cord and a curtain drops inside the opening; the lower part consists of an old piece of sailcloth, the upper part of a piece of fishing net. The floor of the attic is now concealed) There! Now perhaps I can have a little peace!

GINA: Must he go messing about in there again?

HJALMAR: Would you rather he'd run off to Mrs. Eriksen's? *(Sits down)* What is it you want? I thought you said—

GINA: I wanted to ask—will it be all right to lay the table for lunch in here?

HJALMAR: Why not? There aren't any appointments, are there?

GINA: Just that engaged couple; you know—the two that want to be photographed together.

HJALMAR: Why the devil can't they be photographed together some *other* day?

GINA: It's all right, Hjalmar dear. I told them to come in the late afternoon; you'll be taking your nap by then.

HJALMAR: That's good; we'll eat in here then.

GINA: Very well; but there's no hurry—you can go on using the table for a good while yet.

HJALMAR: I'm using it—don't worry! I'm using it for all I'm worth!

GINA: Then, later on—you'll be free, you see. *(She goes into the kitchen. A short pause.)*

EKDAL *(In the doorway of the attic, behind the net)*: Hjalmar!

HJALMAR: Well?

EKDAL: Afraid we'll have to move that water trough—

HJALMAR: I said so all along.

EKDAL: Hm-hm-hm. *(Goes away from the door again.* HJALMAR *goes on working a little, then glances toward the attic and starts to rise.* HEDVIG *comes in from the kitchen.)*

HJALMAR *(Sits down again hurriedly)*: What do you want?

HEDVIG: Just to be with you, Father.

HJALMAR: What are you snooping about in here for? Were you told to keep an eye on me?

HEDVIG: Of course not.

HJALMAR: What's your mother up to now?

HEDVIG: She's busy making the herring salad. *(Goes over to the table)* Father—isn't there anything I can do to help?

HJALMAR: No, no. I'll carry on alone as long as my strength holds out. Never you fear, Hedvig; while your father keeps his health—

HEDVIG: Father! I won't have you say such awful things! *(She wanders about the room a little, stops by the doorway, and looks into the attic.)*

HJALMAR: What's he doing? Can you see?

HEDVIG: Making a new runway to the water trough, I think.

HJALMAR: He'll never manage that alone! And here I have to sit—*chained* to this—!

HEDVIG *(Goes to him)*: Give me the brush, Father. I do it quite well, you know.

HJALMAR: Nonsense! You'd only hurt your eyes.

HEDVIG: No, I wouldn't—really! Please give me the brush.

HJALMAR *(Rises)*: It'll only take a minute—

HEDVIG: What's the harm, then? *(Takes the brush)* There! *(Sits down)* I'll use this one as a model.

HJALMAR: Don't strain your eyes, do you hear? And remember, I'm not responsible; you're doing this on your own responsibility you understand!

HEDVIG *(Starts retouching)*: Of course.

HJALMAR: You're very good at it. I'll only be a minute. *(He slips through the side of the curtain into the attic.* HEDVIG *sits at her work.* HJALMAR *and* EKDAL *are heard arguing.)*

HJALMAR *(Appears behind the net)*: Hedvig—would you hand me those pincers on the shelf; and the chisel, too. *(Turning back to the attic)* You'll see, Father—Now just let me show you what I mean! *(*HEDVIG *has fetched the tools from the shelf and hands them in to him.)* Thanks. It's a good thing I got here when I did! *(Goes away from the opening; they can be heard carpentering and talking inside.* HEDVIG *stands watching them. A moment later there's a knock at the hall door; she doesn't hear it.)*

GREGERS *(Bareheaded and without an overcoat comes in and stops near the door)*: Hm—!

HEDVIG *(Turns and goes toward him)*: Good morning. Do come in.

GREGERS: Thanks. *(Looks toward the attic)* Have you workmen in the house?

HEDVIG: No; it's only Father and Grandfather. I'll call them.

GREGERS: No, don't. I'd rather wait a little. *(Sits down on the sofa.)*

HEDVIG: It's so untidy here—*(Starts clearing away the photographs.)*

GREGERS: Never mind—don't bother! Are those the prints that need retouching?

HEDVIG: Yes; I was just helping Father with them.

GREGERS: Don't let me disturb you.

HEDVIG: No—you won't. *(She gathers the things together and sits down to work;* GREGERS *watches her in silence.)*

GREGERS: Did the wild duck sleep well last night?

HEDVIG: Yes, thank you; I think so.

GREGERS *(Turning and looking toward the attic)*: How different it looks by day; quite different than by moonlight.

HEDVIG: Yes—it changes all the time. In the morning it's not a bit the same as it is in the afternoon; and it looks quite different on rainy days from the way it looks when the sun shines.

GREGERS: You've noticed that, have you?

HEDVIG: Of course; how could I help it?

GREGERS: Do you spend much time in there with the wild duck?

HEDVIG: I go in whenever I can manage it—

GREGERS: I expect you're pretty busy. You go to school, I suppose?

HEDVIG: No—not any more; Father's afraid I'll hurt my eyes.

GREGERS: Does he give you lessons himself then?

HEDVIG: He promised to; but so far he hasn't had time.

GREGERS: Is there nobody else who could help you with your studies?

HEDVIG: There's Mr. Molvik; but he's not always—

GREGERS: Sober, you mean?

HEDVIG: Yes—I suppose that's it.

GREGERS: Then you've a good deal of spare time, haven't you? I should think it must be a world all to itself in there.

HEDVIG: Oh, it is! And it's full of the most wonderful things too!

GREGERS: Is it really?

HEDVIG: Yes. There are great big cupboards filled with books; and lots of them have pictures in them.

GREGERS: Aha!

HEDVIG: And there's an old desk with drawers and pigeon-holes; and a great big clock with figures that used to pop in and out. But the clock's stopped—so they don't work any more.

GREGERS: Time has ceased to exist in the wild duck's world.

HEDVIG: And there's an old paintbox too—and lots of other things. And all the books, of course.

GREGERS: And you read the books, I suppose?

HEDVIG: Whenever I can I do. But most of them are in English, and I don't understand English, you see. Still—I look at the pictures. There's one very large book—*Harrison's History of London* it's called—it must be a hundred years old, I should think. It has lots of pictures in it. On the front page there's a picture of death holding an hour-glass—and he has a lady with him. That one's horrid, I think. But there are heaps of others; pictures of

238

churches, and castles, and streets, and great ships sailing on the sea.

GREGERS: Where did all these wonderful things come from?

HEDVIG: An old sea captain lived here once, and he must have brought them home with him. They used to call him "The Flying Dutchman"; and that was funny, because he wasn't Dutch at all, you know.

GREGERS: Wasn't he?

HEDVIG: No. Then he went away, and never came back—and the things just stayed here.

GREGERS: Tell me—when you sit in there looking at those pictures—don't you ever long to travel, and see something of the world yourself?

HEDVIG: Oh, no! I want to stay home always and help Father and Mother.

GREGERS: To retouch photographs?

HEDVIG: No—not only that. Do you know what I'd *really* like to do? I'd like to learn engraving; then I could make pictures like the ones in all those books.

GREGERS: Hm. What does your father say to that?

HEDVIG: He doesn't like the idea at all. Father's funny in some ways. He keeps talking about my learning basketweaving and wickerwork! I don't think that'd be much fun, do you?

GREGERS: No—I shouldn't think so.

HEDVIG: Still—in a way he's right; he says if I'd learned basketwork I could have made the wild duck its new basket.

GREGERS: That's true enough; you'd have been the logical one to do it, after all.

HEDVIG: Yes—because it's *my* wild duck, you see.

GREGERS: Of course it is.

HEDVIG: Yes, it belongs to me. But when Father and Grandfather want it, I don't mind lending it to them, you
know.

GREGERS: What do they do with it?

HEDVIG: Oh, they look after it, and build things for it; all that
sort of thing.

GREGERS: I'm not surprised; she's the most important creature
in there!

HEDVIG: Indeed she is! After all, she's a *real* wild bird. And it
must be so sad for her to be there all by herself.

GREGERS: She has no family, like the rabbits—

HEDVIG: No. And the hens, too; lots of them were hatched at
the same time and were little chicks together. But she
has no one belonging to her, poor thing. She's a complete stranger; no one knows where she came from—no
one knows anything about her.

GREGERS: And then, too—she was rescued from the boundless
deep, remember!

HEDVIG *(Glances at him swiftly and represses a smile)*: What makes
you call it the boundless deep?

GREGERS: What would you have me call it?

HEDVIG: Most people would say "from under the water" or
"from the bottom of the sea."

GREGERS: But *I* prefer the boundless deep.

HEDVIG: It sounds funny to hear somebody else say that.

GREGERS: Why? What do you mean?

HEDVIG: Nothing. You'd only laugh at me.

GREGERS: Of course I wouldn't. Tell me—what made you
smile? Go on!

HEDVIG: It's just that whenever I think of that place in there—
suddenly—unexpectedly, you know—I think of it as the
boundless deep. It *feels* like that, somehow. You must
think me awfully silly!

GREGERS: No—don't say that!

HEDVIG: After all—it's only an old attic.

GREGERS *(Looks at her intently)*: Are you so sure?

HEDVIG *(Astonished)*: That it's an attic?

GREGERS: Yes. How can you be so certain?

(HEDVIG is silent and looks at him open-mouthed. GINA comes in from the kitchen with a tablecloth.)

GREGERS *(Rising)*: I'm afraid I came too early.

GINA: You have to be somewhere, I suppose. We're nearly ready now. Clear off the table, Hedvig.

(HEDVIG obeys; she and GINA lay the table during the following. GREGERS sits in the armchair looking through a photograph album.)

GREGERS: I hear you've done quite a bit of retouching, Mrs. Ekdal.

GINA *(With a sidelong glance)*: Yes, I have.

GREGERS: A lucky coincidence, wasn't it?

GINA: Why lucky?

GREGERS: Since Hjalmar's a photographer, I mean.

HEDVIG: And Mother can take pictures too.

GINA: I more or less *had* to take it up.

GREGERS: Then I suppose it's you who really runs the business?

GINA: When Hjalmar has too many other things to do, I—

GREGERS: I dare say his father takes up a good deal of his time.

GINA: Yes; and this is no fit job for Hjalmar anyway—wasting his time taking pictures of a lot of silly people!

GREGERS: I quite agree; but once having chosen it as his profession—

GINA: He's no *ordinary* photographer, mind you! I'm sure you understand that, Mr. Werle.

GREGERS: Yes, of course, but still—

(A shot is heard from the attic.)

241

GREGERS *(Starting up)*: What's that?

GINA: There they go—at that shooting again!

GREGERS: Do you mean to say they shoot in there?

HEDVIG: They're out hunting, you see.

GREGERS: What! *(Goes to the door of the attic)* Are you out hunting, Hjalmar?

HJALMAR *(From inside the net)*: Oh, you've come. I didn't know. I was so taken up with—*(To* HEDVIG*)* Why didn't you call us? *(Comes into the studio.)*

GREGERS: Do you mean to tell me you go shooting in the attic?

HJALMAR *(Showing a double-barreled pistol)*: Only with this old thing.

GINA: You and Grandfather'll get into trouble one of these days—fooling with that gun.

HJALMAR *(Irritably)*: How often have I told you—this weapon is a *pistol.*

GINA: I don't see that that makes it any better.

GREGERS: Well, Hjalmar—so you've become a hunter too!

HJALMAR: We do a little rabbit-shooting now and then. It pleases the old man, you know.

GINA: Men are a queer lot! Must have their divergence!

HJALMAR *(Angrily)*: Diversion—I suppose you mean!

GINA: That's what I said, isn't it?

HJALMAR: Well—! Hm. *(To* GREGERS*)* It works out very well; the attic's so high up, no one can hear the shooting. *(Lays the pistol on the top shelf of the bookcase)* Mind you don't touch the pistol, Hedvig. One of the barrels is still loaded; remember that.

GREGERS *(Peering through the net)*: You have a rifle too, I see.

HJALMAR: It's an old gun of Father's. But there's something wrong with the lock—it won't fire any more. It's fun to have it, though; we take it apart, grease it, give it a good cleaning—and then put it together again. That is—*Father* does; he likes puttering about with things like that.

HEDVIG *(Beside* GREGERS*)*: Look! You can see the wild duck clearly now.

GREGERS: Yes—I was just looking at her. She seems to drag her wing a bit.

HJALMAR: That's not strange; that's the broken wing, you see.

GREGERS: And she's lame in one foot, isn't she?

HJALMAR: Yes—perhaps a little.

HEDVIG: That's the foot the dog caught hold of.

HJALMAR: But she's all right otherwise; it's quite amazing—considering she had a charge of shot in her, and the dog grabbed her with his teeth—

GREGERS *(With a glance at* HEDVIG*)*:—and she was down in the boundless deep, as well.

HEDVIG *(Smiling)*: Yes.

GINA *(Goes on setting the table)*: That blessed wild duck! She gets enough fuss made over her!

HJALMAR: Hm—Will lunch be ready soon?

GINA: Yes, in a minute. Now, Hedvig—come and help me. *(*GINA *and* HEDVIG *go out into the kitchen.)*

HJALMAR *(In a low voice)*: I wouldn't stand there watching Father; he doesn't like it. *(*GREGERS *moves away from the attic door)* I'd better close up before the others come. *(Claps his hands to drive the birds back)* Shoo! Get back there! *(Draws up the net and pulls the door panels together)* These contraptions are all my own invention. It's rather fun to fiddle about with things like that. Gina doesn't like the hens and rabbits to get into the studio, so it's important to keep all this in running order.

GREGERS: Yes, I see. It's your wife who really runs the business then?

HJALMAR: I leave the routine part of it to her. It gives me a chance to work on more important things; I use the sitting room, you see.

GREGERS: What kind of things?

HJALMAR: I'm surprised you haven't asked me that before. But you haven't heard about the invention, I suppose?

GREGERS: Invention? No.

HJALMAR: You haven't, eh? Of course—I know you've been living in the wilds—

GREGERS: Have you invented something?

HJALMAR: I haven't quite solved it yet; but I'm working on it constantly. I didn't become a photographer in order to spend my life taking commonplace pictures of commonplace people—I need hardly tell you that.

GREGERS: Just what your wife was saying.

HJALMAR: When I chose the photographic medium, I swore to myself that I would raise it to the level of a science and an art combined; so I set to work on this invention.

GREGERS: What kind of an invention is it? What does it consist of?

HJALMAR: My dear fellow, you mustn't try to pin me down to details yet; these things take time, you know. And, believe me, it's not a question of self-glorification—I'm not working on it for my own sake, I assure you! I have a fixed purpose in life—a sacred duty; and I consider this work part of it.

GREGERS: What is this "purpose in life" you speak of?

HJALMAR: Are you forgetting that white-haired old man in there?

GREGERS: Your poor father—yes. What exactly do you plan to do for him?

HJALMAR: I plan to give him back his self-respect by restoring the name of Ekdal to its former dignity and honor.

GREGERS: I see.

HJALMAR: Yes—I shall rescue him! Poor, broken old man! Do you know that from the moment the trouble started—from the very beginning—he went all to pieces, and he seemed unable to recover. In those terrible days—all

244

during the trial—he was so changed, I hardly knew him—That pistol over there—the one we use to shoot rabbits with—that played its part in the Ekdal tragedy too!

GREGERS: The pistol! Really?

HJALMAR: Oh, yes! When he was found guilty, and they sentenced him to prison—he stood with that pistol in his hand—

GREGERS: You mean—he was going to—?

HJALMAR: Yes. But his courage failed him; he dared not use it. That shows you how broken and demoralized he was. Imagine! He, a soldier! A great hunter with nine bears to his credit. A man directly descended from two lieutenant colonels—in successive generations, naturally—and yet his courage failed him! Can you understand that, Gregers?

GREGERS: Yes; I understand that very well.

HJALMAR: I don't. But that pistol was to turn up again in the Ekdal Saga. When I thought of him in his prison clothes—under lock and key—in that gloomy prison cell—! Those were agonizing days for me! I kept all the shades down in my room. I'd look out now and then, and I couldn't understand how the sun could still be shining. I couldn't understand how people could still be walking through the streets—laughing and chatting about trivial things. It seemed to me as though the world had come to a standstill—as though life itself were under an eclipse.

GREGERS: I felt like that when Mother died.

HJALMAR: And there came a moment when Hjalmar Ekdal seized that pistol and aimed it at his own breast.

GREGERS: You, too, thought of—!

HJALMAR: Yes.

GREGERS: But you didn't fire?

HJALMAR: No—I didn't fire. By a supreme effort I conquered the temptation—and I went on living. It takes courage to choose life under such circumstances, I can tell you.

GREGERS: That depends on how you look at it.

HJALMAR: No, my dear fellow—it's indisputable. And I'm glad I managed to find the necessary strength, for now I shall be able to finish my invention. And when it's ready, Dr. Relling thinks—and I agree with him—that Father may get permission to wear his uniform again. I shall demand that as my sole reward.

GREGERS: Does that mean so much to him—?

HJALMAR: It's his dearest wish. Oh, Gregers—my heart bleeds for him! Whenever we have a little family celebration—Gina's and my wedding anniversary, whatever it may be—in comes the old man wearing the lieutenant's uniform he wore in happier days. But if there's a knock at the door, or if he hears someone in the hall—back he runs to his room as fast as his poor old legs will carry him; for he dare not be caught wearing it in public. It breaks my heart to see him!

GREGERS: When do you expect to finish the invention?

HJALMAR: Good heavens—that's impossible to say! An invention is not a matter of routine, you know. It depends on inspiration—on a sudden intuition—on factors beyond one's immediate control.

GREGERS: But you're making progress with it?

HJALMAR: Of course I'm making progress! I wrestle with it every day—my mind is full of it. Every afternoon, as soon as I've had lunch, I lock myself in the sitting room in there, where I can work in peace. But it's no use *hounding* me about it; as Relling says, that does more harm than good!

GREGERS: What about all this business in the attic? Don't you find that distracting? Doesn't it waste a great deal of your time?

246

HJALMAR: On the contrary! You mustn't think that for a moment! I must have *some* relaxation, after all; something to relieve the strain of incessant concentration. And, anyhow, inspiration is quite unpredictable; when it comes it comes—that's all!

GREGERS: You know, Hjalmar—I think you and the wild duck have quite a lot in common.

HJALMAR: The wild duck! What on earth do you mean?

GREGERS: You dived to the bottom too, and got yourself trapped down there.

HJALMAR: You mean that I was wounded too—by the blow that almost killed my father?

GREGERS: No, not exactly. It's not that you're wounded, Hjalmar; but you've lost your way in a poisonous swamp. You've become infected with an insidious disease, and you've sunk to the bottom to die in the dark.

HJALMAR: Die in the dark? I? Really, Gregers—how can you talk such nonsense!

GREGERS: But don't worry—I'll bring you back. I have a purpose in life too, you see. One I discovered yesterday.

HJALMAR: That's all very well—but kindly leave *me* out of it! I assure you that—apart from a perfectly justifiable melancholy—I'm as content and happy as any man could be.

GREGERS: That's part of the illness, you see. It's all part of the poison.

HJALMAR: My dear Gregers—please don't go on about illnesses and poisons any more! I dislike that kind of talk. In my house no one ever speaks to me about unpleasant things.

GREGERS: That I can well believe.

HJALMAR: I dislike it and it's bad for me—And I don't care what you say—there are no swamps or poisons here! My surroundings may be modest—my home may be humble; but I'm an inventor and the breadwinner of a family, and I assure you this exalts me above any petty material concerns—Ah! Here comes lunch!

(GINA *and* HEDVIG *enter bringing bottles of beer, a decanter of brandy, glasses, etc. At the same time* RELLING *and* MOLVIK *enter from the hall, both without hats or overcoats;* MOLVIK *is dressed in black.)*

GINA *(Placing dishes on the table)*: You're just in time!

RELLING: Molvik got a whiff of herring salad and there was no holding him!

HJALMAR: I'd like you to meet Mr. Molvik, Gregers; and Dr.—oh, but you know Dr. Relling, don't you?

GREGERS: Slightly, yes.

RELLING: Mr. Werle, Jr., of course. We had a few little skirmishes up at the Höjdal Works. Did you just move in?

GREGERS: This morning.

RELLING: Molvik and I live just below you; so if you should happen to need a doctor or a clergyman, you won't have far to go.

GREGERS: I might have to take you up on that: we were thirteen at table yesterday.

HJALMAR: I do wish you'd stop talking about unpleasant things!

RELLING: Your time hasn't come yet, Hjalmar! No need to worry!

HJALMAR: For the sake of my family I hope you're right. But let's sit down now—and eat, drink and be merry!

GREGERS: Shouldn't we wait for your father?

HJALMAR: No; he'll have lunch in his own room presently. Come on! *(The men seat themselves at table and start eating and drinking.* GINA *and* HEDVIG *go in and out waiting on them.)*

RELLING: Molvik was drunk as a lord yesterday, Mrs. Ekdal.

GINA: Was he? Again?

RELLING: Didn't you hear him when I brought him home last night?

GINA: Can't say I did.

RELLING: Just as well; last night he was downright disgusting.

GINA: Is that true, Molvik?

MOLVIK: Let us draw a veil over last night's proceedings; they have no connection with my better self.

RELLING: He becomes like one possessed; then he insists on dragging me out with him. He's demonic—that's what it is.

GREGERS: Demonic?

RELLING: Yes; Molvik is demonic.

GREGERS: Hm.

RELLING: And people with demonic natures can't be expected to go through life on an even keel, you know. They're obliged to run amok now and then—they *have* to. Are you still slaving away at those horrible grimy works?

GREGERS: I have been until now.

RELLING: Did you ever get anyone to honor that claim you made such a fuss about up there?

GREGERS: Claim? *(Understands him)* Oh, I see.

HJALMAR: Claim? What sort of a claim, Gregers?

GREGERS: Nothing. A lot of nonsense.

RELLING: Not at all! He carried on a regular crusade! He went from house to house preaching about something—what was it you called it?—the Claim of the Ideal?

GREGERS: I was young then.

RELLING: Yes! You were young all right! But did you ever get anyone to honor it? You hadn't while I was there, as I remember.

GREGERS: And not since, either.

RELLING: Have you perhaps learned to compromise a little?

GREGERS: Compromise? Never in dealing with a man who really *is* a man.

HJALMAR: No! I should hope not!—More butter, Gina.

RELLING: And a bit of pork for Molvik.

MOLVIK: Ugh! Not *pork!*

(There's a knock at the attic door.)

HJALMAR: Father wants to come out; open up for him, Hedvig.

(HEDVIG goes and slides the door open a little way; EKDAL comes in carrying a fresh rabbit skin; HEDVIG closes the door after him.)

EKDAL: Good morning, gentlemen! Good hunting today! Shot a big one!

HJALMAR: And you skinned it without waiting for me—!

EKDAL: Salted it, too. Good *tender* meat, is rabbit meat. And sweet; tastes like sugar. Enjoy your lunch, gentlemen! *(Goes into his room.)*

MOLVIK *(Getting up)*: Excuse me—I can't—I must get downstairs at once—

RELLING: Take some soda water, man!

MOLVIK: Ugh—Ugh! *(Hurries out by the hall door.)*

RELLING *(To HJALMAR)*: Let's drink a toast to the old hunter.

HJALMAR *(Clinks glasses with him)*: To the gallant old sportsman on the brink of the grave.

RELLING: To the old gray-haired—*(Drinks)* By the way, is his hair gray or white?

HJALMAR: A little of both, I think. As a matter of fact, he hasn't much hair left.

RELLING: Well—you can get on just as well in a wig! You know—you really are a lucky man, Hjalmar; you have a definite purpose in life to strive for—

HJALMAR: And, believe me, I *am* striving for it—!

RELLING: And there's your good, capable wife—padding about

so quietly in her old felt slippers, making everything cozy and comfortable for you—

HJALMAR: Yes, Gina—*(Nods to her)* You're a good companion on life's journey, Gina dear.

GINA: Don't go making a fool of me!

RELLING: And then, there's your Hedvig, Hjalmar—

HJALMAR *(Moved)*: Yes—best of all, my child! My Hedvig! Come here to me, my darling! *(Strokes her hair)* What day is it tomorrow, eh?

HEDVIG *(Shakes him)*: Don't say anything about that, Father.

HJALMAR: It cuts me to the heart to think how meager it will be; just a little ceremony in the attic—

HEDVIG: But I like that best of all!

RELLING: Just you wait till the invention's finished, Hedvig!

HJALMAR: Yes!—*Then* you'll see! Your future will be taken care of; you shall live in comfort all your life—I shall make sure of that! I shall demand—well—something or other on your behalf. It will be the poor inventor's sole request.

HEDVIG *(In a whisper, her arms round his neck)*: Dear, darling Father!

RELLING *(To GREGERS)*: Isn't it pleasant for a change to sit here with this happy family—eating delicious food at a well-spread table?

HJALMAR: It's a joy to share a meal with such good friends!

GREGERS: Personally—I don't like the smell of poison.

RELLING: Poison?

HJALMAR: Oh, don't start *that* again!

GINA: I'd have you know, Mr. Werle, there's no smell of poison here; I air this room out every single day!

GREGERS: No amount of airing can ever get rid of the stench I mean.

HJALMAR: Stench!

GINA: Well—I must say—!

RELLING: Perhaps you brought the stench with *you*, from those mines of yours up there!

GREGERS: You *would* call what I have to bring a stench! That would be like you, Dr. Relling.

RELLING: Now listen, Mr. Werle, Jr.—! Unless I'm very much mistaken you're still obsessed by that blasted *Claim of the Ideal* of yours. I'll bet you have a copy on you now—hidden in some pocket.

GREGERS: You're wrong. I have it hidden in my heart.

RELLING: Well—wherever it is don't produce it here! Not while *I'm* around at any rate.

GREGERS: And what if I produce it all the same?

RELLING: Then I give you fair warning, I shall kick you down-stairs head first.

HJALMAR *(Rising)*: Why, Relling!

GREGERS: All right! Why don't you try it—!

GINA *(Coming between them)*: Dr. Relling! Please! That's enough of that—! But I'd like to tell *you* something, Mr. Werle. After that filthy mess you made with your stove in there, you've no business to come talking about stenches and poisons to *me!*

(There's a knock at the hall door.)

HEDVIG: Mother, there's someone at the door.

HJALMAR: What *is* this! Now we're to be overrun with visitors, I suppose!

GINA: Never mind—I'll go. *(She goes and opens the door, starts and draws back)* Ah!—Oh, no!

(WERLE, wearing a fur coat, steps into the room.)

WERLE: I beg your pardon; I'm told my son is living here.

GINA *(With a gasp)*: Why—yes.

HJALMAR *(Goes toward him)*: Won't you do us the honor, Mr. Werle—

WERLE: Thank you; I merely wish to see my son.

GREGERS: I'm here; what is it?

WERLE: May we go to your room?

GREGERS: My room? Yes—very well—

GINA: Oh! But it's in no fit state—!

WERLE: Out here in the hall will do; but I'd like to speak to you alone.

HJALMAR: You can have this room to yourselves, Mr. Werle. Come, Relling—we'll go in here. (HJALMAR *and* RELLING *go into the sitting room;* GINA *takes* HEDVIG *with her into the kitchen.*)

GREGERS: (*After a short pause*): Well? Now that we're alone, what is it?

WERLE: I gather from something you said last night—and your moving here to the Ekdals' seems to confirm it—that you're bent on causing me some mischief.

GREGERS: I intend to open Hjalmar Ekdal's eyes; he must be made to see his position in its true light.

WERLE: I suppose this is the "purpose in life" you spoke of yesterday?

GREGERS: You've left me no other.

WERLE: Why hold *me* responsible for your warped mind, Gregers?

GREGERS: I hold you responsible for the fact that my whole *life* has been warped. I'm not referring now to what happened to my mother—But I have you to thank for the burden of guilt that weighs on my conscience.

WERLE: So it's your conscience that torments you, is it?

GREGERS: I knew you were laying a trap for old Lt. Ekdal, and I should have been man enough to face you with it. I should at least have warned him. I guessed what you were up to.

WERLE: Then why didn't you speak out?

GREGERS: I was too much of a coward; I didn't dare. At that time I was so dreadfully afraid of you. I went on being afraid of you for years.

WERLE: But you're no longer afraid now, it seems.

GREGERS: No—thank God. I know the wrong done to old Ekdal—by me and others—can never be undone. But I can at least save Hjalmar. I can prevent his life from being ruined by a mass of lies.

WERLE: What good do you think that would do? You don't imagine you'd be doing him a service?

GREGERS: I know I would.

WERLE: And Hjalmar Ekdal will agree with you, you think? You actually believe he's man enough to *thank* you for it?

GREGERS: I know he is.

WERLE: Hm—we'll see.

GREGERS: Besides—if I'm to go on living—I must try to find a cure for my sick conscience.

WERLE: You'll never find a cure; your conscience has been sick, as you choose to call it, ever since you were a little child. That's a legacy from your mother, Gregers; that's all she had to leave you.

GREGERS *(With a scornful smile)*: You haven't got over it yet, have you? You expected her to bring you a fortune when you married her—you've never recovered from the shock of having been mistaken!

WERLE: Let's stick to the point, shall we? You still insist on guiding young Ekdal back to, what is in your opinion, the right path?

GREGERS: That is my intention.

WERLE: Then I might have spared myself this visit; for I suppose it's no good asking whether you'll change your mind and come back home again?

GREGERS: No.

WERLE: And you won't consider joining the firm either?

GREGERS: No.

WERLE: Very well. But, since I'm marrying again, I'll arrange to have your part of the estate transferred to you at once.

GREGERS: No; I don't want it.

WERLE: You don't want it?

GREGERS: My conscience won't allow me to accept it.

WERLE *(After a pause)*: Are you going up to the works again?

GREGERS: No; I've resigned from your employ.

WERLE: What do you plan to do?

GREGERS: I only want to fulfill my purpose in life—that's all.

WERLE: But what do you propose to live on?

GREGERS: I've saved up a little money from my wages.

WERLE: How long will *that* last!

GREGERS: Long enough for me, I expect.

WERLE: What does that mean?

GREGERS: I'll answer no more questions.

WERLE: Very well then, Gregers. Good-bye.

GREGERS: Good-bye.

(WERLE *goes out by the hall door.*)

HJALMAR *(Sticks his head around the sitting-room door)*: Has he gone?

GREGERS: Yes.

(HJALMAR *and* RELLING *come in.* GINA *and* HEDVIG *come from the kitchen.*)

RELLING: That certainly put an end to the lunch party, didn't it!

GREGERS: Put on your things, Hjalmar. I want you to come for a long walk with me.

HJALMAR: All right, I'd be glad to. What did your father want? Was it anything to do with me?

GREGERS: Come along. We've got to have a talk. I'll go and get my coat. *(Goes out by the hall door.)*

GINA *(To* HJALMAR*)*: I wouldn't go with him if I were you.

RELLING: No, don't! Stay where you are.

HJALMAR *(Getting his hat and overcoat)*: What! When an old friend wants to pour out his heart to me in private—!

RELLING: But, damn it! Can't you see the fellow's mad? He's a crackpot—a lunatic!

GINA: You hear that, Hjalmar? His mother was a bit queer too at times.

HJALMAR: All the more reason his friend should keep a watchful eye on him. *(To* GINA*)* Be sure to have dinner ready in good time. Good-bye for the present. *(He goes out by the hall door.)*

RELLING: Too bad that fellow didn't fall right into hell down one of the Höjdal mine shafts!

GINA: Good gracious! What makes you say that?

RELLING *(Mutters)*: I have my reasons.

GINA: Do you think young Werle's really mad?

RELLING: No, worse luck; I don't suppose he's any madder than most people. But he's a sick man all the same.

GINA: What do you think's the matter with him?

RELLING: Well—I'll tell you, Mrs. Ekdal: I'd say he had integrity fever—a particularly bad case of it.

GINA: Integrity fever?

HEDVIG: Is that a kind of illness?

RELLING: Yes; it's a national disease, but it only breaks out sporadically. *(Nods to* GINA*)* Thanks for lunch. *(He goes out by the hall door.)*

GINA *(Pacing restlessly up and down)*: Ugh! That Gregers Werle! He's always been a troublemaker.

HEDVIG *(Stands by the table, gives her mother a searching look)*: Mother, this all seems very strange.

CURTAIN

Act Four

SCENE: HJALMAR EKDAL's *studio. A photograph has just been taken; a camera covered with its cloth, a pedestal, two chairs and a console table stand forward in the room. It is late afternoon, the sun is setting; during the act dusk falls.* GINA *stands at the hall door with a slide and a wet photographic plate in her hand; she is talking to somebody outside.*

GINA: Without fail! Don't worry, I never break a promise. I'll have the first dozen ready for you Monday. Good afternoon. *(Someone is heard going down the stairs.* GINA *closes the door, slips the plate into the slide and puts it into the camera.)*

HEDVIG *(Comes in from the kitchen)*: Have they gone?

GINA *(Tidying up)*: Yes, thank God, I got rid of them at last.

HEDVIG: It's funny Father isn't back yet.

GINA: You're sure he's not in Relling's room?

HEDVIG: No, he's not there; I just ran down the back stairs to see.

GINA: And his dinner's getting cold too.

HEDVIG: That's funny—Father's never late for dinner.

GINA: He'll be here soon—you'll see.

HEDVIG: I wish he'd come: things seem so queer today.

GINA *(Calls out)*: Here he is now!

*(*HJALMAR EKDAL *comes in by the hall door.)*

HEDVIG *(Runs to him)*: We thought you'd *never* come back, Father!

GINA *(Gives him a sidelong look)*: You were out a long time, Hjalmar.

HJALMAR *(Doesn't look at her)*: A fairly long time, yes.

GINA: Did you have something to eat with Werle?

HJALMAR *(Hanging up his coat)*: No.

GINA *(Going toward the kitchen)*: I'll bring your dinner at once then.

HJALMAR: Never mind about dinner. I don't want anything to eat.

HEDVIG *(Goes nearer to him)*: Don't you feel well, Father?

HJALMAR: Well? Yes; well enough. We had a very tiring walk, Gregers and I.

GINA: You shouldn't have gone with him, Hjalmar. You know you're not used to long walks.

HJALMAR: There are many things one has to get used to in this world. *(He wanders about the room)* Has anyone been here while I was out?

GINA: Only that engaged couple.

HJALMAR: No new orders, I suppose?

GINA: No, not today.

HEDVIG: But tomorrow there are sure to be some, Father!

HJALMAR: Let's hope so. For tomorrow I mean to set to work in earnest.

HEDVIG: Tomorrow! Have you forgotten what day it is tomorrow, Father?

HJALMAR: Ah, yes—of course. The day after tomorrow, then. I intend to take personal charge of everything. From now on I shall do all the work myself.

GINA: Why should you bother to do that, Hjalmar? You know it only makes you miserable. I can take the pictures well enough; and that sets you free to work on your invention.

HEDVIG: And then there's the wild duck, Father—and all the hens and rabbits—

HJALMAR: I won't hear another word about that childish nonsense! From tomorrow on I shall never set foot in there again.

HEDVIG: But, Father, tomorrow you promised we'd have our celebration—

HJALMAR: Hm. Yes, that's true. From the day *after* tomorrow, then. As for that wild duck; I'd like to wring its neck!

HEDVIG *(Cries out)*: The wild duck!

GINA: I never heard of such a thing!

HEDVIG *(Shakes him)*: But, Father! It's *my* wild duck! You can't—!

HJALMAR: That's the only thing that stops me. I haven't the heart to do it, Hedvig—for your sake. But I ought to do it, I'm convinced of that. No creature that has been in that man's hands should be allowed to stay under my roof.

GINA: Good Lord! what if Grandfather did get it from poor old Pettersen—

HJALMAR: One has certain moral obligations; there are laws— one might call them the laws of the ideal. A man may jeopardize his soul by failing to obey them.

HEDVIG: But the poor wild duck, Father! Think of the wild duck!

HJALMAR: I told you—I intend to spare it for your sake. Not a hair of its head—I mean—it shall be spared. I've other things to deal with—far more important things than that. Now that it's dusk, Hedvig, you'd better run along and take your walk as usual.

HEDVIG: Must I, Father? I don't much feel like going out.

HJALMAR: I think you'd better go. You seem to be blinking your eyes a lot—it's this foul air in here. It's bad for you.

HEDVIG: Very well. I'll go by the back stairs. My hat and coat—? They must be in my room. But, Father—promise me you won't hurt the wild duck while I'm gone?

HJALMAR: Not a feather on it shall be harmed, I promise you. *(Clasps her to him)* You and I, Hedvig—we two—! Run along now.

(HEDVIG nods to her parents and goes out through the kitchen.)

HJALMAR *(Walks about the room with downcast eyes)*: Gina.

GINA: Yes?

HJALMAR: From tomorrow on—from the day *after* tomorrow,

rather—I wish to take charge of the household accounts myself.

GINA: You want to look after the accounts as well?

HJALMAR: I intend to check all the receipts at any rate.

GINA: Lord knows *that* won't take you very long.

HJALMAR: I wonder. It seems to me our money stretches a surprisingly long way. *(Stops and looks at her)* How do you manage it?

GINA: It's because Hedvig and I use so very little, I suppose.

HJALMAR: What about Father's work for Mr. Werle? Is it true that he gets very generously paid for it?

GINA: I don't know how generous it is. I don't know what other people get, you see.

HJALMAR: Well—how much *do* they pay him? Tell me!

GINA: It varies; he gets enough to cover his expenses here and maybe a little pocket money besides.

HJALMAR: Enough to cover his expenses! Why have you never told me this?

GINA: I didn't like to; I knew it made you happy to think he owed everything to you.

HJALMAR: And instead he owes it all to Mr. Werle!

GINA: Well, God knows, Mr. Werle can afford it.

HJALMAR: Light the lamp!

GINA *(Lighting the lamp)*: Anyway—how do we know it *does* come from Mr. Werle? It might be Graaberg who—

HJALMAR: Don't try to evade matters by dragging Graaberg into this!

GINA: Well, I mean—I only thought—

HJALMAR: Hm!

GINA: I didn't get Grandfather that copying to do: it was Bertha—in the days when she still used to come and see us—

HJALMAR: Why is your voice trembling?

GINA *(Putting on the lamp shade)*: My voice—?

HJALMAR: Yes; and your hands are shaking too. Don't tell me I'm mistaken!

GINA *(Firmly)*: What's he been saying about me, Hjalmar? You might just as well come out with it.

HJALMAR: Is it true—*can* it be true, that—that there was something between you and Werle, while you were in service there?

GINA: No. It wasn't true then, at any rate. Mr. Werle wouldn't leave me alone, *that's* true enough. His wife got suspicious, and fussed and fumed and made a lot of scenes; made my life miserable, she did. And then I gave my notice.

HJALMAR: And after that?

GINA: Then I went home, and Mother—well, she wasn't the kind of woman you took her for, Hjalmar; she kept on at me all the time—you see Mr. Werle had become a widower by then.

HJALMAR: Well?

GINA: I suppose I'd better tell you; he gave me no peace until I let him have his way.

HJALMAR *(Clasps his hands together)*: So this is the mother of my child! How could you hide this from me!

GINA: It was wrong of me, I know; I should have told you long ago.

HJALMAR: You should have told me at the very start; then I'd have known what kind of woman I was dealing with.

GINA: But if you'd known—would you have married me?

HJALMAR: What do you think? Of course not!

GINA: That's why I couldn't bring myself to tell you. I'd grown so fond of you, you see. I'd have been so miserable—I couldn't bear the thought of it.

HJALMAR *(Paces about)*: So this is my Hedvig's mother! And to

261

think that I owe all I possess—*(Kicks a chair)* my home and everything that's in it, to a man who was your former lover! To that damned scoundrel Werle!

GINA: Hjalmar, do you regret these years we've been together?

HJALMAR *(Stands in front of her)*: Tell me! Haven't your days been filled with remorse at the thought of the web of deceit you've spun around me? Answer me! Hasn't it been a constant source of agony and shame to you?

GINA: Hjalmar dear—I've had so much to do. My days have been so full—what with the house and all—

HJALMAR: So you've never even given a moment's thought to your past life!

GINA: It's a long time ago—to tell you the truth I'd almost forgotten the whole stupid business.

HJALMAR: It's this crude, sluggish content that I find so shocking—so revolting! Not a twinge of remorse—incredible!

GINA: I'd like you to tell *me* something, Hjalmar; what would have become of you if you hadn't found a wife like me?

HJALMAR: Like you—!

GINA: Yes. You know I was always more practical and more efficient than you were; I suppose that's only natural— I'm a couple of years older, after all.

HJALMAR: What would have become of *me!*

GINA: You were getting into some pretty wild habits when you first met me. You can't deny that, can you?

HJALMAR: Wild habits! That's what you call them, do you? But how could *you* understand what a man goes through when he's on the brink of despair, as I was! Especially a man with my ardent, sensitive nature.

GINA: Maybe that's true. Anyway—I don't hold it against you; you made a real good husband once we got married and settled down. And things were beginning to be so cozy and comfortable here. Hedvig and I were thinking we might even start spending a bit more on ourselves—get ourselves a few clothes, perhaps—and a little extra food.

HJALMAR: In this swamp of deceit, you could actually think of things like that!

GINA: Oh, God! I wish that awful man had never set foot inside this house!

HJALMAR: I was happy here too; I loved my home. But it was all a delusion! How I shall ever find the necessary inspiration now to bring my invention to fruition, heaven knows! It will die with me, I expect. And it will be your fault—it will be your past, Gina, that will have killed it.

GINA *(On the verge of tears)*: You mustn't say that, Hjalmar! Please don't say things like that! All I've ever wanted was to serve you—to do the best I could for you. You must know that!

HJALMAR: What's become of the poor breadwinner's dream now! As I lay in there on the sofa, incessantly brooding over my invention, I realized only too well that the effort of creation was fast sapping my strength. I had a premonition: I knew that the day when I finally held the patent in my hand—I knew that day would be my last! I saw you in my dream—the proud widow of the inventor—sad, but prosperous and grateful.

GINA *(Drying her tears)*: Hjalmar, you *mustn't* say such things! God forbid that I should ever be a widow.

HJALMAR: It makes no difference now one way or the other. The dream is over now—all over!

(GREGERS WERLE opens the hall door cautiously and looks in.)

GREGERS: May I come in?

HJALMAR: Yes; come in.

GREGERS *(Comes forward, his face beaming with joy, and holds out both his hands to them)*: Well, my dear friends! *(Looks from one to the other and says to* HJALMAR *in a whisper)* Perhaps you haven't had your talk yet?

HJALMAR *(Loudly)*: Yes—we have.

GREGERS: You *have?*

HJALMAR: I've just been through the bitterest moments of my life.

GREGERS: But, surely, the most uplifting too?

HJALMAR: Anyway—we've got it over with; at least for the time being.

GREGERS *(In great surprise)*: But—I don't understand—

HJALMAR: What don't you understand?

GREGERS: This crisis was to have been a turning point; the basis for a whole new way of life. No more falsehood and deception, but a union based on confidence and truth—

HJALMAR: Yes, I know; I know all that.

GREGERS: I expected to find you both radiant—transfigured. But you seem sad and gloomy—

GINA: Yes—well. *(Takes off the lamp shade)*

GREGERS: I don't expect you to understand me, Mrs. Ekdal. It's only natural that you should need time to—But *you,* Hjalmar? You must feel like a man newly dedicated to higher things.

HJALMAR: Yes, of course I do. To some extent—that is.

GREGERS: Surely there can be no greater joy than to forgive a poor erring creature; to rehabilitate her through love and understanding.

HJALMAR: It's not so easy to recover from the bitter experience I've just lived through!

GREGERS: Perhaps not for an *ordinary* man; but for a man like *you*—

HJALMAR: Yes—I realize that. But don't *hound* me about it, Gregers. These things take time, you know.

GREGERS: There's a lot of the wild duck in you, Hjalmar. (RELLING *enters through the hall door.*)

RELLING: Well, well! So we're on the subject of the wild duck again!

HJALMAR: Yes: Mr. Werle's poor wounded victim—

GREGERS: Mr. Werle? Were you talking about *him?*

HJALMAR: Him—and *us;* yes.

RELLING (*To* GREGERS *in an undertone*): You damned interfering fool!

HJALMAR: What did you say?

RELLING: Nothing. I was just expressing my feelings about this quack here. (*To* GREGERS) Why don't you get out before you ruin both their lives?

GREGERS: Their lives won't be ruined, I assure you, Dr. Relling. I needn't speak of Hjalmar—we know him. But I feel sure that, fundamentally, she too possesses the necessary qualities of decency and loyalty—

GINA (*Almost in tears*): Then why couldn't you have let me be?

RELLING: May I ask you, Mr. Werle, Jr., what you think you're doing in this house?

GREGERS: Laying the foundations of a true marriage.

RELLING: I see; so you think the Ekdals' marriage wasn't good enough?

GREGERS: I suppose it was as good as the majority of marriages—unfortunately! But it certainly was never based on truth.

HJALMAR (*To* RELLING): I'm afraid you've never given much thought to the Ideal.

RELLING: Rubbish, my friend! Tell me, Mr. Werle—roughly speaking—how many true marriages have you encountered in your life?

GREGERS: Hardly any—now I come to think of it.

RELLING: Neither have I.

GREGERS: But I've seen all too many of the other kind. And I know only too well how harmful such marriages can be to both people concerned.

HJALMAR: A man's spiritual integrity can be totally destroyed—that's the appalling part of it!

RELLING: I've never actually been married—so perhaps I'm not competent to judge. But one thing I *do* know: the child is part of the marriage too; and I advise you to leave the child alone.

HJALMAR: Hedvig!—My poor Hedvig!

RELLING: Yes; you'd better damn well leave Hedvig out of this! You two are grown-up people; if you want to make a mess of your lives, that's up to you. But I warn you to be careful about Hedvig. You might cause her irreparable harm.

HJALMAR: Harm?

RELLING: Yes. Or she might try to harm herself—and others too.

GINA: What makes you think that, Relling?

HJALMAR: You mean—? There's no immediate danger to her eyesight, is there?

RELLING: I'm not talking about her eyesight! Hedvig's at a difficult age. Heaven knows *what* she might get into her head.

GINA: You're right—she's had some queer ideas of late. She's taken to messing about with the kitchen stove, for instance. Playing at "house-on-fire" she calls it. I've been afraid she might really set fire to the place one of these days.

RELLING: There, you see! I knew it.

GREGERS *(To* RELLING*)*: But how do you explain that kind of thing?

RELLING *(Curtly)*: Adolescence—Mr. Werle, Jr.

HJALMAR: As long as she has her father—! As long as I'm this side of the grave—!

(There's a knock at the door.)

GINA: Hush, Hjalmar; there's someone in the hall. *(Calls out)* Come in!

(MRS. SÖRBY enters; she wears a hat and a warm coat.)

MRS. SÖRBY: Good evening!

GINA *(Goes toward her)*: Why, Bertha! Is it you?

MRS. SÖRBY: Yes. I hope I'm not disturbing you?

HJALMAR: Good heavens, no! How could an emissary from *that* house—!

MRS. SÖRBY *(To GINA)*: Actually—I'd hoped to find you alone, at this time of day. I just ran over to have a little chat with you, and say good-bye.

GINA: Good-bye? Are you going away?

MRS. SÖRBY: Early tomorrow morning—up to Höjdal. Mr. Werle left this afternoon. *(To GREGERS, casually)* He told me to say good-bye to you for him.

GINA: Well—fancy!

HJALMAR: So Mr. Werle's gone, has he? And you're going after him?

MRS. SÖRBY: Yes. What do you say to that, Ekdal?

HJALMAR: I say, be careful!

GREGERS: Let me explain; my father is going to marry Mrs. Sörby.

HJALMAR: Marry her!

GINA: Oh, Bertha! So it's really happened at last!

RELLING *(With a slight quiver in his voice)*: This surely can't be true?

MRS. SÖRBY: Yes, dear Dr. Relling, it's true enough.

RELLING: You're really going to marry again?

MRS. SÖRBY: It looks like it! Mr. Werle got a special license, and we're to have a very quiet wedding, up at the works.

GREGERS: Then let me be a dutiful stepson, and wish you happiness.

MRS. SÖRBY: Thanks very much—if you really mean it. I hope it will bring happiness to both of us.

RELLING: I don't see why it shouldn't. Mr. Werle never gets drunk, as far as I know—and, unlike the late-lamented horse doctor, he's not in the habit of beating his wives either.

MRS. SÖRBY: Oh, let poor Sörby rest in peace. He had his good points too.

RELLING: But I expect Mr. Werle has even better ones.

MRS. SÖRBY: At least he hasn't wasted all that was best in him; when a man does that, he must face the consequences.

RELLING: Tonight I shall go out with Molvik.

MRS. SÖRBY: Don't do that, Relling. Please—for my sake!

RELLING: What else is there to do? *(To* HJALMAR*)* If you feel like joining us, Hjalmar—come along!

GINA: No, thank you. Hjalmar doesn't go to places of *that* sort!

HJALMAR *(In an angry undertone)*: Oh, do be quiet!

RELLING: Goodbye Mrs.—Werle. *(Goes out by the hall door.)*

GREGERS *(To* MRS. SÖRBY*)*: You seem to be on very intimate terms with Dr. Relling.

MRS. SÖRBY: We've known each other for many years. At one time it looked as though something might have come of it.

GREGERS: It's just as well for you it didn't.

MRS. SÖRBY: Yes, you're right. But then, I've never been one to act on impulse. A woman can't afford to throw herself away.

GREGERS: Aren't you afraid I might say something to my father about this former friendship?

MRS. SÖRBY: I've naturally told him all about it.

GREGERS: Oh?

MRS. SÖRBY: Yes; I've told him everything that anyone could possibly find to say against me. The moment I realized what was in his mind, I made a point of doing so.

GREGERS: Then you're more than usually frank, it seems to me.

MRS. SÖRBY: I've always been frank. I think for a woman it's the best policy.

HJALMAR: What do you say to that, Gina?

GINA: We can't all be alike. Some women are one way, and some another.

MRS. SÖRBY: You know, Gina—I believe my way is best. And Mr. Werle has no secrets from me either. He can sit and talk to me quite openly—just like a child. It's the first time he's ever been able to do that. It's all wrong that a man of his type—full of health and vigor—should have had to spend the best years of his life listening to interminable lectures on his sins! And mostly imaginary sins too—as far as I can make out.

GINA: Lord knows *that's* true enough!

GREGERS: If you ladies intend to pursue this topic, I think I'd better go.

MRS. SÖRBY: No—you needn't go; I shan't say any more. I just wanted you to know that my dealings have been honorable and aboveboard from the start. I dare say many people will envy me and think me very lucky—and in a way I am. But I shall give as good as I get, I promise you. I shall never fail him. And now that he'll soon be helpless, I'll be able to repay him by serving him and caring for him always. I can do that better than anyone else, I think.

HJALMAR: What do you mean—helpless?

GREGERS *(To* MRS. SÖRBY*)*: Don't say anything about that here.

MRS. SÖRBY: It's no use trying to hide it any longer; he's going blind.

HJALMAR *(With a start)*: Blind? He's going blind you say? That's very strange.

GINA: Lots of people do, unfortunately.

MRS. SÖRBY: You can imagine what that means to a man in his position. I shall simply have to use my eyes for both of us, and do the best I can—But I really can't stay any longer—I have so much to do—By the way, I was to give you a message, Mr. Ekdal: If there's anything Werle can ever do for you, just mention it to Graaberg.

GREGERS: An offer that Hjalmar Ekdal will most certainly refuse.

MRS. SÖRBY: Really? He didn't used to be so—

GINA: No, Bertha. Hjalmar doesn't need anything from Mr. Werle now.

HJALMAR *(Slowly and forcefully)*: Be so good as to give my regards to your future husband, and tell him I intend to call on Mr. Graaberg very shortly—

GREGERS: What! You don't mean you—?

HJALMAR: —call on Mr. Graaberg, I say, and demand a full accounting of the money I owe to his employer. I intend to pay this debt of honor—ha! ha! ha! debt of honor is a good name for it!—but no more of that—I intend to pay it in full with interest at five percent.

GINA: But, Hjalmar dear—where will we ever get the money?

HJALMAR: You may tell your fiancé that I am forging ahead with my invention. Tell him that I am sustained in this laborious task by the desire to rid myself once and for all of this painful debt. That is my chief motive in pursuing the work on my invention so relentlessly. I plan to devote the profits to freeing myself from all obligation to your future husband.

MRS. SÖRBY: What has been happening here?

HJALMAR: You may well ask!

MRS. SÖRBY: Well, I'll say good-bye. There were a couple of

other things I wanted to talk to you about, Gina—but they must wait till some other time—Good-bye.

(HJALMAR *and* GREGERS *bow silently;* GINA *takes* MRS. SÖRBY *to the door.*)

HJALMAR: Not beyond the threshold, Gina!

(MRS. SÖRBY *goes out;* GINA *closes the door after her.*)

HJALMAR: There, Gregers! That burden of debt is off my mind!

GREGERS: It soon will be, at any rate.

HJALMAR: I think my behavior might be described as suitably correct?

GREGERS: Your behavior was admirable, as I knew it would be.

HJALMAR: There are times when one cannot possibly disregard the claim of the Ideal. But it will be a long hard struggle. It's not easy for a man without a penny to his name, and with a family to support, to pay off a long-standing debt of this sort—on which, one might say, the dust of oblivion has settled. But it must be faced; my integrity as a human being demands it.

GREGERS (*Puts his hands on* HJALMAR'S *shoulders*): My dear Hjalmar—wasn't it a good thing that I came?

HJALMAR: Ye-es.

GREGERS: Don't you feel happier, now that you see your position clearly?

HJALMAR (*Somewhat impatiently*): Yes—of course I do. But there's one thing that offends my sense of justice.

GREGERS: What thing?

HJALMAR: It's just that—but perhaps I shouldn't speak of your father in this way—

GREGERS: Say anything you like as far as I'm concerned.

HJALMAR: It shocks me to think that he has succeeded where I have failed. His marriage will be a *true* marriage, you see.

GREGERS: How can you say a thing like that!

HJALMAR: But it's so, isn't it? Your father's marriage to Mrs. Sörby is based on truth and mutual confidence. They've kept nothing back; they hold no secrets from each other. They've reached a complete agreement. It's as though they'd each confessed their sins and given each other absolution.

GREGERS: Well—what then?

HJALMAR: That's the whole point—don't you see? You said yourself that no true marriage could exist unless these problems had been faced and cleared away.

GREGERS: But this is quite different, Hjalmar. You surely don't compare yourself—or Gina here—with *those* two—? You know quite well what I mean.

HJALMAR: All the same—there's something about this that offends my sense of justice. If things like this are allowed to happen, there's obviously no such thing as a Divine Power ruling the universe!

GINA: Hjalmar! For God's sake don't say such things!

GREGERS: Hm. Don't let's embark on that subject.

HJALMAR: Yet—now I come to think of it—it's possible to see the hand of Destiny at work in this: he's going blind.

GINA: But perhaps that isn't true.

HJALMAR: I'm positive it's true; if there *is* such a thing as Divine Justice it *must* be true. Look at all the unsuspecting people he's hoodwinked in his time—!

GREGERS: A great many, unfortunately.

HJALMAR: And now he's being made to pay for it by going blind himself: it's retribution.

GINA: You frighten me when you say such dreadful things.

HJALMAR: It's sometimes salutary to examine the darker sides of life.

(HEDVIG, *in her hat and coat, comes in by the hall door. She is breathless and excited.*)

GINA: Back already?

HEDVIG: Yes; I didn't want to stay out any longer. And it was just as well, because I met someone at the front door as I came in—

HJALMAR: That Mrs. Sörby, I suppose.

HEDVIG: That's right.

HJALMAR *(Pacing up and down)*: I hope that's the last time you'll ever lay eyes on *her*.
(A pause. HEDVIG *glances from one to the other as if trying to gauge their mood.)*

HEDVIG *(Coaxingly, going up to* HJALMAR*)*: Father.

HJALMAR: Well—what is it?

HEDVIG: Mrs. Sörby brought me something.

HJALMAR: Something for you?

HEDVIG: Yes—it's something for tomorrow.

GINA: Bertha always has some little present for you on your birthday.

HJALMAR: What is it?

HEDVIG: Oh, we're not supposed to see it yet. Mother's to bring it in to me early tomorrow morning.

HJALMAR: What *is* this? A conspiracy behind my back?

HEDVIG *(Rapidly)*: No, of course not! You can see it if you like! Look—it's this great big letter. *(She takes it out of her coat pocket.)*

HJALMAR: So there's a letter too.

HEDVIG: That's all she gave me; the rest'll come later, I suppose. But, just think—a letter! It's the first one I've ever had. And there's "Miss" written on the envelope. *(Reads)* "Miss Hedvig Ekdal." Just think of it—that's *me!*

HJALMAR: Let me see that letter.

HEDVIG *(Hands it to him)*: There you are.

HJALMAR: This is Mr. Werle's handwriting.

GINA: Are you sure, Hjalmar?

HJALMAR: Look for yourself.

273

GINA: I don't know about such things.

HJALMAR: May I open it, and read it, Hedvig?

HEDVIG: Of course, Father, if you want to.

GINA: Not this evening, Hjalmar; we're supposed to save it till tomorrow.

HEDVIG *(Softly)*: Oh, let him read it, Mother. I'm sure it's something nice. Father will be pleased and things will be all right again.

HJALMAR: I may open it then?

HEDVIG: Yes, Father, do! It'll be such fun to see what's in it!

HJALMAR: Very well. *(He opens the envelope, takes out a paper, reads it through, and seems bewildered)* What does this mean—?

GINA: What does it say?

HEDVIG: Do tell us, Father dear!

HJALMAR: Be quiet. *(Reads it through again; he turns pale but speaks with self-control)* It's a deed of gift.

HEDVIG: Really? What do I get?

HJALMAR: Here—read it yourself. (HEDVIG *takes it and goes over to the lamp to read it.)*

HJALMAR *(In an undertone, clenching his hands)*: The eyes! The eyes—and now, *this!*

HEDVIG: But—isn't this for Grandfather?

HJALMAR *(Takes the paper from her)*: Gina—what do you make of it?

GINA: I wouldn't understand anything about it. Just tell me what it is.

HJALMAR: It's a letter to Hedvig from Mr. Werle, informing her that in the future her grandfather need trouble himself no further with any copying work; but instead—he may draw on Mr. Werle's office for a hundred crowns a month.

GREGERS: Aha!

HEDVIG: A hundred crowns, Mother! That's what I thought it said!

GINA: That's nice for Grandfather.

HJALMAR: —a hundred crowns a month as long as he may need it; which means as long as he lives, of course.

GINA: Poor old man—so he's provided for at least.

HJALMAR: Wait. There's more to come. You probably didn't read this, Hedvig. Afterwards the gift reverts to you.

HEDVIG: To me! All that money to *me!*

HJALMAR: For the rest of your life you will receive a hundred crowns a month, he writes. Do you hear that, Gina?

GINA: Yes, I hear it.

HEDVIG: All that money, Father! Think of it! *(Shakes him)* Father, Father—aren't you glad?

HJALMAR *(Shakes her off)*: Glad! *(Paces up and down)* God! What perspectives—what vistas all this opens up to me! So— it's Hedvig! Why should he shower gifts on her!

GINA: Well, I suppose—it's Hedvig's birthday after all—

HEDVIG: But it will all belong to you, Father! You know I'll give it all to you and Mother!

HJALMAR: To your mother, yes! Of course—that's as it should be!

GREGERS: Hjalmar—this is a trap he's laid for you.

HJALMAR: Another one of his traps, you think?

GREGERS: He said to me only this morning, "Hjalmar Ekdal is not the man you take him for."

HJALMAR: Not the man—!

GREGERS: "You'll soon find out," he said.

HJALMAR: So he wants to show you he can bribe me—

HEDVIG: Mother, what does all this mean?

GINA: Go and take off your things.

(HEDVIG goes out through the kitchen, on the verge of tears.)

GREGERS: Well, Hjalmar—? Was *he* right about you, or am I?

HJALMAR *(Slowly tears the paper in two and lays the pieces on the table)*: There is my answer.

GREGERS: Just what I expected.

HJALMAR *(Goes over to* GINA *who is standing by the stove and says in a low voice)*: I want no more lies, I warn you, Gina. If things were really over between you and Werle when you became "fond of me"—as you choose to put it—why did he make it possible for us to marry?

GINA: He perhaps thought he'd be able to come and go as he liked, here in our house.

HJALMAR: Was that all? Mightn't he have been afraid? Wasn't it something to do with your condition at the time?

GINA: I don't know what you mean.

HJALMAR: I must know—Has your child the right to live under my roof?

GINA *(Draws herself up; her eyes flash)*: You ask *me* that!

HJALMAR: Answer me! Does Hedvig belong to me—or—? Well?

GINA *(Looks at him coldly and defiantly)*: I don't know.

HJALMAR *(Trembling slightly)*: You don't know?

GINA: No. How should I? A creature like *me*—?

HJALMAR *(Quietly, turning away from her)*: Then I have nothing more to do in this house.

GREGERS: Consider what you're doing, Hjalmar!

HJALMAR *(Putting on his overcoat)*: What is there to consider? For a man like me there can be no alternative.

GREGERS: There are many things to be considered. You three must stay together. How else can you start afresh in a spirit of forgiveness and self-sacrifice?

HJALMAR: I don't want to. Never, never! My hat! *(Takes his hat)* My home is nothing but a mass of ruins! *(Bursts into tears)* Gregers! I have no child!

HEDVIG *(Who has opened the kitchen door)*: Father! What are you saying! *(Runs to him)* Father!

GINA: There, you see!

HJALMAR: Don't touch me, Hedvig! Keep away from me—I can't bear to look at you! Oh! Those eyes—! Good-bye. *(Starts toward the door.)*

HEDVIG *(Clings to him, screaming)*: No! No! Don't leave me!

GINA *(Cries out)*: The poor child, Hjalmar! Look at the child!

HJALMAR: I won't! I can't! I must get out of here—away from this! *(He tears himself away from HEDVIG and goes out through the hall door.)*

HEDVIG *(Her eyes full of despair)*: He's going away from us, Mother! He's going away! He'll never come back—never!

GINA: Don't cry, Hedvig. Father will come back—you'll see.

HEDVIG *(Flings herself down on the sofa sobbing)*: No he won't! He won't! He'll never come home to us anymore!

GREGERS: I meant it all for the best, Mrs. Ekdal. You do believe that, don't you?

GINA: Yes—I suppose so. But God forgive you all the same.

HEDVIG: I shall die if he doesn't come back, Mother—I shall die! What have I done to him? Go and find him, Mother, and bring him home again!

GINA: Yes, darling—yes! Try and be calm now. I'll go and look for him. *(Puts on her outdoor things)* Perhaps he's down at Relling's. Don't cry any more—promise!

HEDVIG *(Sobbing convulsively)*: I won't—I won't! I promise! If only he'll come back!

GREGERS: You don't think it would be better to let him fight it out alone?

GINA: Let him do that later! We must get the child quieted down first. *(Goes out by the hall door.)*

HEDVIG *(Sits up and dries her tears)*: Please! What is it all about?

You've got to tell me! Why doesn't Father want me any more?

GREGERS: You must wait till you're grown-up before asking about that.

HEDVIG: But I can't wait till I'm grown-up and go on being miserable like this!—I think I know what it's all about—Perhaps I'm not really Father's child.

GREGERS *(Uneasily)*: How could *that* be?

HEDVIG: Mother may have picked me up somewhere; and Father's just discovered it. I've read about things like that.

GREGERS: But even if that were so—

HEDVIG: I don't see why he should stop being fond of me on that account; I should think he'd love me even more. The wild duck came to us as a present too—and I love it very dearly all the same.

GREGERS *(Switches the conversation)*: The wild duck—yes! Let's talk about the wild duck for a while.

HEDVIG: Poor wild duck. He can't bear to look at her either anymore. Just think—he said he'd like to wring her neck!

GREGERS: But I'm sure he'd never do it!

HEDVIG: He said he'd like to! I thought it was horrid of him. I say a prayer for the wild duck every night. I ask God to protect it from death and everything that's evil.

GREGERS *(Looking at her)*: Do you say your prayers every night?

HEDVIG: Yes, I do.

GREGERS: Who taught you to do that?

HEDVIG: I taught myself. Father was terribly ill once—they had to put leeches on his chest. He kept saying death was staring him in the face.

GREGERS: Well?

HEDVIG: So that night when I went to bed, I said a prayer for him. And I've kept on with it ever since.

GREGERS: And now you pray for the wild duck too?

HEDVIG: Yes, I thought I'd better; she was so very weak at first, you know.

GREGERS: Do you say your prayers in the morning too?

HEDVIG: No—of course not!

GREGERS: Why not? Aren't morning prayers any good?

HEDVIG: Well—in the morning it's light, you see; there's nothing to be afraid of then.

GREGERS: And this wild duck you're so fond of—You say your father wanted to wring its neck?

HEDVIG: He said he'd *like* to—but that he'd spare her for my sake. That was kind of him, I thought.

GREGERS *(Coming a little nearer)*: What if you were to offer up the wild duck as a sacrifice? For *his* sake?

HEDVIG *(Rises)*: The wild duck!

GREGERS: Yes. Supposing you were to sacrifice to him the thing you love most dearly in the world?

HEDVIG: Would that do any good—do you think?

GREGERS: Try it, Hedvig.

HEDVIG *(Softly, with shining eyes)*: Very well—I *will*.

GREGERS: Do you think you'll really have the courage?

HEDVIG: The wild duck! I'll ask Grandfather to shoot it for me.

GREGERS: Yes, do that. But don't say a word to your mother about it.

HEDVIG: Why not?

GREGERS: She doesn't understand us.

HEDVIG: The wild duck! I'll try and do it the first thing in the morning.

(GINA comes in from the hall door.)

HEDVIG *(Goes to her)*: Did you find him, Mother?

GINA: No. But he went to fetch Relling, and they went out together.

GREGERS: Are you sure?

GINA: The porter's wife told me—she saw them. Molvik was with them too, she said.

GREGERS: That's strange! I should have thought he'd want to fight things out alone—!

GINA *(Taking off her things)*: Men are queer creatures! God knows *where* Relling's dragged him off to. I ran over to Mrs. Eriksen's—but they weren't there.

HEDVIG *(Fighting back her tears)*: What if he *never* comes back to us, Mother!

GREGERS: He'll come back. I'll send him word tomorrow. You'll see—he'll come. Go to sleep now, Hedvig—and don't worry. Good night. *(He goes out by the hall door.)*

HEDVIG *(Sobbing, throws herself into her mother's arms)*: Mother! Mother!

GINA *(Pats her shoulder and sighs)*: Ah, yes! Relling was right. That's what happens when people come around with all this crazy talk of claims and idols!

CURTAIN

Act Five

SCENE: HJALMAR EKDAL'S *studio. Cold, gray morning light; patches of snow lie on the large panes of the studio window.*

GINA enters from the kitchen wearing an apron with a bib and carrying a broom and a duster; she goes toward the sitting-room door. At the same moment HEDVIG comes in quickly from the hall.

GINA *(Stops)*: Well?

HEDVIG: Mother, you know, I think he's down at Relling's—

GINA: There, you see!

HEDVIG: Because the porter's wife says there were two people with Relling when he came home last night.

GINA: Just what I thought.

HEDVIG: But what good does it do, if he won't come up to us?

GINA: At least I can go down and have a talk with him.

(OLD EKDAL in his slippers and a dressing gown, and smoking his pipe, appears at the door of his room.)

EKDAL: Oh, Hjalmar—Isn't Hjalmar home?

GINA: No, he's gone out.

EKDAL: What—so early? And in all this snow? Well—never mind. I'll take my morning walk alone.

(He slides open the attic door; HEDVIG helps him; he goes in; she closes it after him.)

HEDVIG: Mother, what will poor Grandfather do, when he hears that Father's going to leave us?

GINA: Nonsense! Grandfather mustn't know anything about it. Thank God he was out yesterday—during all the rumpus.

HEDVIG: Yes, but—

(GREGERS comes in from the hall.)

GREGERS: Well? Any news of him?

GINA: They say he's down at Relling's.

GREGERS: Relling's! Did he *really* go out with those two?

GINA: It looks like it.

GREGERS: How could he! When it was so important for him to be alone—to collect his thoughts in solitude!

GINA: Yes. That's what he should have done.

(RELLING *comes in from the hall.*)

HEDVIG *(Going to him)*: Is Father down with you?

GINA *(Simultaneously)*: Is he down there?

RELLING: Yes, of course he is.

HEDVIG: You might have let us know!

RELLING: Yes—I'm a swine, I know. But I had that other swine on my hands—our demonic friend, I mean. And I got so tired, I fell into a stupor—

GINA: What has Hjalmar got to say today?

RELLING: Nothing whatever.

HEDVIG: Hasn't he said anything at all?

RELLING: Not a blessed word.

GREGERS: Well—that's understandable enough.

GINA: Then what's he doing?

RELLING: Lying on the sofa snoring.

GINA: Is he? He's a great one for snoring, Hjalmar is.

GREGERS: You mean—he's actually asleep?

RELLING: He certainly appears to be.

GREGERS: I expect it's only natural; after the spiritual crisis he's been through—

GINA: And then, he's not used to gadding about at night.

HEDVIG: It'll do him good to get some sleep, Mother.

GINA: That's what I think. We'd better not wake him up too early. Thanks, Relling. I'll see about getting the house cleaned up a bit—come and help me, Hedvig.

(GINA *and* HEDVIG *go into the sitting room.*)

GREGERS *(Turning to* RELLING*)*: How would you explain this spiritual upheaval that Hjalmar Ekdal's going through?

RELLING: Damned if I saw anything resembling a spiritual upheaval—!

GREGERS: Come now! At a turning point like this? When he's about to start on a whole new way of life—? You must realize that a man of Hjalmar's character—

RELLING: Did you say *character?* Hjalmar? If he ever possessed a vestige of that rare attribute, it was crushed in him, I assure you—thoroughly extirpated—while he was still a child.

GREGERS: That seems hardly likely—considering the loving care with which he was brought up.

RELLING: By those doting, hysterical maiden aunts of his you mean?

GREGERS: Let me tell you they were women who never lost sight of the Ideal—now, I suppose, you'll start jeering again!

RELLING: No—I'm in no mood for that. I happen to know a lot about these ladies; he's often waxed eloquent on the subject of his two "soul-mothers"—as he calls them! Hjalmar has had the great misfortune of always being looked on as a shining light in his own particular circle—

GREGERS: And don't you think he is? Deep down—I mean?

RELLING: I've certainly never noticed it. That his father should have thought so—that's understandable enough; the old lieutenant's always been something of an ass.

GREGERS: He's a man who has never lost his childlike nature—that's what you fail to understand.

RELLING: All right—have it your own way! Then, when our dear sweet Hjalmar went to college, his fellow students looked on him as the great hope of the future, too. He was handsome enough—the scoundrel! Pink and white—the kind the girls all go for. And then he had a facile mind, and a romantic voice which he used to good

---

effect declaiming other people's poetry, and other people's thoughts—

GREGERS *(Indignantly)*: It can't be Hjalmar Ekdal you're talking about like this—?

RELLING: Yes—with your permission. This is the truth about that idol of yours to whom you bow the knee.

GREGERS: It never occurred to me I could be quite *that* blind.

RELLING: You are though—pretty nearly. You're a sick man too, you see.

GREGERS: You're right about that, at least.

RELLING: Yes. Yours is a complicated case. First you've got that blasted integrity fever to contend with; then—what's worse—you live in a constant delirium of hero worship; it's absolutely necessary for you to look up to and adore something outside yourself.

GREGERS: It would inevitably have to be something outside myself.

RELLING: But you make such ridiculous mistakes about these imaginary paragons of yours! Why do you persist in presenting your Claim of the Ideal to people who are totally insolvent?

GREGERS: Why do you spend so much time with Hjalmar Ekdal, if this is your opinion of him?

RELLING: I'm a doctor of sorts, you know—God help me! I feel obliged to look after the sick people who live under the same roof with me.

GREGERS: So you think Hjalmar Ekdal is sick too?

RELLING: Most people are sick, unfortunately.

GREGERS: May I ask what cure you're using in Hjalmar's case?

RELLING: My usual one. I try to discover the basic lie—the pet illusion—that makes life possible; and then I foster it.

GREGERS: The basic lie? Surely—I misunderstood—?

RELLING: No, no; that's what I said: the basic lie that makes life possible.

GREGERS: And what "basic lie" do you suppose Hjalmar to be suffering from?

RELLING: I don't betray secrets like that to quacks. You've made enough mess of the case for me already. But my method is infallible; I've used it on Molvik too; I've convinced him he's demonic—that did the trick for him.

GREGERS: You mean—he's *not* demonic?

RELLING: What the hell does it mean: to be demonic? It's a lot of nonsense I invented to make life possible for him. Without that the poor harmless wretch would have gone under years ago—in an agony of despair and self-contempt. And what about the old lieutenant? But that's different: he discovered the cure for himself, you see.

GREGERS: Lt. Ekdal? What do you mean?

RELLING: Just think of it! The mighty bear-hunter shooting rabbits in the attic. And there's no happier hunter in the world than that old man fooling about in there in all that rubbish. He's saved four or five withered old Christmas trees, and to him they're just as beautiful and green and fresh as the whole of the great Höjdal forest. To him the rooster and the hens are wild birds in the treetops; and the rabbits that lope about the attic floor are the bears he used to grapple with out in the wilds, when he was young and vigorous.

GREGERS: Poor old Lt. Ekdal; he's gone a long way from the ideals of his youth.

RELLING: While I think of it, Mr. Werle, Jr.—I wish you'd stop using that foreign word: *ideals*. We have a perfectly good one of our own: lies.

GREGERS: You seem to think the two things are related!

RELLING: They are: they're as alike as typhoid and malignant fever.

GREGERS: I shall never give up until I've rescued Hjalmar from your clutches, Dr. Relling.

RELLING: So much the worse for *him*. Rob the average man of his basic lie and you rob him of his happiness as well. *(To* HEDVIG *who comes in from the sitting room)* And now, little wild-duck mother, I'll just run down and see how your father's getting on; I expect he's lying there meditating on that wonderful invention. *(He goes out through the hall door.)*

GREGERS *(Going up to* HEDVIG*)*: You haven't done it yet, have you? I can see it in your face.

HEDVIG: What? Oh, you mean—about the wild duck? No.

GREGERS: When it actually came to the point, I suppose your courage failed you.

HEDVIG: No—it wasn't that. But when I woke up this morning and remembered what we'd talked about, it seemed queer to me somehow.

GREGERS: Queer?

HEDVIG: Yes; I don't know—Last night, right at the time, I thought it was a very beautiful idea; but I didn't think so much of it—after I'd slept on it, you see.

GREGERS: I see that growing up in the atmosphere of this house has unfortunately had its effect on you.

HEDVIG: I don't care about that—if only Father would come back to us—

GREGERS: If only your eyes had been opened to the true values in life; if you only had the joyous, courageous spirit of self-sacrifice, you'd see how quickly your father would come back to you—But I still have faith in you, Hedvig—don't forget that. *(He goes out into the hall.)*
*(*HEDVIG *paces about the room; she is about to go into the kitchen when a knock is heard at the attic door;* HEDVIG *goes over and opens it a little way;* OLD EKDAL *comes out. She slides the door closed again.)*

EKDAL: Hm. Not much fun going for your morning walk alone.

HEDVIG: Didn't you feel like going hunting, Grandfather?

EKDAL: Weather's not right for hunting; it's so dark you can hardly see.

HEDVIG: Do you ever feel like shooting anything besides the rabbits?

EKDAL: Why? Aren't the rabbits good enough?

HEDVIG: Yes, of course; but what about the wild duck?

EKDAL: Ho! ho! You're afraid I'll shoot your wild duck, are you? I'd never do that. Never.

HEDVIG: No. I don't suppose you could, could you? It's very difficult to shoot wild ducks, they say.

EKDAL: What do you mean I *couldn't*? I should rather think I *could!*

HEDVIG: How would you go about it, Grandfather?—Not with *my* wild duck, of course; I mean with others?

EKDAL: I'd shoot at the breast, you see; that's the surest place. And then you must always shoot *against* the feathers, you understand—not *with* them.

HEDVIG: And then do they die, Grandfather?

EKDAL: They die all right—if you shoot properly. I'll go in and brush up a bit. Hm—you see—hm. *(Goes into his room.)*
*(*HEDVIG *waits a moment or two, glances toward the sitting-room door, goes over to the bookcase, stands on tiptoe, takes the double-barreled pistol down from the shelf and looks at it.* GINA *carrying her broom and duster comes in from the sitting room.* HEDVIG *puts down the pistol hastily without being seen.)*

GINA: Don't stand there messing about with your father's things, Hedvig.

HEDVIG *(Going away from the bookcase)*: I was just trying to tidy up a bit.

GINA: You'd better go in the kitchen and see if the coffee's keeping hot. I'll take a tray down to him when I go.
*(*HEDVIG *goes out;* GINA *begins sweeping and cleaning up the studio. After a while the hall door opens cautiously and* HJALMAR EKDAL *looks in; he wears his overcoat but no hat; he is*

unwashed and his hair is dishevelled and unkempt. His eyes are dull and heavy.)

GINA *(Stands with the broom in her hand and looks at him)*: Well now, Hjalmar—you came back after all.

HJALMAR *(Comes in and answers in a gloomy voice)*: I've come back—but only to go away again immediately.

GINA: Yes—I suppose so. But, my goodness! What a state you're in!

HJALMAR: A state?

GINA: And it's your good overcoat too! That's done for, I'm afraid!

HEDVIG *(At the kitchen door)*: Mother, shall I—? *(Sees* HJALMAR, *gives a cry of joy and runs toward him)* Father, Father!

HJALMAR *(Turns away with a gesture of repulsion)*: Keep away from me! *(To* GINA*)* Keep her away, I tell you!

GINA *(In an undertone)*: Go into the sitting room, Hedvig. *(*HEDVIG *silently obeys.)*

HJALMAR *(Making a show of being busy opens the table drawer)*: I want my books—I'll need them with me. Where are my books?

GINA: What books?

HJALMAR: My scientific books, of course—All those technical periodicals I need for my invention.

GINA *(Looking in the bookcase)*: Are they these things—without a binding?

HJALMAR: Yes—naturally.

GINA *(Lays a pile of magazines on the table)*: Don't you want Hedvig to cut the pages for you?

HJALMAR: I want no pages cut for me.
(A short pause.)

GINA: So you still intend to leave us, Hjalmar?

HJALMAR *(Rummaging among the books)*: I should think that was obvious.

GINA: Well, well!

HJALMAR: I don't intend to stay here to be stabbed through the heart each hour of the day!

GINA: God forgive you for believing all those dreadful things about me!

HJALMAR: Then prove—!

GINA: I think you're the one who ought to prove!

HJALMAR: After a past like yours? There are certain claims— I'm tempted to call them Claims of the Ideal—

GINA: What about Grandfather? What's going to happen to him—poor old man?

HJALMAR: I know my duty. The poor helpless old man shall go with me. I'll go out presently and make arrangements— Hm. *(Hesitating)* Did anyone find my hat on the stairs?

GINA: No. Have you lost your hat?

HJALMAR: I naturally had it on when I came in last night; there's no doubt about that. But this morning I couldn't find it.

GINA: Dear Lord! Where on earth did you go with those two good-for-nothings?

HJALMAR: Don't bother me with trifles. I'm in no mood to remember details.

GINA: I do hope you haven't caught cold, Hjalmar! *(Goes out into the kitchen.)*

HJALMAR *(Mutters to himself in a low angry tone as he empties the table drawer)*: You're a scoundrel, Relling; an infamous, treacherous scoundrel! I wish to God someone would wring your neck!

(He lays aside some old letters, catches sight of the torn document from the day before, picks it up and examines the two pieces; puts it down hurriedly as GINA enters.)

GINA *(Puts a tray with coffee, etc. down on the table)*: You might like a drop of something hot. And there's some bread and butter and a bit of that smoked tongue.

HJALMAR *(Glancing at the tray)*: Smoked tongue, you say? No! Nothing under this roof! I haven't eaten a morsel of food for nearly twenty-four hours, that's true enough—but never mind! My notes! And the preliminary chapters of my autobiography! What has become of my diary—and all my important papers? *(Opens the door to the sitting room but draws back)* There she is again!

GINA: The poor child has to be somewhere!

HJALMAR: Come out. *(He stands aside.* HEDVIG, *terrified, comes into the studio.* HJALMAR, *his hand on the door knob, says to* GINA*)* During these last few moments in my former home I wish to be spared all contact with intruders—*(Goes into the sitting room.)*

HEDVIG *(Runs to her mother and says softly in a trembling voice)*: Does he mean me?

GINA: Stay in the kitchen, Hedvig; or, no—perhaps you'd better go to your own room. *(Speaks to* HJALMAR *as she goes in to him)* Wait a minute, Hjalmar. Don't rummage about in all the drawers; I know where everything is.

HEDVIG *(Stands motionless for a moment, confused and terrified; she bites her lips to prevent herself from crying. Then she clenches her hands convulsively and says softly)*: The wild duck!
(She steals over and takes the pistol from the shelf, slides open the attic door a little way, creeps in, and draws the door closed after her. HJALMAR *and* GINA *begin to argue in the sitting room.)*

HJALMAR *(Comes in with some notebooks and old loose sheets of paper and lays them on the table)*: What's the good of that portmanteau! That won't hold anything—I've *hundreds* of things to take with me!

GINA *(Follows him carrying the portmanteau)*: Why not leave everything here for the time being, and just take a clean shirt and a pair of extra underdrawers?

HJALMAR: Phew! These exhausting preparations—! *(He pulls off his overcoat and throws it on the sofa.)*

GINA: Look! Your coffee's getting cold!

HJALMAR: Hm. *(Drinks a gulp without thinking and then another.)*

GINA *(Dusting the backs of the chairs)*: You'll have a hard time finding a big enough place for all those rabbits.

HJALMAR: Good God! You don't expect me to drag all those rabbits with me!

GINA: Grandfather could never get along without his rabbits.

HJALMAR: He'll just have to get used to it. After all *I'm* sacrificing far more important things than rabbits!

GINA *(Dusting the bookcase)*: I'd better pack your flute, hadn't I?

HJALMAR: No. No flute for me. But I shall need my pistol.

GINA: Are you going to take that gun along?

HJALMAR: My loaded pistol—yes.

GINA *(Looks for it)*: It isn't here. He must have taken it in there with him.

HJALMAR: Is he in the attic?

GINA: Of course he is.

HJALMAR: Hm. Poor lonely old man. *(He takes some bread and butter and smoked tongue, eats it, and finishes his cup of coffee.)*

GINA: If we hadn't rented that room, you could have moved in there.

HJALMAR: And go on living under the same roof as—! Never! Never!

GINA: I suppose you couldn't manage in the sitting room for a day or two? You could have it all to yourself; I'd see to that.

HJALMAR: No! I can't breathe inside these walls!

GINA: Why not down with Relling and Molvik, then?

HJALMAR: Never mention their names to me again! The very thought of them is enough to take away my appetite— No—I shall simply have to go out into the storm; go from house to house, seeking shelter for my old father and myself.

GINA: But you have no hat, Hjalmar! You've gone and lost it, you know.

HJALMAR: Those two scoundrels! Vicious, infamous brutes! I'll have to pick up a hat somewhere on the way. *(Takes some more bread and tongue)* Something'll have to be done about it; I've no desire to risk my life. *(Looks for something on the tray.)*

GINA: What are you looking for?

HJALMAR: Butter.

GINA: I'll get you some at once. *(She goes out into the kitchen.)*

HJALMAR *(Shouting after her)*: Oh, never mind; dry bread is good enough for me.

GINA *(Bringing in a dish of butter)*: There you are; it's freshly churned.
(She pours him a fresh cup of coffee; he sits on the sofa, spreads more butter on the already-buttered bread, and eats and drinks for a while in silence.)

HJALMAR: Would it be possible for me, without being annoyed by anyone—anyone at all—to stay in the sitting room in there, just for a day or two?

GINA: Why, of course. I only wish you would.

HJALMAR: I don't see how I can possibly get Father moved in such a hurry.

GINA: No. And then, you ought to prepare him too. Tell him you don't want to live here with us anymore.

HJALMAR *(Pushing away his coffee cup)*: Yes, there is that. It's awful to think of having to broach this difficult subject with him. I must have a breathing spell—a chance to think things out. I can't cope with all these problems in a single day!

GINA: Of course not; and it's such awful weather too.

HJALMAR *(Touching WERLE's letter)*: I see that paper is still hanging about.

GINA: Yes. *I* haven't touched it.

HJALMAR: Well—it's no concern of mine—

GINA: *I* certainly never thought of using it.

HJALMAR: Still—there's no sense in throwing it away; in all the commotion of my moving, it might easily—

GINA: I'll take good care of it, Hjalmar.

HJALMAR: In the first place, the gift was made to Father; it's really up to him to decide whether he'll make use of it or not.

GINA *(Sighs)*: Yes—poor old Father—

HJALMAR: Just as a matter of precaution, I think—have you any paste?

GINA *(Goes to the bookcase)*: There's a pot of paste right here.

HJALMAR: And a brush?

GINA: Here's a brush too. *(Brings him the things.)*

HJALMAR *(Takes a pair of scissors)*: Just a strip of paper on the back—Far be it from me to lay hands on other people's property—especially when it belongs to a penniless old man. And to—that other one as well. There! Leave it there for now, and when it's dry, put it away. I never want to lay eyes on that document again. Never!

(GREGERS WERLE comes in from the hall.)

GREGERS *(Somewhat surprised)*: Oh—you're sitting in here, are you?

HJALMAR *(Rises hurriedly)*: I just sat down for a moment; out of sheer exhaustion.

GREGERS: You seem to have had breakfast too.

HJALMAR: The body has its claims too, you know—occasionally.

GREGERS: Well—what have you decided?

HJALMAR: For a man like me there can be only one possible decision. I was busy gathering a few of my most important things together; but it's bound to take a little time.

GINA *(With a touch of impatience)*: Which shall I do? Get the room ready, or pack your bag for you?

HJALMAR *(With an irritated look at* GREGERS*)*: Pack the bag!—and get the room ready too!

GINA *(Picks up the portmanteau)*: Very well; I'll just put in the shirt and those other things we spoke of. *(She goes into the sitting room and closes the door after her.)*

GREGERS *(After a short pause)*: It never occurred to me that things would come to this. Is it really necessary for you to leave your home?

HJALMAR *(Wandering about restlessly)*: What would you have me do? I wasn't made to bear unhappiness, Gregers. I need security; I must be surrounded by peace and comfort.

GREGERS: But you could find all that here, couldn't you? Why not try it? You have a splendid opportunity now to start afresh; why not begin again from here? And there's your invention to consider too; don't forget that.

HJALMAR: My invention! Don't even speak of that. That's a very doubtful proposition, I'm afraid.

GREGERS: Really? What do you mean?

HJALMAR: What on earth do you expect me to invent? Other people have invented practically everything already. It gets more difficult every day—

GREGERS: But I thought you'd worked so hard on it.

HJALMAR: It's all that damned Relling's fault!

GREGERS: Relling?

HJALMAR: Yes. He kept on telling me I had great inventive talent—that I would undoubtedly discover something to revolutionize photography.

GREGERS: I see! So it was Relling!

HJALMAR: But it's been a source of great happiness to me. Not so much the invention itself, but the fact that Hedvig had such faith in it. She believed in it as only a child can

believe—unreservedly, wholeheartedly—At least, I was
fool enough to *think* she did.

GREGERS: Hedvig couldn't possibly deceive you—you *must*
know that.

HJALMAR: I know nothing any more! She's the obstacle, you
see. Hedvig's the one who's plunged my whole life into
darkness.

GREGERS: Hedvig! Are you talking about *Hedvig?* How could
she possibly plunge your life into darkness?

HJALMAR *(Without answering)*: I've loved that child more than
anything on earth. Each time I came back to this humble
room, she would run to meet me—and it was such a joy
to see her blinking up at me with those sweet little eyes
of hers so full of happiness. I loved her with all my
heart—fool that I was! And I imagined that she loved me
just as deeply in return.

GREGERS: You *imagined* it, you say?

HJALMAR: What else *can* I say now? I can get nothing out of
Gina. Besides—she's totally unaware of the part the Ideal
plays in this whole business. But I must open my heart
to you, Gregers: I'm tormented by the thought that perhaps Hedvig never really cared for me at all.

GREGERS: And supposing she were to give you a great proof of
her love? *(Listens)* What's that? It sounded like the wild
duck—

HJALMAR: Yes—it's the wild duck quacking; Father's in the
attic.

GREGERS: Is he! *(His face lights up with joy)* You'll see—you may
soon have proof of how much your poor misunderstood
Hedvig loves you.

HJALMAR: What proof could she possibly give me? I'd never
dare believe any assurances of hers.

GREGERS: I'm positive Hedvig doesn't even know the meaning
of deceit.

HJALMAR: I wouldn't count too much on that, Gregers. Heaven knows what Gina and Mrs. Sörby have sat here scheming and plotting. And Hedvig's no fool—she has sharp ears. That gift may not have been such a surprise to her after all. As a matter of fact, I thought I noticed something in her manner—

GREGERS: What's got into you, Hjalmar? What makes you say such things?

HJALMAR: I've had my eyes opened—that's all. You'll see—this deed of gift may be only the beginning; Mrs. Sörby has always had a great fondness for Hedvig, and now she's in a position to do anything she wants to for the child. They could snatch her away from me whenever they chose to do so.

GREGERS: Nonsense! Hedvig would never consent to leave you.

HJALMAR: Don't be so sure. Just think of all *they* have to offer her! And *I* who have loved her so deeply—! My greatest happiness would have been to take her hand and lead her through life, as one might lead a frightened child through a dark, empty room. But—I'm convinced of it now!—the poor photographer up in his garret has never meant anything to her at all. She was just being shrewd; trying to keep on the good side of him until something better came along.

GREGERS: Come, Hjalmar—you know you don't believe that yourself.

HJALMAR: I don't know *what* to believe—that's the dreadful part of it—and I shall *never* know. You rely too much on the Ideal, my dear Gregers—otherwise you couldn't possibly doubt the truth of what I say. If those others were to come—laden with all their riches—and call out to the child: Leave him! You'll have a better life with us—

GREGERS: Yes? What then?

HJALMAR: And if I were to ask her: Hedvig, are you willing to give up that better life for me? *(With a scornful laugh)*

You'd find out soon enough what her answer would be!
(A pistol shot is heard in the attic.)

GREGERS *(Loudly and joyfully)*: Hjalmar!

HJALMAR: There! He's at his shooting again!

GINA *(Comes in)*: Oh, Hjalmar—I wish Grandfather wouldn't bang away in there all by himself!

HJALMAR: I think I'll just look in—

GREGERS *(Eagerly, with emotion)*: Wait, Hjalmar. Do you know what that was?

HJALMAR: Of course I do.

GREGERS: No you don't; but *I* know. That was the proof!

HJALMAR: What proof?

GREGERS: That was the child's sacrifice to you. She's persuaded your father to shoot the wild duck.

HJALMAR: The wild duck!

GINA: Good gracious!

HJALMAR: What's the point of that?

GREGERS: She's sacrificed the thing she loved best in the world to *you*. She thought, if she did that, you'd come to love her again, you see.

HJALMAR *(Tenderly, with emotion)*: Poor child!

GINA: The things she thinks of!

GREGERS: All she wants is your love, Hjalmar. She can't live without it.

GINA *(Fighting back her tears)*: You see, Hjalmar!

HJALMAR: Where is she, Gina?

GINA *(Sniffs)*: She's in the kitchen, I suppose—poor little thing!

HJALMAR *(Tears open the kitchen door and says)*: Hedvig, come! Come to me, Hedvig! *(Looks around)* No—she's not in here.

GINA: Then she must be in her room.

HJALMAR *(From outside)*: She's not here either. *(Comes in again)* She must have gone out.

GINA: Well, you wouldn't have her anywhere about the house.

HJALMAR: I hope she'll come home soon—so that I can tell her—Everything's going to be all right now, Gregers. I believe we'll be able to start a new life after all.

GREGERS *(Quietly)*: Thanks to the child; I knew it would be so. *(OLD EKDAL appears at the door of his room; he is in full uniform and is busy buckling on his sword.)*

HJALMAR *(In astonishment)*: Why, Father! Were you in there?

GINA: Don't tell me you've been shooting in your room?

EKDAL *(Approaching, resentfully)*: So you go hunting by yourself now, do you, Hjalmar?

HJALMAR *(Anxious and bewildered)*: I thought you were in the attic; wasn't it you who fired that shot in there?

EKDAL: Fired a shot? I? Hm.

GREGERS *(Calls out to HJALMAR)*: She's shot the wild duck herself!

HJALMAR: What can it mean! *(Rushes to the attic door, tears it open, looks in, and cries out)* Hedvig!

GINA *(Runs to the door)*: God! What's happened?

HJALMAR *(Goes into the attic)*: She's lying on the floor!

GREGERS: What! Hedvig? *(Goes in to HJALMAR.)*

GINA *(Simultaneously)*: Hedvig! *(Inside the attic)* No, no, no!

EKDAL: Ho! ho! Is she going shooting too?

(HJALMAR, GINA and GREGERS carry HEDVIG into the studio; her right hand hangs down with the pistol still clasped tightly in its fingers.)

HJALMAR *(Distracted)*: The pistol must have gone off—she's wounded herself! Call for help! Help!

GINA *(Rushes out into the hall and calls down the stairs)*: Relling! Relling! Dr. Relling! Come quickly!

(HJALMAR and GREGERS lay HEDVIG down on the sofa.)

EKDAL *(Quietly)*: The forest takes revenge.

HJALMAR *(On his knees beside her)*: She's beginning to come to. She's coming to—yes, yes.

GINA *(Who has come in again)*: Where is she wounded? I don't see anything—
(RELLING comes in hurriedly followed by MOLVIK; the latter without his waistcoat and necktie, and with his coat open.)

RELLING: What's happening here?

GINA: They say Hedvig has shot herself.

HJALMAR: Quickly! Help us!

RELLING: Shot herself! *(He pushes the table aside and starts to examine her.)*

HJALMAR *(Still kneeling, looks up at him anxiously)*: It can't be serious, can it? Eh, Relling? She's hardly bleeding at all; it can't be serious?

RELLING: How did it happen?

HJALMAR: We don't know—!

GINA: She wanted to shoot the wild duck.

RELLING: The wild duck?

HJALMAR: The pistol must have gone off.

RELLING: Hm. I see.

EKDAL: The forest takes revenge. But I'm not afraid! Not I!
(Goes into the attic and slides the door shut after him.)

HJALMAR: Relling—why don't you say something?

RELLING: The bullet entered the breast.

HJALMAR: Yes—but she's coming to—

RELLING: Can't you see that Hedvig's dead?

GINA *(Bursts into tears)*: My child! My little child!

GREGERS *(Huskily)*: In the boundless deep—

HJALMAR *(Jumps up)*: She must live, she *must!* For God's sake, Relling—if only for a moment. Just long enough for me to tell her how deeply I've loved her all the time!

RELLING: The bullet pierced her heart. Internal hemorrhage. Death must have been instantaneous.

HJALMAR: Oh, God! And I drove her from me like a dog! She died for love of me: she crept into the attic, filled with grief and terror, and died for love of me! *(Sobs)* Never to be able to tell her! Never to be able to atone! *(Clenches his fists and looks upward shouting)* You, up there—! If You *are* there—! Why have You done this thing to me!

GINA: Hush, hush! You mustn't go on like that! We didn't deserve to keep her, I suppose.

MOLVIK: The child is not dead; it sleepeth.

RELLING: Rubbish.

HJALMAR *(Becomes calm, goes over to the sofa, folds his arms, and looks down at HEDVIG)*: She's so stiff—so still.

RELLING *(Tries to loosen the hand holding the pistol)*: She's holding it so tightly—so very tightly—

GINA: No, Relling—don't force her fingers. Let the gun be.

HJALMAR: She shall take it with her.

GINA: Yes; let her. But the child mustn't lie here—on show like this. She shall go to her own room. Help me, Hjalmar.

(HJALMAR and GINA carry HEDVIG between them.)

HJALMAR *(As they carry her)*: Gina, Gina! How can you ever bear it!

GINA: We must try and help each other. At least *now* she belongs to both of us.

MOLVIK *(Stretching out his arms and muttering)*: Blessed be the Lord; to earth thou shalt return; to earth thou shalt return—

RELLING *(In a whisper)*: Shut up, you fool—you're drunk.

(HJALMAR and GINA carry the body out through the kitchen door. RELLING shuts it after them. MOLVIK slinks out into the hall.)

RELLING *(Goes over to GREGERS and says)*: No one will ever make me believe this was an accident.

GREGERS *(Who has been standing horrified, his face twitching)*: How could this dreadful thing have happened? No one will ever know.

RELLING: The front of her dress was burned. She must have aimed the pistol at her heart and fired.

GREGERS: Hedvig has not died in vain. Didn't you see? His sorrow brought out all that is noblest in him.

RELLING: Most people are noble in the presence of death. One wonders how long this nobility of his will last.

GREGERS: Why shouldn't it last? Why shouldn't it increase and grow stronger with the years?

RELLING: The years! Before this year is out, little Hedvig will be no more to him than a theme on which to exercise his eloquence!

GREGERS: How dare you say that of Hjalmar Ekdal!

RELLING: We'll talk of this again when this year's grass has withered on her grave. You'll see. He'll be spouting about "the child snatched from her father's loving arms by an untimely death"; he'll be wallowing in a sea of self-pity and maudlin sentimentality. You wait. You'll see.

GREGERS: All I can say is—if *you* are right and *I* am wrong, then life is not worth living.

RELLING: Life would be quite pleasant all the same—if it were not for certain lunatics, certain fanatics, who hammer at our doors, insisting on some nonsense they call the Claim of the Ideal.

GREGERS *(Gazing before him)*: Then I'm glad my fate is what it is.

RELLING: And what *is* it, may I ask?

GREGERS *(Starts to go)*: To be thirteenth at table.

RELLING: The hell it is. I wish I could believe it!

CURTAIN

Hedda Gabler

A Play in Four Acts

Characters

JÖRGEN TESMAN,
*holder of a scholarship for research
in the History of Civilization*

MRS. HEDDA GABLER TESMAN,
his wife

MISS JULIANE TESMAN,
his aunt

MRS. THEA RYSING ELVSTED

JUDGE BRACK

EJLERT LÖVBORG

BERTE,
maid at the Tesmans'

The action takes place in TESMAN'S *villa
on the west side of Oslo.*

Act One

SCENE: *A large, handsomely furnished drawing room, decorated in dark colors. In the back wall a wide opening with portières that are drawn back. This opening leads to a smaller room decorated in the same style as the drawing room. In the right-hand wall of the front room is a folding door leading to the hall. In the wall opposite, on the left, a glass door, its hangings also drawn back. Through the panes can be seen part of a veranda and trees covered in autumn foliage. Standing well forward is an oval table, with a cover on it and surrounded by chairs. By the wall on the right stands a wide stove of dark porcelain, a high-backed armchair, an upholstered footstool and two tabourets. A small sofa fits into the right-hand corner with a small round table in front of it. Down left, standing slightly away from the wall, another sofa. Above the glass door, a piano. On either side of the opening in the back wall two étagères with terra-cotta and majolica ornaments. Against the back wall of the inner room a sofa, a table, and a couple of chairs. Above the sofa hangs the portrait of a handsome elderly man in the uniform of a general. Over the table a hanging lamp with an opalescent glass shade. A number of bouquets of flowers are arranged about the drawing room, in vases and glasses. Others lie on the various tables. The floors in both rooms are covered with thick carpets. It is morning. The sun shines through the glass door.*

MISS JULIANE TESMAN, wearing a hat and carrying a parasol, enters from the hall followed by BERTE, who carries a bouquet wrapped in paper. MISS TESMAN is a good and pleasant-looking lady of about sixty-five. Simply but nicely dressed in a gray tailor-made suit. BERTE is a maid getting on in years, plain and rather countrified in appearance.

MISS TESMAN *(Stops just inside the door, listens, and says softly):* Good gracious! They're not even up—I do believe!

BERTE *(Also speaks softly):* That's what I told you, Miss Juliane. The steamer got in so late last night; and the young mistress had such a lot of unpacking to do before she could get to bed.

MISS TESMAN: Well—let them sleep as long as they like. But when they do get up, they'll certainly need a breath of fresh air. *(She goes to the glass door and opens it wide.)*

BERTE *(At the table, uncertain what to do with the bouquet in her hand)*: There's not a bit of room left anywhere. I'll just put them down here, Miss Juliane. *(Puts the bouquet down on the piano.)*

MISS TESMAN: So now you have a new mistress, Berte. Heaven knows it was hard enough for me to part with you.

BERTE *(On the verge of tears)*: Don't think it wasn't hard for me too, Miss Juliane; after all those happy years I spent with you and Miss Rina.

MISS TESMAN: We'll just have to make the best of it, Berte. Master Jörgen needs you—he really does. You've looked after him ever since he was a little boy.

BERTE: That's true, Miss Juliane; but I can't help worrying about Miss Rina lying there helpless, poor thing; how *will* she manage? That new maid will never learn to take proper care of an invalid!

MISS TESMAN: I'll soon be able to train her; and until then, I'll do most of the work myself—so don't you worry about my poor sister, Berte.

BERTE: But, there's something else, Miss Juliane—you see, I'm so afraid I won't be able to please the young mistress.

MISS TESMAN: Well—there may be one or two things, just at first—

BERTE: She'll be very particular, I expect—

MISS TESMAN: That's only natural—after all, she's General Gabler's daughter. She was used to being spoiled when her father was alive. Do you remember how we used to see her galloping by? How smart she looked in her riding clothes!

BERTE: Indeed I do remember, Miss Juliane! Who would ever

have thought that she and Master Jörgen would make a match of it!

MISS TESMAN: God moves in mysterious ways—! But, by the way, Berte—before I forget—you mustn't say Master Jörgen any more—it's Doctor Tesman!

BERTE: I know, Miss Juliane. That was one of the very first things the young mistress told me last night. So it's really true, Miss Juliane?

MISS TESMAN: Yes, it is indeed! He was made a doctor by one of the foreign universities while he was abroad. It was a great surprise to me; I knew nothing about it until he told me last night on the pier.

BERTE: Well—he's clever enough for anything, he is! But I never thought he'd go in for doctoring people!

MISS TESMAN: It's not *that* kind of a doctor, Berte! *(Nods significantly)* But later on, you may have to call him something even grander!

BERTE: Really, Miss Juliane? Now what could that be?

MISS TESMAN *(Smiles)*: Wouldn't you like to know! *(Moved)* I wonder what my poor brother would say if he could see what a great man his little boy has become. *(Looking around)* But, what's this, Berte? Why have you taken all the covers off the furniture?

BERTE: The young mistress told me to. She said she couldn't bear them.

MISS TESMAN: Perhaps she intends to use this as the living room?

BERTE: I think maybe she does, Miss Juliane; though Master Jörgen—I mean the Doctor—said nothing about it.
(JÖRGEN TESMAN enters the inner room from right, singing gaily. He carries an unstrapped empty suitcase. He is a young-looking man of thirty-three, medium height. Rather plump, a pleasant, round, open face. Blond hair and beard, wears spectacles. Rather carelessly dressed in comfortable lounging clothes.)

MISS TESMAN: Good morning—good morning, my dear Jörgen!

TESMAN *(At the opening between the rooms)*: Aunt Juliane! Dear Aunt Juliane! *(Goes to her and shakes her warmly by the hand)* Way out here—so early in the morning—eh?

MISS TESMAN: I had to come and see how you were getting on.

TESMAN: In spite of going to bed so late?

MISS TESMAN: My dear boy—as if that mattered to me!

TESMAN: You got home all right from the pier—eh?

MISS TESMAN: Quite all right, dear, thank you. Judge Brack was kind enough to see me safely to my door.

TESMAN: We were so sorry we couldn't give you a lift—but Hedda had such a fearful lot of luggage—

MISS TESMAN: Yes—she did seem to have quite a bit!

BERTE *(To* TESMAN*)*: Should I ask the Mistress if there's anything I can do for her, sir?

TESMAN: No thank you, Berte—there's no need. She said she'd ring if she wanted anything.

BERTE *(Starting right)*: Very good, sir.

TESMAN *(Indicates suitcase)*: You might just take that suitcase with you.

BERTE *(Taking it)*: Yes, sir. I'll put it in the attic. *(She goes out by the hall door.)*

TESMAN: Do you know, Aunt Juliane—I had that whole suitcase full of notes? It's unbelievable how much I found in all the archives I examined; curious old details no one had any idea existed.

MISS TESMAN: You don't seem to have wasted your time on your wedding trip!

TESMAN: Indeed I haven't!—But do take off your hat, Aunt Juliane—let me help you—eh?

MISS TESMAN *(While he does so)*: How sweet of you! This is just like the old days when you were still with us!

TESMAN *(He turns the hat around in his hands, looking at it admir-*

ingly from all sides): That's a very elegant hat you've treated yourself to.

MISS TESMAN: I bought that on Hedda's account.

TESMAN: On Hedda's account—eh?

MISS TESMAN: Yes—I didn't want her to feel ashamed of her old aunt—in case we should happen to go out together.

TESMAN *(Patting her cheek):* What a dear you are, Aunt Juliane—always thinking of everything! *(Puts the hat down on a chair near the table)* And now let's sit down here on the sofa and have a cozy little chat till Hedda comes. *(They sit down. She leans her parasol in the corner of the sofa.)*

MISS TESMAN *(Takes both his hands and gazes at him):* I can't tell you what a joy it is to have you home again, Jörgen.

TESMAN: And it's a joy for me to see you again, dear Aunt Juliane. You've been as good as a father and mother to me—I can never forget that!

MISS TESMAN: I know, dear—you'll always have a place in your heart for your poor old aunts.

TESMAN: How *is* Aunt Rina—eh? Isn't she feeling a little better?

MISS TESMAN: No, dear. I'm afraid she'll never be any better, poor thing! But I pray God I may keep her with me a little longer—for now that I haven't you to look after anymore, I don't know what will become of me when she goes.

TESMAN *(Pats her on the back):* There, there, there!

MISS TESMAN *(With a sudden change of tone):* You know, I can't get used to thinking of you as a married man, Jörgen. And to think that you should have been the one to carry off Hedda Gabler—the fascinating Hedda Gabler—who was always surrounded by so many admirers!

TESMAN *(Hums a little and smiles complacently):* Yes—I wouldn't be surprised if some of my friends were a bit jealous of me—eh?

MISS TESMAN: And then this wonderful wedding trip! Five—nearly six months!

TESMAN: Of course you must remember the trip was also of great value to me in my research work. I can't begin to tell you all the archives I've been through—and the many books I've read!

MISS TESMAN: I can well believe it! *(More confidentially, lowering her voice)* But, Jörgen dear, are you sure you've nothing—well—nothing *special* to tell me?

TESMAN: About our trip?

MISS TESMAN: Yes.

TESMAN: I can't think of anything I didn't write you about. I had a doctor's degree conferred on me—but I told you that last night.

MISS TESMAN: Yes, yes—you told me about that. But what I mean is—haven't you any—well—any expectations?

TESMAN: Expectations?

MISS TESMAN: Yes, Jörgen. Surely you can talk frankly to your old aunt?

TESMAN: Well, of course I have expectations!

MISS TESMAN: Well?

TESMAN: I have every expectation of becoming a professor one of these days!

MISS TESMAN: A professor—yes, yes, I know dear—but—

TESMAN: In fact, I'm certain of it. But you know that just as well as I do, Aunt Juliane.

MISS TESMAN *(Chuckling)*: Of course I do, dear—you're quite right. *(Changing the subject)* But we were talking about your journey—it must have cost a great deal of money, Jörgen!

TESMAN: Well, you see, the scholarship I had was pretty ample—that went a good way.

MISS TESMAN: Still—I don't see how it could have been ample

enough for two—especially traveling with a lady—they say that makes it ever so much more expensive.

TESMAN: It does make it a bit more expensive—but Hedda simply had to have this trip—she really had to—it was the fashionable thing to do.

MISS TESMAN: I know—nowadays it seems a wedding has to be followed by a wedding trip. But tell me, Jörgen—have you been over the house yet?

TESMAN: I have indeed! I've been up since daybreak!

MISS TESMAN: What do you think of it?

TESMAN: It's splendid—simply splendid! But it seems awfully big—what on earth shall we do with all those empty rooms?

MISS TESMAN *(Laughingly)*: Oh, my dear Jörgen—I expect you'll find plenty of use for them—a little later on.

TESMAN: Yes, you're right, Aunt Juliane—as I get more and more books—eh?

MISS TESMAN: Of course, my dear boy—it was your books I was thinking of!

TESMAN: I'm especially pleased for Hedda's sake. She had her heart set on this house—it belonged to Secretary Falk, you know—even before we were engaged, she used to say it was the one place she'd really like to live in.

MISS TESMAN: But I'm afraid you'll find all this very expensive, my dear Jörgen—very expensive!

TESMAN *(Looks at her a little despondently)*: Yes, I suppose so. How much do you really think it will cost? I mean approximately—eh?

MISS TESMAN: That's impossible to say until we've seen all the bills.

TESMAN: Judge Brack wrote Hedda that he'd been able to secure very favorable terms for me.

MISS TESMAN: But you mustn't worry about it, my dear boy—

for one thing, I've given security for all the furniture and the carpets.

TESMAN: Security? You, dear Aunt Juliane? What sort of security?

MISS TESMAN: A mortgage on our annuity.

TESMAN *(Jumps up)*: What!

MISS TESMAN: I didn't know what else to do.

TESMAN *(Standing before her)*: You must be mad, Aunt Juliane— quite mad. That annuity is all that you and Aunt Rina have to live on!

MISS TESMAN: Don't get so excited about it! It's only a matter of form, Judge Brack says. He was kind enough to arrange the whole matter for me.

TESMAN: That's all very well—but still—!

MISS TESMAN: And from now on you'll have your own salary to depend on—and even if we should have to help out a little, just at first—it would only be the greatest pleasure to us!

TESMAN: Isn't that just like you, Aunt Juliane! Always making sacrifices for me.

MISS TESMAN *(Rises and places her hands on his shoulders)*: The only happiness I have in the world is making things easier for you, my dear boy. We've been through some bad times, I admit—but now we've reached the goal and we've nothing to fear.

TESMAN *(Sits down beside her again)*: Yes—it's amazing how everything's turned out for the best!

MISS TESMAN: Now there's no one to stand in your way—even your most dangerous rival has fallen. Well, he made his bed—let him lie on it, poor misguided creature.

TESMAN: Has there been any news of Ejlert—since I went away, I mean?

MISS TESMAN: They say he's supposed to have published a new book.

TESMAN: Ejlert Lövborg! A new book? Recently—eh?

MISS TESMAN: That's what they say—but I shouldn't think any book of his would be worth much. It'll be a very different story when *your* new book appears. What's it to be about, Jörgen?

TESMAN: It will deal with the domestic industries of Brabant during the Middle Ages.

MISS TESMAN: Fancy being able to write about such things!

TESMAN: Of course it'll be some time before the book is ready—I still have to arrange and classify all my notes, you see.

MISS TESMAN: Yes—collecting and arranging—no one can compete with you in that! You're not your father's son for nothing!

TESMAN: I can't wait to begin! Especially now that I have my own comfortable home to work in.

MISS TESMAN: And best of all—you have your wife! The wife you longed for!

TESMAN *(Embracing her)*: Yes, you're right, Aunt Juliane— Hedda! She's the most wonderful part of it all! *(Looks toward opening between the rooms)* But here she comes—eh? *(*HEDDA *enters from the left through the inner room. She is a woman of twenty-nine. Her face and figure show breeding and distinction. Her complexion is pale and opaque. Her eyes are steel-gray and express a cold, unruffled repose. Her hair is an agreeable medium-brown, but not especially abundant. She wears a tasteful, somewhat loose-fitting negligee.)*

MISS TESMAN *(Goes to meet* HEDDA*)*: Good morning, Hedda dear—and welcome home!

HEDDA *(Gives her her hand)*: Good morning, my dear Miss Tesman. What an early visitor you are—how kind of you!

MISS TESMAN *(Seems slightly embarrassed)*: Not at all. And did the bride sleep well in her new home?

HEDDA: Thank you—fairly well.

TESMAN *(Laughing)*: Fairly well! I like that, Hedda! You were sleeping like a log when I got up!

HEDDA: Yes—fortunately. You know, Miss Tesman, one has to adapt oneself gradually to new surroundings. *(Glancing toward the left)* Good heavens—what a nuisance! That maid's opened the window and let in a whole flood of sunshine!

MISS TESMAN *(Starts toward door)*: Well—we'll just close it then!

HEDDA: No, no—don't do that! Jörgen dear, just draw the curtains, will you? It'll give a softer light.

TESMAN *(At the door)*: There, Hedda! Now you have both shade and fresh air!

HEDDA: Heaven knows we need some fresh air, with all these stacks of flowers! But do sit down, my dear Miss Tesman.

MISS TESMAN: No—many thanks! Now that I know everything's all right here, I must be getting home to my poor sister.

TESMAN: Do give her my best love, Aunt Juliane—and tell her I'll drop in and see her later in the day.

MISS TESMAN: Yes, dear, I'll do that. . . . Oh! I'd almost forgotten *(Feeling in the pocket of her dress)* I've brought something for you!

TESMAN: What can that be, Aunt Juliane—eh?

MISS TESMAN *(Produces a flat parcel wrapped in newspaper and presents him with it)*: Look, dear!

TESMAN *(Opens the parcel)*: Oh, Aunt Juliane! You really kept them for me! Isn't that touching, Hedda—eh?

HEDDA *(By the étagère on the right)*: Well, what is it, dear?

TESMAN: My slippers, Hedda! My old bedroom slippers!

HEDDA: Oh, yes—I remember. You often spoke of them on our journey.

TESMAN: I can't tell you how I've missed them! *(Goes up to her)* Do have a look at them, Hedda—

HEDDA *(Going toward stove)*: I'm really not very interested, Jörgen—

TESMAN *(Following her)*: Dear Aunt Rina embroidered them for me during her illness. They have so many memories for me—

HEDDA *(At the table)*: Scarcely for me, Jörgen.

MISS TESMAN: Of course not, Jörgen! They mean nothing to Hedda.

TESMAN: I only thought, now that she's one of the family—

HEDDA *(Interrupting)*: We shall never get on with this servant, Jörgen!

MISS TESMAN: Not get on with Berte?

TESMAN: Hedda dear, what do you mean?

HEDDA *(Pointing)*: Look! She's left her old hat lying about on the table.

TESMAN *(Flustered—dropping the slippers on the floor)*: Why— Hedda—!

HEDDA: Just imagine if someone were to come in and see it!

TESMAN: But, Hedda! That's Aunt Juliane's hat!

HEDDA: Oh! Is it?

MISS TESMAN *(Picks up the hat)*: Yes, indeed it is! And what's more it's not old—little Mrs. Tesman!

HEDDA: I really didn't look at it very closely, Miss Tesman.

MISS TESMAN *(Puts on the hat)*: This is the very first time I've worn it!

TESMAN: And it's a lovely hat, too—quite a beauty!

MISS TESMAN: Oh, it isn't as beautiful as all that. *(Looking around)* Where's my parasol? *(Takes it)* Ah—here it is! *(Mutters)* For this is mine too—not Berte's.

TESMAN: A new hat and a new parasol—just think, Hedda!

HEDDA: Most handsome and lovely, I'm sure!

TESMAN: Yes—isn't it, eh? But do take a good look at Hedda—see how lovely *she* is!

MISS TESMAN: Hedda was always lovely, my dear boy—that's nothing new. *(She nods and goes toward the right.)*

TESMAN *(Following her)*: But don't you think she's looking especially well? I think she's filled out a bit while we've been away.

HEDDA *(Crossing the room)*: Oh, do be quiet . . . !

MISS TESMAN *(Who has stopped and turned toward them)*: Filled out?

TESMAN: Of course, you can't notice it so much in that loose dress—but I have certain opportunities—

HEDDA *(Stands at the glass door—impatiently)*: You have no opportunities at all, Jörgen—

TESMAN: I think it must have been the mountain air in the Tyrol—

HEDDA *(Curtly interrupting)*: I'm exactly as I was when we left!

TESMAN: That's what you say—but I don't agree with you! What do you think, Aunt Juliane?

MISS TESMAN *(Gazing at her with folded hands)*: Hedda is lovely—lovely! *(Goes to her, takes her face in her hands and gently kisses the top of her head)* God bless and keep you, Hedda Tesman, for Jörgen's sake!

HEDDA *(Quietly freeing herself)*: Please! Oh, please let me go!

MISS TESMAN *(With quiet emotion)*: I shan't let a day pass without coming to see you!

TESMAN: That's right, Aunt Juliane!

MISS TESMAN: Good-bye, dearest Hedda—good-bye!

(She goes out by the hall door. TESMAN *sees her out. The door remains half open.* TESMAN *can be heard repeating his greetings to* AUNT RINA *and his thanks for the bedroom slippers. Meanwhile,* HEDDA *paces about the room, raises her arms and clenches*

her hands as though in desperation. She flings back the curtains of the glass door and stands gazing out. In a moment TESMAN *returns and closes the door behind him.)*

TESMAN *(Picking up the slippers from the floor)*: What are you looking at, Hedda?

HEDDA *(Once more calm and controlled)*: I'm just looking at the leaves—they're so yellow—so withered.

TESMAN *(Wraps up the slippers and puts them on the table)*: Well, we're well into September now.

HEDDA *(Again restless)*: God, yes! September—September already!

TESMAN: Didn't you think Aunt Juliane was a little strange? Almost solemn, I thought. What do you suppose was the matter with her—eh?

HEDDA: Well, you see, I scarcely know her. Isn't she always like that?

TESMAN: No, not as she was today.

HEDDA *(Leaving the glass door)*: Perhaps she was annoyed about the hat.

TESMAN: Oh, not specially—perhaps just for a moment—

HEDDA *(Crosses over toward the fireplace)*: Such a peculiar way to behave—flinging one's hat about in the drawing room—one doesn't do that sort of thing.

TESMAN: I'm sure Aunt Juliane won't do it again.

HEDDA: I shall manage to make my peace with her. When you see her this afternoon, Jörgen, you might ask her to come and spend the evening here.

TESMAN: Yes, I will, Hedda. And there's another thing you could do that would give her so much pleasure.

HEDDA: Well—what's that?

TESMAN: If you could only be a little more affectionate with her—just for my sake—eh?

HEDDA: I shall try to call her Aunt—but that's really all I can do.

TESMAN: Very well. I just thought, now that you belong to the family—

HEDDA: I really don't see why, Jörgen—*(She goes up toward the center opening.)*

TESMAN *(After a short pause)*: Is there anything the matter with you, Hedda, eh?

HEDDA: No, nothing. I'm just looking at my old piano. It doesn't seem to fit in with the rest of the furniture.

TESMAN: The first time I draw my salary, we'll see about exchanging it.

HEDDA: Exchange it! Why exchange it? I don't want to part with it. Why couldn't we put it in the inner room and get a new one for here? That is, of course, when we can afford it.

TESMAN *(Slightly taken back)*: Yes, I suppose we could do that.

HEDDA *(Takes up the bouquet from the piano)*: These flowers weren't here last night when we arrived.

TESMAN: I expect Aunt Juliane brought them for you.

HEDDA *(Examines the bouquet)*: Here's a card. *(Takes out a card and reads it)* "Shall return later in the day." Can you guess who it's from?

TESMAN: No. Tell me.

HEDDA: From Mrs. Elvsted.

TESMAN: Really! Sheriff Elvsted's wife. The former Miss Rysing.

HEDDA: Exactly. The girl with that irritating mass of hair—she was always showing off. I've heard she was an old flame of yours, Jörgen?

TESMAN *(Laughs)*: Oh, that didn't last long, and it was before I met you, Hedda. Fancy her being in town.

HEDDA: Funny that she should call on us. I haven't seen her for years. Not since we were at school together.

TESMAN: I haven't seen her, either, for ever so long. I wonder how she can stand living in that remote, dreary place.

HEDDA: I wonder! *(After a moment's thought, says suddenly)* Tell me, Jörgen, doesn't Ejlert Lövborg live somewhere near there?

TESMAN: Yes, I believe he does. Somewhere in that neighborhood.

BERTE *(Enters by the hall door)*: That lady, ma'am, who left some flowers a little while ago is back again. *(Pointing)* The flowers you have in your hand, ma'am.

HEDDA: Oh, is she? Very well, ask her to come in.

(BERTE *opens the door for* MRS. ELVSTED *and exits.* MRS. ELVSTED *is a fragile woman with soft, pretty features. Her large, round, light-blue eyes are slightly prominent and have a timid, questioning look. Her hair is unusually fair, almost white-gold and extremely thick and wavy. She is a couple of years younger than* HEDDA. *She wears a dark visiting dress, in good taste but not in the latest fashion.)*

HEDDA *(Graciously goes to meet her)*: How do you do, my dear Mrs. Elvsted? How delightful to see you again after all these years.

MRS. ELVSTED *(Nervously, trying to control herself)*: Yes, it's a very long time since we met.

TESMAN *(Gives her his hand)*: And we haven't met for a long time, either, eh?

HEDDA: Thank you for your lovely flowers.

MRS. ELVSTED: Oh, don't mention it. I would have come to see you yesterday, but I heard you were away.

TESMAN: Have you just arrived in town, eh?

MRS. ELVSTED: Yes, I got here yesterday morning. I was so upset not to find you at home.

HEDDA: Upset! But why, my dear Mrs. Elvsted?

TESMAN: But, my dear Mrs. Rysing—eh, Mrs. Elvsted, I mean—

HEDDA: I hope you're not in any trouble.

MRS. ELVSTED: Well, yes, I am, and I know no one else in town that I could possibly turn to—

HEDDA *(Puts the bouquet down on the table)*: Come, let's sit down here on the sofa—

MRS. ELVSTED: I'm really too nervous to sit down.

HEDDA: Of course you're not. Come along now—*(She draws* MRS. ELVSTED *down to the sofa and sits beside her.)*

TESMAN: Well, Mrs. Elvsted?

HEDDA: Has anything gone wrong at home?

MRS. ELVSTED: Well, eh—yes, and no. I do hope you won't misunderstand me.

HEDDA: Perhaps you'd better tell us all about it, Mrs. Elvsted.

TESMAN: I suppose that's what you've come for, eh?

MRS. ELVSTED: Yes, of course. Well, first of all—But perhaps you've already heard—Ejlert Lövborg is in town, too.

HEDDA: Lövborg!

TESMAN: What! Ejlert Lövborg has come back! Think of that, Hedda!

HEDDA: Good heavens, yes, I heard it!

MRS. ELVSTED: He's been here for a week. A whole week. I'm so afraid he'll get into trouble—

HEDDA: But, my dear Mrs. Elvsted, why should you be so worried about him?

MRS. ELVSTED *(Gives her a startled look and speaks hurriedly)*: Well, you see—he's the children's tutor.

HEDDA: Your children's?

MRS. ELVSTED: No. My husband's. I have none.

HEDDA: Oh, your stepchildren's then?

MRS. ELVSTED: Yes.

TESMAN *(With some hesitation)*: Was he—I don't quite know how to put it—was he dependable enough to fill such a position, eh?

324

MRS. ELVSTED: For the last two years his conduct has been irreproachable.

TESMAN: Has it, really? Think of that, Hedda!

HEDDA: Yes, yes, yes! I heard it.

MRS. ELVSTED: Irreproachable in every respect, I assure you, but still I know how dangerous it is for him to be here in town all alone, and he has quite a lot of money with him. I can't help being worried to death about him.

TESMAN: But why did he *come* here? Why didn't he stay where he was? With you and your husband, eh?

MRS. ELVSTED: After his book was published he felt too restless to stay on with us.

TESMAN: Oh, yes, of course. Aunt Juliane told me he had published a new book.

MRS. ELVSTED: Yes, a wonderful book. A sort of outline of civilization. It came out a couple of weeks ago. It's sold marvelously. Made quite a sensation.

TESMAN: Has it really? Then I suppose it's something he wrote some time ago—during his better years.

MRS. ELVSTED: No, no. He's written it all since he's been with us.

TESMAN: Well, isn't that splendid, Hedda? Think of that!

MRS. ELVSTED: Yes, if only he'll keep it up.

HEDDA: Have you seen him here in town?

MRS. ELVSTED: Not yet. I had great trouble finding out his address, but this morning I got it at last.

HEDDA *(Gives her a searching look)*: But doesn't it seem rather odd of your husband to—

MRS. ELVSTED *(With a nervous start)*: Of my husband—what?

HEDDA: Well—to send you on such an errand. Why didn't he come himself to look after his friend?

MRS. ELVSTED: Oh, no. My husband is much too busy. And besides, I had some shopping to do.

HEDDA *(With a slight smile)*: Oh, I see!

MRS. ELVSTED *(Rising quickly and uneasily)*: I implore you, Mr. Tesman, be good to Ejlert Lövborg if he should come to see you. I'm sure he will. You were such great friends in the old days, and after all, you're both interested in the same studies. You specialize in the same subjects—as far as I can understand.

TESMAN: Yes, we used to, at any rate.

MRS. ELVSTED: That's why I'd be so grateful if you too would—well—keep an eye on him. You will do that, won't you, Mr. Tesman?

TESMAN: I'd be delighted to, Mrs. Rysing.

HEDDA: Elvsted!

TESMAN: I'd be delighted to do anything in my power to help Ejlert. You can rely on me.

MRS. ELVSTED *(Presses his hands)*: Oh, how very kind of you! I can't thank you enough. . . . *(Frightened)* You see, my husband is so very fond of him.

HEDDA *(Rises)*: Yes—I see. I think you should write to him, Jörgen. He may not care to come of his own accord.

TESMAN: Perhaps that would be the right thing to do, Hedda, eh?

HEDDA: Yes. The sooner the better. Why not at once?

MRS. ELVSTED *(Imploringly)*: Oh, yes, please do!

TESMAN: I'll write him this minute. Have you his address, Mrs. Ry—Elvsted?

MRS. ELVSTED *(Takes a slip of paper from her pocket and gives it to him)*: Here it is.

TESMAN: Splendid. Then I'll go in. *(Looks around)* Oh—I mustn't forget my slippers. Ah! Here they are. *(Takes the parcel and starts to go.)*

HEDDA: Mind you write him a nice friendly letter, Jörgen, and a good long one, too.

TESMAN: I most certainly will.

MRS. ELVSTED: But don't let him know that I suggested it!

TESMAN: Of course not! That goes without saying, eh? *(He goes out right, through the inner room.)*

HEDDA *(Smilingly goes to* MRS. ELVSTED *and says in a low voice):* There! Now we've killed two birds with one stone.

MRS. ELVSTED: What do you mean?

HEDDA: Couldn't you see that I wanted to get rid of him?

MRS. ELVSTED: Yes, to write the letter.

HEDDA: And so that I could talk to you alone.

MRS. ELVSTED *(Bewildered):* About the same thing?

HEDDA: Precisely.

MRS. ELVSTED *(Apprehensively):* But there's nothing else to tell, Mrs. Tesman. Absolutely nothing.

HEDDA: Of course there is. I can see that. There's a great *deal* more to tell. Come along. Sit down. We'll have a nice friendly talk. *(She forces* MRS. ELVSTED *down into the armchair by the stove and seats herself on one of the tabourets.)*

MRS. ELVSTED *(Anxiously looking at her watch):* But, really, Mrs. Tesman, I was just thinking of going—

HEDDA: Oh, you can't be in such a hurry. Come along, now—I want to know all about your life at home.

MRS. ELVSTED: I prefer not to speak about that.

HEDDA: But to me, dear! After all, we went to school together.

MRS. ELVSTED: Yes, but you were in a higher class, and I was always so dreadfully afraid of you then.

HEDDA: Afraid of me!

MRS. ELVSTED: Yes, dreadfully. When we met on the stairs you always used to pull my hair.

HEDDA: Did I, really!

MRS. ELVSTED: Yes. And once you said you were going to burn it all off.

HEDDA: I was just teasing you, of course!

MRS. ELVSTED: I was so silly in those days, and afterward we drifted so far apart. We lived in different worlds. . . .

HEDDA: Well, then we must drift together again. At school we always called each other by our first names. Why shouldn't we now?

MRS. ELVSTED: I think you're mistaken—

HEDDA: Of course not. I remember it distinctly. We were *great* friends! *(Draws her stool near to* MRS. ELVSTED *and kisses her on the cheek)* So you must call me Hedda.

MRS. ELVSTED *(Pressing her hands and patting them)*: You're so kind and understanding. I'm not used to kindness.

HEDDA: And I shall call you my darling little Thora.

MRS. ELVSTED: My name is Thea.

HEDDA: Yes, yes, of course, I meant Thea! *(Looking at her compassionately)* So my darling little Thea—you mean they're not kind to you at home?

MRS. ELVSTED: If only I had a home! But I haven't. I never had one.

HEDDA *(Gives her a quick look)*: I suspected something of the sort.

MRS. ELVSTED *(Gazing helplessly before her)*: Ah!

HEDDA: Tell me, Thea—I'm a little vague about it. When you first went to the Elvsteds' you were engaged as housekeeper, weren't you?

MRS. ELVSTED: I was supposed to go as governess, but Mrs. Elvsted—the first Mrs. Elvsted, that is—was an invalid, and rarely left her room, so I had to take charge of the house as well.

HEDDA: And, eventually, you became mistress of the house?

MRS. ELVSTED *(Sadly)*: Yes, I did.

HEDDA: How long ago was that?

MRS. ELVSTED: That I married him?

HEDDA: Yes.

MRS. ELVSTED: Five years ago.

HEDDA: Yes, that's right.

MRS. ELVSTED: Oh, those five years, especially the last two or three of them—If only you knew, Mrs. Tesman!

HEDDA *(Slaps her lightly on the hand)*: Mrs. Tesman! Thea!

MRS. ELVSTED: I'll try—You have no idea, Hedda—

HEDDA *(Casually)*: Ejlert Lövborg's lived near you about three years, hasn't he?

MRS. ELVSTED *(Looks at her doubtfully)*: Ejlert Lövborg? Why, yes, he has.

HEDDA: Had you met him before, here in town?

MRS. ELVSTED: No, not really—I knew him by his name, of course.

HEDDA: But I suppose up there you saw a good deal of him.

MRS. ELVSTED: Yes, he came to our house every day. He gave the children lessons, you see. I had so much to do; I couldn't manage that, as well.

HEDDA: No. Of course not. And I suppose your husband's away from home a good deal.

MRS. ELVSTED: Yes. Being sheriff, he often has to travel about his district.

HEDDA *(Leans against the arm of the chair)*: Now, my dear darling little Thea, I want you to tell me everything—exactly as it is.

MRS. ELVSTED: Well, then you must question me.

HEDDA: Tell me—what sort of a man is your husband, Thea? To live with, I mean. Is he kind to you?

MRS. ELVSTED *(Evasively)*: He probably thinks he is.

HEDDA: But isn't he much too old for you, dear? There must be at least twenty years between you.

MRS. ELVSTED *(Irritably)*: Yes, that makes it all the harder. We haven't a thought in common. Nothing, in fact.

HEDDA: But, I suppose he's fond of you in his own way.

329

MRS. ELVSTED: Oh, I don't know. I think he finds me useful. And then it doesn't cost much to keep me. I'm not expensive.

HEDDA: That's stupid of you.

MRS. ELVSTED *(Shakes her head)*: It couldn't be otherwise. Not with him. I don't believe he really cares about anyone but himself. And perhaps a little for the children.

HEDDA: And for Ejlert Lövborg, Thea?

MRS. ELVSTED *(Looking at her)*: Ejlert Lövborg? What makes you say that?

HEDDA: Well, it's obvious!—After all, he's sent you all this way into town, simply to look for him!—*(With the trace of a smile)* Wasn't that what you told Jörgen?

MRS. ELVSTED *(With a nervous twitch)*: Yes, I suppose I did. *(Vehemently but in a low voice)* Oh, I might as well tell you the truth. It's bound to come out sooner or later.

HEDDA: What—?

MRS. ELVSTED: Well, then—my husband knew nothing about my coming here.

HEDDA: Your husband didn't know!

MRS. ELVSTED: No, of course not. He was away himself at the time. I couldn't stand it any longer, Hedda. I simply couldn't. I felt so alone, so deserted—

HEDDA: Yes, yes—well?

MRS. ELVSTED: So I packed a few of my things—just those I needed most—I didn't say a word to anyone. I simply left the house.

HEDDA: Just like that!

MRS. ELVSTED: Yes, and took the next train to town.

HEDDA: But, Thea, my darling! How did you dare do such a thing?

MRS. ELVSTED *(Rises and walks about the room)*: What else could I possibly do?

HEDDA: But what will your husband say when you go home again?

MRS. ELVSTED *(At the table, looks at her)*: Back to him!

HEDDA: Well, of course.

MRS. ELVSTED: I shall never go back to him again.

HEDDA *(Rises and goes toward her)*: You mean you've actually left your home for *good?*

MRS. ELVSTED: I saw nothing else to do.

HEDDA: But to leave like that, so openly—

MRS. ELVSTED: You can't very well *hide* a thing like that!

HEDDA: But what will people say about you, Thea?

MRS. ELVSTED: They can say whatever they like. *(Sits on the sofa wearily and sadly)* I only did what I had to do.

HEDDA *(After a short silence)*: What are your plans now?

MRS. ELVSTED: I don't know yet. All I know is that I must live near Ejlert Lövborg, if I'm to live at all.

HEDDA *(Takes a chair from the table, sits down near MRS. ELVSTED and strokes her hands)*: Tell me, Thea—how did this friendship start between you and Ejlert Lövborg?

MRS. ELVSTED: It grew gradually. I began to have a sort of power over him.

HEDDA: Really?

MRS. ELVSTED: Yes. After a while he gave up his old habits. Oh, not because I asked him to—I never would have dared do that. But I suppose he realized how unhappy they made me, and so he dropped them.

HEDDA *(Concealing a scornful smile)*: So, my darling little Thea, you've actually reformed him!

MRS. ELVSTED: Well, *he* says so, at any rate, and in return he's made a human being out of me. Taught me to think and understand so many things.

HEDDA: Did he give you lessons, too, then?

MRS. ELVSTED: Not lessons, exactly, but he talked to me, explained so much to me—and the most wonderful thing of all was when he finally allowed me to share in his work. Allowed me to help him.

HEDDA: He did, did he?

MRS. ELVSTED: Yes. He wanted me to be a part of everything he wrote.

HEDDA: Like two good comrades!

MRS. ELVSTED *(Brightly)*: Comrades! Why, Hedda, that's exactly what *he* says! I ought to be so happy, but somehow I'm not. I'm so afraid it may not last.

HEDDA: You're not very sure of him, then?

MRS. ELVSTED *(Gloomily)*: I sometimes feel a shadow between Lövborg and me—a woman's shadow.

HEDDA *(Looks at her intently)*: Who could that be?

MRS. ELVSTED: I don't know. Someone he knew long ago. Someone he's never been able to forget.

HEDDA: Has he told you anything about her?

MRS. ELVSTED: He spoke of her once—quite vaguely.

HEDDA: What did he say?

MRS. ELVSTED: He said that when they parted she threatened to shoot him.

HEDDA *(With cold composure)*: What nonsense! No one does that sort of thing here!

MRS. ELVSTED: I know. That's why I think it must have been that red-haired cabaret singer he was once—

HEDDA: Very likely.

MRS. ELVSTED: They say she used to go about with loaded pistols.

HEDDA: Then of course it must have been she.

MRS. ELVSTED *(Wringing her hands)*: But, Hedda, they say she's here now—in town, again! I'm so worried I don't know what to do!

HEDDA *(With a glance toward inner room)*: Sh! Here comes Tesman. Not a word to him. All this is between us.

MRS. ELVSTED *(Jumps up)*: Yes, yes, of course.

(JÖRGEN TESMAN, a letter in his hand, enters from the right through the inner room.)

TESMAN: Well, here is the letter signed and sealed!

HEDDA: Splendid! Mrs. Elvsted was just leaving, Jörgen. Wait a minute! I'll go with you as far as the garden gate.

TESMAN: Do you think Berte could post this for me, dear?

HEDDA *(Takes the letter)*: I'll tell her to.

(BERTE enters from the hall.)

BERTE: Judge Brack wishes to know if you will see him, ma'am.

HEDDA: Yes. Show him in. And post this letter, will you?

BERTE *(Taking the letter)*: Certainly, ma'am.

(She opens the door for JUDGE BRACK and goes out. The JUDGE is a man of forty-five. Thick-set but well-built and supple in his movements. His face is rounded and his profile aristocratic. His short hair is still almost black and carefully dressed. His eyes are bright and sparkling. His eyebrows thick. His mustache also thick with short-cut ends. He wears a smart walking suit, slightly youthful for his age. He uses an eyeglass, which he lets drop from time to time.)

BRACK *(Bowing, hat in hand)*: May one venture to call so early in the day?

HEDDA: Of course one may.

TESMAN *(Shakes hands with him)*: You know you're always welcome. *(Introduces him.)* Judge Brack, Miss Rysing.

HEDDA: Ah!

BRACK *(Bows)*: Delighted.

HEDDA *(Looks at him and laughs)*: What fun to have a look at you by daylight, Judge.

BRACK: Do you find me—altered?

HEDDA: A little younger, I think.

BRACK *(Laughs and goes down to fireplace)*: I thank you, most heartily.

TESMAN: But what do you say to Hedda, eh? Doesn't she look flourishing? She's positively—

HEDDA: For heaven's sake, leave me out of it, Jörgen! You'd far better thank Judge Brack for all the trouble he's taken.

BRACK: Oh, don't mention it. It was a pleasure, I assure you.

HEDDA: Yes, you're a loyal soul; but I mustn't keep Mrs. Elvsted waiting. Excuse me, Judge. I'll be back directly. *(Exchange of greetings.* MRS. ELVSTED *and* HEDDA *go out through the hall door.)*

BRACK: Well, I hope your wife's pleased with everything.

TESMAN: We really can't thank you enough. Of course she wants to rearrange things a bit, and she talks of buying a few additional trifles.

BRACK: Is that so?

TESMAN: But you needn't bother about that. Hedda will see to that herself. Why don't we sit down, eh?

BRACK *(Sits at table)*: Thanks. Just for a moment—There's something I must talk to you about, my dear Tesman.

TESMAN: Yes, the expenses, eh? *(Sits down)* I suppose it's time we got down to business.

BRACK: Oh, that's not so very pressing. Though perhaps it would have been wiser to be a bit more economical.

TESMAN: But that would have been out of the question. You know Hedda, Judge. After all, she's been used to a certain standard of living—

BRACK: Yes, that's just the trouble.

TESMAN: Fortunately, it won't be long before I receive my appointment.

BRACK: Well, you see—such things sometimes hang fire.

TESMAN: Have you heard anything further, eh?

BRACK: Nothing really definite. *(Interrupts himself)* But, by the way, I have one bit of news for you.

TESMAN: Well?

BRACK: Your old friend Ejlert Lövborg is back in town.

TESMAN: I've heard that already.

BRACK: Really? Who told you?

TESMAN: That lady who went out with Hedda.

BRACK: Oh, yes, what was her name? I didn't quite catch it.

TESMAN: Mrs. Elvsted.

BRACK: Oh, yes, the sheriff's wife. Of course. Lövborg's been living near them these past few years.

TESMAN: And, just think, I'm delighted to hear he's quite a reformed character.

BRACK: Yes, so they say.

TESMAN: And he's published a new book, eh?

BRACK: Indeed he has.

TESMAN: I hear it's made quite a sensation.

BRACK: A most unusual sensation.

TESMAN: Think of that. I'm delighted to hear it. A man of such extraordinary gifts. I felt so sorry to think he'd gone completely to wrack and ruin!

BRACK: Well—everybody thought so.

TESMAN: I wonder what he'll do now—how on earth will he manage to make a living?
(During these last words HEDDA *has reentered by the hall door.)*

HEDDA *(To* BRACK *with a scornful laugh)*: Isn't that just like Tesman, Judge? Always worrying about how people are going to make their living.

TESMAN: We were just talking about Ejlert Lövborg, dear.

HEDDA *(Giving him a quick glance. Seats herself in the armchair by the stove and asks casually)*: What's the matter with him?

TESMAN: That money he inherited—he's undoubtedly squandered that long ago. And he can't very well write a new book every year, eh? So why shouldn't I wonder what's to become of him?

BRACK: Perhaps I can give you some information on the subject.

TESMAN: Indeed?

BRACK: You must remember that his relatives have a great deal of influence.

TESMAN: But they washed their hands of him long ago.

BRACK: At one time he was considered the hope of the family.

TESMAN: At one time, perhaps. But he soon put an end to that.

HEDDA: Who knows? *(With a slight smile)* I hear they've quite reformed him up at the Elvsteds'.

BRACK: And then there's his new book, of course.

TESMAN: Yes, that's true. Let's hope things will turn out well for him. I've just written him a note. I asked him to come and see me this evening, Hedda dear.

BRACK: But you're coming to my stag party this evening. You promised me last night on the pier.

HEDDA: Had you forgotten, Tesman!

TESMAN: Yes, I really had.

BRACK: In any case, I think you can be pretty sure he won't come.

TESMAN: Why shouldn't he?

BRACK *(With a slight hesitation, rises and leans against the back of the chair)*: My dear Tesman, and you, too, Mrs. Tesman, I think it's only right that I should inform you of something that—

TESMAN: That concerns Ejlert, eh?

BRACK: Yes, you as well as him.

TESMAN *(Jumps up anxiously)*: But, my dear Judge, what is it?

BRACK: I think you should be prepared to find your appointment deferred—rather longer than you desired or expected.

TESMAN: Has anything happened to prevent it, eh?

BRACK: The nomination may depend on the result of a competition.

TESMAN: A competition! Think of that, Hedda. But who would my competitor be? Surely not—?

BRACK: Yes. Ejlert Lövborg. Precisely. *(HEDDA leans farther back in the armchair with an ejaculation.)*

TESMAN: No, no! It's impossible! It's utterly inconceivable, eh?

BRACK: It may come to that, all the same.

TESMAN: But, Judge Brack, this would be incredibly unfair to me. *(Waving his arms)* Just think, I'm a married man! We married on these prospects, Hedda and I. Think of the money we've spent, and we've borrowed from Aunt Juliane, too! Why, they practically promised me the appointment, eh?

BRACK: Don't get so excited. You'll probably get the appointment all the same, only you'll have to compete for it.

HEDDA *(Sits motionless in the armchair)*: Just think, Jörgen, it will have quite a sporting interest.

TESMAN: Dearest Hedda, how can you be so indifferent about it?

HEDDA *(As before)*: Indifferent! I'm not in the least indifferent. I can hardly wait to see which of you will win.

BRACK: In any case, I thought it better to warn you, Mrs. Tesman! Perhaps under the circumstances, you'd better go easy on those "additional trifles" you're thinking of buying.

HEDDA: I don't see how this could possibly make any difference, my dear Judge.

BRACK: Really? Then I've no more to say. Good-bye. I'll call for you later on my way back from my afternoon walk.

TESMAN: Yes, yes—I'm so upset—my head's in a whirl!

HEDDA *(Still reclining, holds out her hand to him)*: I shall hope to see you later, Judge.

BRACK: Thank you, Mrs. Tesman. Good-bye.

TESMAN *(Accompanies him to the door)*: Good-bye, my dear Judge. You really must excuse me—

(JUDGE goes out by the hall door.)

TESMAN *(Pacing the room)*: Oh, Hedda, Hedda, one should never rush into adventures, eh?

HEDDA *(Looks at him and smiles)*: Do you do that, Jörgen?

TESMAN: What else can you call it? To get married and settle down on mere expectations, eh?

HEDDA: You may be right.

TESMAN: Well, at least we have our lovely home, Hedda, eh? The home we both dreamed of.

HEDDA *(Rises slowly and wearily)*: I'd counted on doing a lot of entertaining. That was part of the agreement, I thought. We were to keep open house.

TESMAN: I'd been so looking forward to it, Hedda dear. To see you, a brilliant hostess, surrounded by distinguished guests—Well, we'll just have to make the best of it for the time being, dear. Be happy in one another. We can always invite Aunt Juliane in now and then. But I wanted it to be so different for you, Hedda. So very different.

HEDDA: I suppose this means I'll have to do without my butler.

TESMAN: Yes, I'm afraid a butler is quite out of the question!

HEDDA: You promised me a saddle horse, remember? I suppose *that's* out of the question, too?

TESMAN: I'm afraid so, Hedda.

HEDDA *(Walks about the room)*: Well, at least I have one thing to amuse myself with.

TESMAN *(Beaming)*: Thank heaven for that. What is it, Hedda, eh?

HEDDA *(At center opening—looks at him with suppressed scorn)*: My pistols, Jörgen.

TESMAN: Your pistols!

HEDDA *(With cold eyes)*: General Gabler's pistols. *(She goes out through the inner room to the left.)*

TESMAN *(Rushes to the center opening and calls after her)*: Oh, Hedda, darling, please don't touch those dangerous things. For my sake, Hedda, eh?

CURTAIN

Act Two

SCENE: *The room at the* TESMANS' *as in the first act. Only the piano has been removed and replaced by an elegant little writing table with bookshelves. A smaller table has been placed by the sofa left. Most of the bouquets have been removed.* MRS. ELVSTED's *bouquet stands on the large table downstage. It is afternoon.*

HEDDA, *dressed to receive callers, is alone in the room. She stands by the open glass door loading a pistol. The matching pistol lies in an open pistol case on the writing table.*

HEDDA *(Looks down into the garden and calls out)*: Welcome back, Judge!
BRACK *(Is heard calling below at a distance)*: Thank you, Mrs. Tesman.
HEDDA *(Raises the pistol and takes aim)*: Now, I'm going to shoot you, Judge!
BRACK *(From below)*: No, no, don't aim at me like that!
HEDDA: That's what you get for sneaking in the back way. *(She fires.)*
BRACK *(Nearer)*: Have you gone quite mad?
HEDDA: So sorry. Did I hit you by any chance?
BRACK *(Still from outside)*: I wish you'd stop all this nonsense.
HEDDA: Come along, Judge, I'll let you pass.
(JUDGE BRACK, dressed as for a men's party, comes in through the glass door. Over his arm he carries a light overcoat.)
BRACK: So you're still fooling with those pistols. What are you shooting at?
HEDDA: Just killing time. Shooting up into the blue.
BRACK *(Gently takes the pistol out of her hand)*: Allow me. *(Examines it)* Hm . . . I know this pistol . . . I've seen it before.

340

(Looks around) Where's the case for it? Ah, here! *(Places the pistol in its case and closes it)* So that game is finished for today.

HEDDA: What in heaven's name am I to do with myself all day long!

BRACK: Haven't you had any visitors?

HEDDA *(Closing the glass door)*: Not one. I suppose all our friends are still out of town.

BRACK: Isn't Tesman home?

HEDDA *(At the writing table, putting the pistol case away in a drawer)*: No. He rushed off to his aunts' directly after lunch. He didn't expect you so early, Judge.

BRACK: Fancy my not thinking of that! That was stupid of me.

HEDDA *(Turns her head and looks at him)*: Why stupid?

BRACK: Because I should have come even earlier.

HEDDA *(Crossing the room)*: Then you'd have found no one to receive you, for I've been dressing ever since lunch.

BRACK: But isn't there a little crack in the door through which one might converse?

HEDDA: No. You forgot to provide one, Judge.

BRACK: Again stupid of me.

HEDDA: We must just sit here and wait until Tesman comes— He may not be back for some time.

BRACK: Never mind. I shan't be impatient.

(HEDDA *sits in the corner of the sofa.* BRACK *lays his overcoat over the back of the nearest chair and sits down, but keeps his hat in his hand. A short pause. They look at each other.)*

HEDDA: Well?

BRACK *(In the same tone)*: Well?

HEDDA: I spoke first.

BRACK *(Slightly bending forward)*: Let's have a really pleasant little talk, Mrs.—Hedda.

HEDDA *(Leaning farther back on the sofa)*: It seems ages since our

last one, doesn't it, Judge? Of course, I don't count the
few words we had last night and this morning.

BRACK: I know—you mean a *real* talk. Just a "twosome."

HEDDA: Yes, that's it.

BRACK: Every single day I've wished you were home again.

HEDDA: I've wished that, too.

BRACK: You have? Really, Mrs. Hedda? And I thought you
were having such a good time on your journey.

HEDDA: Ha!

BRACK: Tesman's letters led me to think so.

HEDDA: Oh, well, Tesman! You know Tesman, my dear Judge!
His idea of bliss is grubbing about in a lot of dirty
bookshops and making endless copies of antiquated
manuscripts.

BRACK *(With a touch of malice)*: Well, after all, that's his vocation in life, you know. Or a large part of it.

HEDDA: Yes, if it's one's vocation, I suppose that makes it
different, but as for me! Oh, my dear Judge, I can't tell
you how bored I've been!

BRACK *(Sympathetically)*: Are you really serious?

HEDDA: Of course. Surely you can understand? How would
you like to spend six whole months without meeting a
soul you could really talk to?

BRACK: I shouldn't like it at all.

HEDDA: But the most unendurable thing of all was—

BRACK: What?

HEDDA: To be everlastingly with one and the same person.

BRACK *(With a nod of agreement)*: Morning, noon, and night, at
all possible times.

HEDDA: I said "everlastingly."

BRACK: But with our good Tesman, I should have thought one
might—

HEDDA: Tesman is a specialist, my dear Judge.

BRACK: Undeniably.

HEDDA: And specialists are not amusing traveling companions—Not for long, at any rate.

BRACK: Not even the specialist you happen to love?

HEDDA: Ugh! Don't use that revolting word!

BRACK *(Startled)*: What? What's that, Mrs. Hedda?

HEDDA *(Half laughing, half in irritation)*: Just you try it! Nothing but the history of civilization morning, noon, and night.

BRACK: Everlastingly.

HEDDA: And then all this business about the domestic industries of Brabant during the Middle Ages. That's the most maddening part of it all.

BRACK *(Looks at her searchingly)*: But, tell me, in that case, how did it happen that you—?

HEDDA: Married Tesman, you mean? Is there anything so very odd in that?

BRACK: Both yes and no, Mrs. Hedda.

HEDDA: I had danced myself tired, my dear Judge—and I wasn't getting any younger. *(With a slight shudder)* But I won't talk about that. I won't even think about it.

BRACK: You certainly have no cause.

HEDDA *(Watching him intently)*: And one must admit that Jörgen Tesman is a thoroughly worthy man.

BRACK: A worthy, dependable man. There can be no question of that.

HEDDA: And I don't see anything especially—*funny* about him, do you?

BRACK: Funny? No—o—not really. No, I wouldn't say that.

HEDDA: After all, he's a distinguished scholar. Who knows? He may still go far.

BRACK *(Looks at her uncertainly)*: I thought you believed like everyone else that some day he'd become a really famous man.

HEDDA *(In a tired voice)*: Yes, so I did. And then since he was so absolutely bent on supporting me, I really didn't see why I shouldn't accept his offer.

BRACK: No, if you look at it from that point of view—

HEDDA: Well, that was more than some of my other admirers were prepared to do, my dear Judge.

BRACK *(Laughs)*: I can't answer for the others, of course. You know that, generally speaking, I have a great respect for the state of matrimony, but I confess, that as an individual—

HEDDA *(Jokingly)*: I never had any hopes as far as you were concerned.

BRACK: All I ask of life is to know a few people intimately. A few nice people whom I can help and advise, in whose houses I can come and go as a trusted friend.

HEDDA: Of the—master of the house, you mean?

BRACK *(With a bow)*: Well, preferably, of the mistress. But of the master, too, of course! I find such a triangular friendship, if I may call it so, a great convenience to all concerned.

HEDDA: Yes, God knows, a third person would have been welcome on our journey. Oh, those infernal tête-à-têtes!

BRACK: Cheer up! Your wedding trip is over now.

HEDDA *(Shaking her head)*: Not by a long shot. No, we've only stopped at a station on the line.

BRACK: Then the thing to do is to jump out and stretch oneself a bit, Mrs. Hedda.

HEDDA: I never jump out.

BRACK: Why not?

HEDDA: There's always someone there waiting to—

BRACK *(Laughing)*: Stare at your legs, you mean?

HEDDA: Precisely.

BRACK: Well, good heavens—

HEDDA *(With a gesture of distaste)*: I don't like that sort of thing. I'd rather keep my seat and continue the tête-à-tête.

BRACK: But if a third person were to jump *in* and join the couple?

HEDDA: Ah! But *that's* quite a different thing!

BRACK: A trusted, understanding friend.

HEDDA: Gay and entertaining in a variety of ways?

BRACK: And not a bit of a specialist.

HEDDA *(With an audible sigh)*: That would certainly be a great relief!

BRACK *(Hears the front door open and glances in that direction)*: The triangle is completed.

HEDDA *(In a half-tone)*: And on goes the train.

(JÖRGEN TESMAN enters from the hall. He wears a gray walking suit and a soft felt hat. He carries a great number of paperbound books under his arm and in his pockets.)

TESMAN *(Goes up to the table beside the corner sofa)*: Pooh! It's a warm job to carry all these books, Hedda. *(Puts them down)* I'm positively perspiring! *(HEDDA makes a scarcely audible ejaculation: "How charming, Jörgen!" TESMAN puts some of the books down on the table)* Oh, you're here already, Judge. Berte didn't tell me.

BRACK *(Rising)*: I came in through the garden.

HEDDA: What are all those books, Jörgen?

TESMAN *(Thumbing through the books)*: They're some new books on my special subject. I simply had to have them.

HEDDA: Your special subject, Jörgen?

BRACK: On his special subject, Mrs. Tesman. *(He and HEDDA exchange a confidential smile.)*

HEDDA: Do you need still more books on your special subject, Jörgen?

TESMAN: One can never have too many, Hedda. One *must* keep up with all the new publications.

HEDDA: Yes, I suppose one must.

TESMAN *(Searching among the books)*: Look, I got Ejlert Lövborg's new book, too. *(Offers it to her)* Would you care to have a look at it, Hedda, eh?

HEDDA: No, thank you—Well, perhaps a little later, Jörgen.

TESMAN: I glanced through it on my way home.

BRACK: What do you think of it? As a specialist, I mean.

TESMAN: He handles his subject with the greatest restraint. That is what struck me most—It's quite remarkable. He never wrote like that before. *(Gathers the books together)* I'll just take these into my study. I'm longing to cut the leaves. And then I suppose I'd better change, though we needn't go just yet, eh?

BRACK: Oh, no. There's not the slightest hurry.

TESMAN: Then I'll take my time. *(Starts to go out with the books but stops and turns at center opening)* Oh, by the way, Hedda, Aunt Juliane is afraid she can't come to see you this evening.

HEDDA: Oh? Why not? Is she still annoyed about the hat?

TESMAN: Of course not. That wouldn't be a bit like her! No, but you see, Aunt Rina's very ill.

HEDDA: She always is.

TESMAN: Yes, but today she's worse than ever, poor thing!

HEDDA: Then she'll need her sister with her. That's only natural. I shall have to try and bear it.

TESMAN: I can't tell you how delighted Aunt Juliane was to see you looking so well, so positively flourishing.

HEDDA *(In a half-tone, rising)*: Oh, those eternal aunts!

TESMAN: What did you say, dear?

HEDDA *(Going to the glass door)*: Nothing—nothing—nothing!

TESMAN: Very well, Hedda—eh? *(He goes out right, through the inner room.)*

BRACK: What was that you said about a hat?

HEDDA: Oh, it was just something that happened this morning. Miss Tesman had taken off her hat and put it down on the table. *(Looks at him and smiles)* And I pretended to think it was the servant's.

BRACK *(Shakes his head)*: Why, my dear Mrs. Hedda. How could you do such a thing to that nice old lady?

HEDDA *(Walks nervously about the room)*: My dear Judge, I really don't know. I suddenly get impulses like that and I simply can't control them. *(Flings herself down in the armchair by the stove)* I don't know how to explain it myself.

BRACK *(Behind the armchair)*: You're not really happy. I think that's the explanation.

HEDDA *(Gazing straight before her)*: I can't imagine why I should be—happy? Can you tell me?

BRACK: Well, to begin with; here you are, in the very house you always longed to live in.

HEDDA *(Looks up at him and laughs)*: You really believe in that fairy tale?

BRACK: Wasn't it true, then?

HEDDA: I'll tell you how it happened: last summer I made use of Tesman to see me home from parties.

BRACK: Unfortunately, my way lay in a different direction.

HEDDA: Yes, you were going in a different direction then, weren't you, Judge?

BRACK *(Laughs)*: Shame on you, Mrs. Hedda! And so you and Tesman—?

HEDDA: Well, one evening we happened to pass by this house. Tesman, poor thing, was turning and twisting and couldn't think of anything to say. I really felt sorry for the poor learned wretch.

BRACK *(Smiles skeptically)*: Sorry! You!

HEDDA: Yes, I really did. I felt sorry for him. And so just to make conversation, to help him out a bit, I was foolish

enough to say what a charming house this was, and how
I should love to live in it.

BRACK: No more than that?

HEDDA: Not *that* evening.

BRACK: But afterward?

HEDDA: Afterward! Afterward my foolishness was not without
consequences, my dear Judge.

BRACK: Yes—Unfortunately, that happens all too often.

HEDDA: Thanks! So, you see it was this fictitious enthusiasm
for Secretary Falk's villa that really brought Tesman and
me together. It was the immediate cause of our engage-
ment, our wedding, our wedding journey, and all the
rest of it. Well, my dear Judge, they say, as you make
your bed, so you must lie.

BRACK: This is really priceless! So I suppose you didn't really
care a rap about the house?

HEDDA: No, God knows, I didn't!

BRACK: Still, now that we've made it so attractive and comfortable for you—

HEDDA: To me it smells of lavender and dried rose leaves.
What might be called the "Aunt Juliane atmosphere."

BRACK *(Laughs)*: No. That's probably a legacy from the late
Mrs. Falk.

HEDDA: Yes! Yes, you're right! There is a touch of decay about
it. *(She clasps her hands behind her head, leans back in the chair
and looks at him)* Oh, my dear Judge, my dear Judge! How
incredibly I shall bore myself here!

BRACK: Why shouldn't you, too, find some sort of vocation in
life, Mrs. Hedda?

HEDDA: A vocation—that would attract me?

BRACK: Preferably, yes.

HEDDA: God only knows what kind of a vocation that would
be! I often wonder whether—*(Breaks off)* But that
wouldn't be any good, either.

BRACK: What? Tell me.

HEDDA: I was wondering whether I could get Jörgen to go into politics.

BRACK *(Laughs)*: Tesman? No, really! I'm afraid political life would be the last thing in the world for him.

HEDDA: I know you're probably right; but I could try and get him into it all the same.

BRACK: But what satisfaction would it be to you unless he were successful at it? Why should you want to drive him into it?

HEDDA: Because I'm *bored*, I tell you. *(After a pause)* So you think it quite out of the question for Jörgen ever to become—let's say—Secretary of State?

BRACK: Ha, ha! Mrs. Hedda. You must remember, apart from anything else, to become anything of that sort he'd have to be a fairly rich man.

HEDDA *(Rises impatiently)*: There you are. Money! Always money! *(Crosses the room)* It's this genteel poverty that makes life so hideous, so utterly ludicrous.

BRACK: Now I should say the fault lies elsewhere.

HEDDA: Where then?

BRACK: I don't believe you've ever really been stirred by anything in life.

HEDDA: Anything serious, you mean?

BRACK: If you like. But I expect it will come.

HEDDA *(Tossing her head)*: If you're thinking about that ridiculous professorship, that's Jörgen's own affair. I assure you I shan't give a thought to that!

BRACK: I dare say. But suppose you should suddenly find yourself faced with what's known in solemn language, as a grave responsibility—*(Smiling)* a *new* responsibility, Mrs. Hedda.

HEDDA *(Angrily)*: Be quiet! Nothing of that sort will ever happen to me.

BRACK *(Cautiously)*: We'll talk of this again a year from now, at the very latest.

HEDDA *(Curtly)*: That sort of thing doesn't appeal to me, Judge. I'm not fitted for it. No responsibilities for me!

BRACK: What makes you think you're less fitted than the majority of women? Why should you deliberately turn away from duties—?

HEDDA *(At the glass door)*: Be quiet, I tell you! I sometimes think there's only one thing in this world I'm really fitted for.

BRACK *(Nearer to her)*: What's that, if I may ask?

HEDDA *(Looking out)*: Boring myself to death! Now you know it. *(Turns, looks toward the inner room, and laughs)* Ah! I thought so—here comes the professor!

BRACK *(Softly, warningly)*: Now, now! Mrs. Hedda!

(JÖRGEN TESMAN, dressed for the party, his gloves and hat in his hands, enters from the right through the inner room.)

TESMAN: Oh, Hedda, has any message come from Ejlert, eh?

HEDDA: No.

TESMAN: Then he'll be here presently, you'll see.

BRACK: You really think he'll come?

TESMAN: I'm almost sure of it. What you told us this morning was probably just a rumor.

BRACK: Do you think so?

TESMAN: At any rate, Aunt Juliane didn't believe for a moment that he would ever stand in my way again. Think of that!

BRACK: Well, then, there's nothing to worry about.

TESMAN *(Puts his hat and gloves down on a chair, right)*: I'd like to wait for him as long as possible, though.

BRACK: We've plenty of time. My guests won't arrive before seven or half-past.

TESMAN: Meanwhile, we can keep Hedda company and see what happens, eh?

HEDDA (*Puts* BRACK'S *overcoat and hat on the corner sofa*): And if the worse comes to the worst, Mr. Lövborg can spend the evening with me.

BRACK: What do you mean by "the worst"?

HEDDA: I mean—if he refuses to go with you and Tesman.

TESMAN (*Looks at her dubiously*): But, Hedda dear, do you think it would be quite the thing for him to stay here with you, eh? Remember, Aunt Juliane isn't coming.

HEDDA: No, but Mrs. Elvsted is. We three can have a cup of tea together.

TESMAN: Oh, well, then it would be *quite* all right.

BRACK (*Smiling*): It might perhaps be the best thing for him, too.

HEDDA: Why the "best thing," Judge?

BRACK: Well, you know how rude you are about my stag parties, Mrs. Tesman. You always say they're only safe for men of the strictest principles.

HEDDA: I'm sure Mr. Lövborg's principles are strict enough now. A converted sinner—

(BERTE *appears at the hall door.*)

BERTE: There's a gentleman asking to see you, ma'am.

HEDDA: Oh, yes—show him in.

TESMAN (*Softly*): It must be Ejlert. Think of that! (EJLERT LÖVBORG *enters from the hall. He is slim and lean. The same age as* TESMAN, *he looks older, as though worn out by life. Hair and beard dark-brown; a long, pale face, but with patches of color on the cheekbones; he wears a well-cut black visiting suit, obviously new. He carries dark gloves and a silk hat. He stands near the door and makes a rapid bow. He seems slightly embarrassed.* TESMAN *goes to him and shakes him by the hand*) Welcome, my dear Ejlert. So at last we meet again!

LÖVBORG (*Speaks in a hushed voice*): Thanks for your letter, Jörgen. (*Approaches* HEDDA) May I shake hands with you, too, Mrs. Tesman?

351

HEDDA *(Takes his hand)*: How do you do, Mr. Lövborg, I'm delighted to see you. *(She motions with her hand)* I don't know if you two gentlemen—

LÖVBORG *(With a slight bow)*: Judge Brack, I believe.

BRACK *(Bows likewise)*: Yes, I've had the pleasure, some years ago.

TESMAN *(To* LÖVBORG, *with his hands on his shoulders)*: And now, Ejlert, you must make yourself at home, mustn't he, Hedda? I hear you're going to settle in town again, eh?

LÖVBORG: Yes, I am.

TESMAN: Well, that's splendid. I just got your new book, Ejlert, but I haven't had time to read it yet.

LÖVBORG: I wouldn't bother to, if I were you.

TESMAN: Why, what do you mean?

LÖVBORG: It's pretty thin stuff.

TESMAN: Just think! How can you say that?

BRACK: It's been enormously praised, I hear.

LÖVBORG: That was exactly what I wanted, so I put nothing in it that anyone could take exception to.

BRACK: Very wise of you.

TESMAN: But, my dear Ejlert—

LÖVBORG: You see, I'm determined to make a fresh start; to win a real position for myself.

TESMAN *(Slightly embarrassed)*: Oh, so that's what you plan to do, eh?

LÖVBORG *(Smiles, puts down his hat, and takes a parcel wrapped in paper from his coat pocket)*: But when this one appears, Jörgen Tesman, you'll have to read it, for this is a real book. Every ounce of my true self is in this.

TESMAN: Really! What's it about?

LÖVBORG: It's the sequel.

TESMAN: Sequel? Sequel of what?

LÖVBORG: Of the other book.

352

TESMAN: You mean, the new one?

LÖVBORG: Yes, of course.

TESMAN: But, my dear Ejlert, surely that comes right down to our time, doesn't it?

LÖVBORG: Yes, but this deals with the future.

TESMAN: With the future. But good heavens, we know nothing about the future!

LÖVBORG: There's a thing or two to be said about it all the same. *(Opens the parcel)* Look here—

TESMAN: That's not your handwriting.

LÖVBORG: No, I dictated it. *(Thumbs through the pages)* It falls into two sections. The first deals with the civilizing forces of the future and the second—*(turning to the pages toward the end)* forecasts the probable lines of development.

TESMAN: How remarkable! I should never have thought of writing anything of that sort.

HEDDA *(At the glass door, drumming on the pane)*: No, I daresay not.

LÖVBORG *(Puts the manuscript back in its wrapping and lays it on the table)*: I brought it with me; I thought I might read you a bit of it this evening.

TESMAN: That was very kind of you, Ejlert, but this evening— *(Glancing at BRACK)* I don't see how we can manage it—

LÖVBORG: Well, then, some other time. There's no hurry.

BRACK: The fact is, Mr. Lövborg, I'm giving a little party this evening to celebrate Tesman's return.

LÖVBORG *(Looking for his hat)*: Oh, then I mustn't detain you.

BRACK: No, but wait. I'd be delighted if you would give me the pleasure of your company.

LÖVBORG *(Curtly and decisively)*: I'm sorry. I can't. Thank you very much.

BRACK: Oh, nonsense! Do come. We shall be quite a select

little circle, and I can assure you, we shall have a "jolly time," as Mrs. Hed—Mrs. Tesman puts it.

LÖVBORG: I don't doubt that, but nevertheless—

BRACK: And you could bring your manuscript with you and read it to Tesman at my house. I could give you a room all to yourselves.

TESMAN: Yes, think of that, Ejlert. Why shouldn't you do that, eh?

HEDDA *(Interposing)*: But, Jörgen dear, if Mr. Lövborg says he doesn't want to go, I'm sure Mr. Lövborg would much prefer to stay here and have supper with me.

LÖVBORG *(Looking at her)*: With you, Mrs. Tesman?

HEDDA: Mrs. Elvsted will be here, too.

LÖVBORG: Oh—*(Casually)* I saw her for a moment today.

HEDDA: Oh, did you? Well, she's spending the evening here. So you see, you're almost obliged to stay, Mr. Lövborg. Otherwise, Mrs. Elvsted will have no one to see her home.

LÖVBORG: That's true. Many thanks. In that case, I will stay, Mrs. Tesman.

HEDDA: Splendid! I'll just give one or two orders to the servant. *(She goes to the hall door and rings. BERTE enters. HEDDA talks to her in a whisper and points to the inner room. BERTE nods and goes out.)*

TESMAN *(During the above, to EJLERT LÖVBORG)*: Tell me, Ejlert, is it this new subject, the future, that you are going to lecture about?

LÖVBORG: Yes.

TESMAN: They told me at the bookstore that you were planning a series of lectures.

LÖVBORG: Yes, I am. I hope you've no objection.

TESMAN: No, of course not, but—

LÖVBORG: I can quite see that it might interfere with your plans.

TESMAN *(Depressed)*: I can't very well expect you, out of consideration for *me*, to—

LÖVBORG: But, of course, I'll wait until you receive your appointment.

TESMAN: What! You'll wait! Then—then you're not going to compete with me, eh?

LÖVBORG: No. I only want people to realize that I *could* have—a sort of moral victory, if you like.

TESMAN: Why, bless my soul, then Aunt Juliane was right after all! I was sure of it. Hedda, just think, Ejlert is not going to stand in our way!

HEDDA *(Curtly)*: Our way! Do please leave me out of it, Jörgen. *(She goes up toward the inner room where* BERTE *is arranging a tray with decanters and glasses on the table.* HEDDA *nods approvingly and comes forward again.* BERTE *goes out.)*

TESMAN *(During the above)*: What do you say to this, Judge, eh?

BRACK: Well, I say a moral victory may be all very fine but—

TESMAN: Yes, certainly, but all the same—

HEDDA *(Looks at* TESMAN *with a cold smile)*: You stand there looking absolutely thunderstruck, Jörgen.

TESMAN: Well, you know, I almost believe I am.

HEDDA *(Pointing to the inner room)*: And now, gentlemen, won't you have a glass of cold punch before you go?

BRACK *(Looks at his watch)*: A sort of stirrup cup, you mean. Yes, that's not a bad idea.

TESMAN: A capital idea, Hedda. Just the thing. Now that a heavy weight has been lifted off my mind—

HEDDA: You'll join them, Mr. Lövborg?

LÖVBORG *(With a gesture of refusal)*: No, thank you, nothing for me.

BRACK: Why, surely, cold punch is not poison.

LÖVBORG: Perhaps not for everyone.

HEDDA: Well, then, you two go in and I'll sit here and keep Mr. Lövborg company.

TESMAN: Yes, do, Hedda dear.

(*TESMAN and* BRACK *go into the inner room, sit down, drink punch, smoke cigarettes, and carry on an animated conversation during the following.* EJLERT LÖVBORG *remains standing by the stove.* HEDDA *goes to the writing table.*)

HEDDA (*In a raised voice*): Perhaps you'd like to look at some snapshots, Mr. Lövborg. You know, Tesman and I did some sightseeing in the Tyrol, on our way home. I'd so love to show you—(*She brings over an album which she lays on the table by the sofa, in the further corner of which she seats herself.* EJLERT LÖVBORG *approaches, then stops and stands looking at her. He then takes a chair and sits on her left with his back to the inner room. She opens the album*) Do you see this group of mountains, Mr. Lövborg? It's the Ortlar group—Oh, yes, Tesman has written the name underneath. "The Ortlar group near Meran."

LÖVBORG (*Who has never taken his eyes off her, says softly and slowly*): Hedda Gabler—

HEDDA (*Gives him a hasty look*): Sh!

LÖVBORG (*Repeats softly*): Hedda Gabler—

HEDDA (*Looking at the album*): That was my name in the old days, when you and I knew each other.

LÖVBORG: Then I must learn never to say Hedda Gabler again? Never as long as I live?

HEDDA (*Turning over the pages*): Yes, I'm afraid you must.

LÖVBORG (*In an indignant tone*): Hedda Gabler married! And married to Jörgen Tesman!

HEDDA: Such is life!

LÖVBORG: Oh, Hedda, Hedda, how could you throw yourself away like that?

HEDDA (*Looks at him sharply*): I won't have you say such things.

LÖVBORG: Why shouldn't I?

(*TESMAN comes into the room and goes toward the sofa.*)

HEDDA (*Hears him coming and says in a casual tone*): And this, Mr.

Lövborg, is a view from the Ampezzo Valley. Just look at those peaks. *(Looks up at* TESMAN *affectionately)* Oh, Jörgen dear, what's the name of these curious peaks?

TESMAN: Let me see—oh, those are the Dolomites.

HEDDA: Oh, yes, those are the Dolomites, Mr. Lövborg.

TESMAN: Hedda dear, are you sure you wouldn't like me to bring some punch. For yourself, at any rate, eh?

HEDDA: Yes, I think I will have some, dear. And perhaps a few biscuits.

TESMAN: A cigarette?

HEDDA: No, I think not, dear.

TESMAN: Very well.

(He goes into the inner room again and out to the right. BRACK *sits in the inner room, occasionally keeping an eye on* HEDDA *and* LÖVBORG.*)*

LÖVBORG *(Softly as before)*: Answer me, Hedda. How could you do it?

HEDDA *(Apparently absorbed in the album)*: If you go on calling me Hedda, I won't talk to you.

LÖVBORG: Can't I say Hedda even when we're alone?

HEDDA: No. You may think it, but you mustn't say it.

LÖVBORG: I understand. It offends your love for Jörgen Tesman.

HEDDA *(Glances at him and smiles)*: Love? How funny you are!

LÖVBORG: It's not love, then?

HEDDA: All the same, no unfaithfulness, remember.

LÖVBORG: Hedda, answer me just one thing.

HEDDA: Sh!

*(*TESMAN *comes from the inner room carrying a small tray.)*

TESMAN: Here you are! Doesn't this look tempting? *(He puts the tray down on the table.)*

HEDDA: Why do you bring it yourself, Jörgen?

TESMAN *(Filling the glasses)*: I think it's such fun to wait on you, Hedda.

HEDDA: But you've poured out two glasses. Mr. Lövborg said he wouldn't have any.

TESMAN: I know. But Mrs. Elvsted will be here soon, won't she?

HEDDA: Oh, yes, of course, Mrs. Elvsted—

TESMAN: Had you forgotten her, eh?

HEDDA: Yes, you know we were so engrossed in these photographs. Oh, Jörgen dear, do you remember this little village?

TESMAN: Yes, of course I do. It's the one just below the Brenner Pass. Don't you remember? We spent the night there.

HEDDA: Oh, yes. And met that gay party of tourists.

TESMAN: Yes, that was the place. Just think, if only we could have had you with us, Ejlert, eh? *(He goes back to the inner room and sits down with* JUDGE BRACK.*)*

LÖVBORG: Answer me this one thing, Hedda.

HEDDA: Well?

LÖVBORG: Was there no love in your feeling for *me*, either? Not the slightest touch of love?

HEDDA: I wonder—To me it seems that we were just two good comrades, two thoroughly intimate friends. *(Smiles)* You especially were exceedingly frank!

LÖVBORG: It was you who made me so.

HEDDA: You know, as I look back on it all, I realize there was something very beautiful, something fascinating, something daring—yes, daring—in that secret intimacy, that comradeship no living soul suspected.

LÖVBORG: Yes, there was, wasn't there, Hedda? Do you remember when I used to come to your home in the afternoon and the General sat over at the window reading his paper, with his back toward us—

HEDDA: We two sat on the corner sofa—

LÖVBORG: Always the same illustrated paper before us—

HEDDA: For want of an album, yes!

LÖVBORG: Do you remember, Hedda, all those wild things I confessed to you? Things no one suspected at the time—my days and nights of passion and frenzy, of drinking and madness—How did you make me talk like that, Hedda? By what power?

HEDDA: Power?

LÖVBORG: Yes. How else can one explain it? And all those devious questions you used to ask—

HEDDA: Questions you understood so perfectly—

LÖVBORG: How could you bring yourself to ask such questions? So candidly, so boldly?

HEDDA: In a devious way, if you please.

LÖVBORG: Yes, but boldly, all the same.

HEDDA: How could you bring yourself to answer them, Mr. Lövborg?

LÖVBORG: That's just what I can't understand. There must have been love at the bottom of it. Perhaps you felt that by making me confess like that you were somehow washing away my sins.

HEDDA: No, not quite.

LÖVBORG: What was your motive, then?

HEDDA: Isn't it quite easy to understand, that a young girl, especially if it can be done in secret—

LÖVBORG: Well?

HEDDA: Should be tempted to investigate a forbidden world? A world she's supposed to know nothing about?

LÖVBORG: So that was it.

HEDDA: That had a lot to do with it, I think.

LÖVBORG: I see; we were both greedy for life. That made us comrades. But why did it end?

HEDDA: You were to blame for that!

LÖVBORG: You broke with me.

HEDDA: I realized the danger; you wanted to spoil our intimacy—to drag it down to reality. You talk of my boldness, my candor—why did you try to abuse them?

LÖVBORG *(Clenching his hands)*: Why didn't you do as you said? Why didn't you shoot me?

HEDDA: Because . . . I have such a fear of scandal.

LÖVBORG: Yes, Hedda, you are a coward at heart.

HEDDA: A terrible coward. *(With a change of tone)* But after all, it was a lucky thing for you. You found ample consolation at the Elvsteds'.

LÖVBORG: I know Thea has confided in you.

HEDDA: And I suppose you've confided in her—about us?

LÖVBORG: Not a word. She's too stupid to understand that.

HEDDA: Stupid?

LÖVBORG: About that sort of thing—yes.

HEDDA: And I am a coward. *(Leans toward him, without looking him in the eye, says softly)* Now I'll confide something to you.

LÖVBORG *(Intensely)*: Well?

HEDDA: My not daring to shoot you—

LÖVBORG: Yes?

HEDDA: That was not my greatest cowardice that evening.

LÖVBORG *(Looks at her a moment, understands, and whispers passionately)*: Oh, Hedda, Hedda Gabler! I begin to understand the real meaning of our comradeship. You and I!—You see, it *was* your craving for life—

HEDDA *(Softly, with a keen look)*: Be careful! Believe nothing of the sort. *(It has begun to get dark. The hall door is opened by* BERTE. HEDDA *closes the album with a bang and calls out smilingly)* At last! Thea darling!—(MRS. ELVSTED *enters from the hall. She is in evening dress. The door is closed behind her.* HEDDA, *still on the sofa, stretches out her arms toward her)*

Darling little Thea, I thought you were never coming! *(In passing,* MRS. ELVSTED *lightly greets the gentlemen in the inner room, then goes to the table and gives* HEDDA *her hand.* EJLERT LÖVBORG *rises. He and* MRS. ELVSTED *greet each other with a silent nod.)*

MRS. ELVSTED: Shouldn't I go and say good evening to your husband?

HEDDA *(Puts her arm around* MRS. ELVSTED *and leads her toward sofa)*: No, we needn't bother about them. I expect they'll soon be off.

MRS. ELVSTED: Are they going out?

HEDDA: Yes. To a wild party!

MRS. ELVSTED *(Quickly. To* LÖVBORG*)*: You're not going, are you?

LÖVBORG: No.

HEDDA: No. Mr. Lövborg is staying here with us.

*(*LÖVBORG *sits down again on the sofa.)*

MRS. ELVSTED *(Takes a chair and starts to sit beside him)*: Oh, how nice it is to be here!

HEDDA: No, no, little Thea, not there! You be a good girl and sit here, next to me. I'll sit between you.

MRS. ELVSTED: Just as you like. *(She goes around the table and sits on the sofa to* HEDDA'S *right.* LÖVBORG *sits down again.)*

LÖVBORG *(To* HEDDA, *after a short pause)*: Isn't she lovely to look at?

HEDDA *(Lightly stroking her hair)*: Only to look at?

LÖVBORG: We're two real comrades, she and I. We have absolute faith in each other. We can talk with perfect frankness.

HEDDA: Not in a devious way, Mr. Lövborg.

LÖVBORG: Well—

MRS. ELVSTED *(Softly, clinging to* HEDDA*)*: Oh, I'm so happy, Hedda! You know—he actually says I've inspired him in his work.

HEDDA *(Looks at her and smiles)*: Does he really, dear?

LÖVBORG: And then she has such courage, Mrs. Tesman.

MRS. ELVSTED: Good heavens, courage!

LÖVBORG: Tremendous courage where your comrade is concerned.

HEDDA: God, yes, courage! If one only had that!

LÖVBORG: What then?

HEDDA: Then life might perhaps be endurable, after all. . . . *(With a sudden change of tone)* Now, my darling little Thea, you must have a nice glass of cold punch.

MRS. ELVSTED: No, thank you. I never take anything like that.

HEDDA: Then how about you, Mr. Lövborg?

LÖVBORG: I don't either, thank you.

MRS. ELVSTED: No, he doesn't either.

HEDDA *(Looks at him intently)*: But if I want you to.

LÖVBORG: It makes no difference.

HEDDA *(Laughs)*: Poor me! Have I no power over you at all, then?

LÖVBORG: Not in that respect.

HEDDA: No, but seriously. I really think you ought to take it for your own sake.

MRS. ELVSTED: Why, Hedda—

LÖVBORG: How do you mean?

HEDDA: People might begin to suspect that you weren't quite sure, quite confident of yourself.

MRS. ELVSTED *(Softly)*: Don't, Hedda.

LÖVBORG: People may suspect whatever they like.

MRS. ELVSTED *(Happily)*: Yes, let them.

HEDDA: You should have seen Judge Brack's face a moment ago. . . .

LÖVBORG: Indeed?

HEDDA: His contemptuous smile when you didn't dare join them in there.

LÖVBORG: Didn't dare! I simply preferred to stay here and talk to you.

MRS. ELVSTED: That's natural enough, Hedda.

HEDDA: That's not what Judge Brack thought. You should have seen him smile and look at Tesman when you didn't dare go to his ridiculous little party.

LÖVBORG: Didn't dare! You say I didn't dare!

HEDDA: No, *I* don't say it—but that's how Judge Brack looks at it.

LÖVBORG: Well, let him.

HEDDA: So you're not going with them?

LÖVBORG: No, I'm staying here with you and Thea.

MRS. ELVSTED: Yes, Hedda, of course he is.

HEDDA *(Smiles and nods approvingly to* LÖVBORG*)*: There, you see! Firm as a rock. Faithful to all good principles now and forever. That's how a man should be. *(Turns to* MRS. ELVSTED *and says with a caress)* What did I tell you this morning, Thea? Didn't I tell you not to be upset?

LÖVBORG *(Amazed)*: Upset?

MRS. ELVSTED *(Terrified)*: Hedda—! Please, Hedda.

HEDDA: You see? Now are you convinced? You haven't the slightest reason to be so anxious and worried. . . . There! Now we can all three enjoy ourselves.

LÖVBORG *(With a start)*: What does all this mean, Mrs. Tesman?

MRS. ELVSTED: Oh, God! What are you doing, Hedda?

HEDDA: Be careful! That horrid Judge is watching you.

LÖVBORG: So you were anxious and worried on my account?

MRS. ELVSTED *(Softly, miserably)*: Oh, Hedda, you've ruined everything.

LÖVBORG *(Looks at her intently for a moment. His face is distorted)*: Well, my comrade! So that's all your faith amounts to!

MRS. ELVSTED *(Imploringly)*: You *must* listen to me, Ejlert—

363

LÖVBORG *(Takes one of the glasses of punch, raises it, and says in a low, hoarse voice)*: Your health, Thea! *(He empties the glass, puts it down, and takes the second one.)*

MRS. ELVSTED *(Softly)*: Hedda, Hedda, how could you do this?

HEDDA: I do it? I? Are you crazy?

LÖVBORG: And your health, too, Mrs. Tesman. Thanks for the truth. Long live the truth! *(He empties the glass and is about to fill it again.)*

HEDDA *(Lays her hand on his arm)*: There, there! No more for the present. You're going to the party, remember.

LÖVBORG *(Putting down the glass)*: Now, Thea, be honest with me.

MRS. ELVSTED: Yes?

LÖVBORG: Did your husband know you came after me?

MRS. ELVSTED *(Wringing her hands)*: Ejlert! . . .

LÖVBORG: It was arranged between you, wasn't it, that you should come to town and keep an eye on me. I dare say the old man suggested it himself. No doubt he needed my help in the office. Or perhaps it was at the card table he missed me.

MRS. ELVSTED *(Softly, in great distress)*: Ejlert! Ejlert!

LÖVBORG *(Seizes the glass and is about to fill it)*: Let's drink to the old sheriff, too!

HEDDA *(Preventing him)*: No more now. Remember you're going to read your manuscript to Jörgen.

LÖVBORG *(Calmly, putting down the glass)*: I'm behaving like a fool, Thea. Try and forgive me, my dear, dear comrade. You'll see—I'll prove to you—I'll prove to everyone, that I'm all right again. I'm back on my feet. Thanks to you, Thea.

MRS. ELVSTED *(Radiant)*: Oh, thank God!

(In the meantime BRACK *has looked at his watch. He and* TESMAN *rise and come into the drawing room.)*

BRACK *(Takes up his hat and overcoat)*: Well, Mrs. Tesman, it's time to go.

HEDDA: I suppose it is, Judge.

LÖVBORG *(Rising)*: I've decided to join you, Judge.

MRS. ELVSTED *(Softly, imploringly)*: Oh, Lövborg, don't!

HEDDA *(Pinching her arm)*: Sh! They'll hear you.

LÖVBORG *(To BRACK)*: Since you were kind enough to invite me.

BRACK: You've changed your mind?

LÖVBORG: Yes, if you don't mind.

BRACK: I'm delighted.

LÖVBORG *(Putting the manuscript in his pocket, to TESMAN)*: I should like to show you one or two things before the manuscript goes to press.

TESMAN: Just think, how delightful! But, Hedda dear, in that case, how is Mrs. Elvsted to get home?

HEDDA: Oh, we shall manage, somehow.

LÖVBORG *(Looking toward the ladies)*: Mrs. Elvsted? Of course, I'll come back and fetch her. *(Comes nearer)* Around ten o'clock, Mrs. Tesman. Will that do?

HEDDA: That will be splendid, Mr. Lövborg.

TESMAN: Well, then, that's settled. But you mustn't expect me so early, Hedda.

HEDDA: Oh, you can stay as long as you like, Jörgen.

MRS. ELVSTED *(With suppressed anxiety)*: Well, then, Mr. Lövborg, I'll wait here till you come.

LÖVBORG *(With his hat in his hand)*: That's understood, Mrs. Elvsted.

BRACK: Well, gentlemen, shall we start? I hope we're going to have a very jolly time, as a certain fair lady puts it.

HEDDA: If only the fair lady could be there, unseen, Judge.

BRACK: Why unseen?

HEDDA: So as to share a little in your unbridled fun.

BRACK *(Laughs)*: I shouldn't advise the fair lady to try it.

TESMAN *(Also laughing)*: Come. You're a nice one, Hedda. Think of that!

BRACK: Well, good-bye. Good-bye, ladies!

LÖVBORG *(Bowing)*: About ten o'clock then.

HEDDA: Yes, Mr. Lövborg!

(BRACK, LÖVBORG, and TESMAN go out by the hall door. Simultaneously, BERTE comes in from the inner room with a lighted lamp which she puts on the drawing-room table; she goes out again through the inner room.)

MRS. ELVSTED *(Who has risen and paces restlessly about the room)*: Hedda, what will come of all this!

HEDDA: At ten o'clock he will be here, with vine leaves in his hair. Flushed and fearless!

MRS. ELVSTED: If I could only believe that—

HEDDA: And then, you see, he will have regained confidence in himself. He'll be a free man forever and ever.

MRS. ELVSTED: Pray God you may be right.

HEDDA: I am right! It will be as I say. *(Rises and approaches her)* Doubt him as much as you like. I believe in him. Now we shall see—

MRS. ELVSTED: You have some hidden reason for all this, Hedda.

HEDDA: Yes, I have. For once in my life I want the power to shape a human destiny.

MRS. ELVSTED: But surely, you have that!

HEDDA: I haven't. I never have had.

MRS. ELVSTED: But what about your husband?

HEDDA: Do you think he's worth bothering about! If you could only understand how poor I am; and that you should be allowed to be so rich!—*(She flings her arms around her passionately)* I think I shall have to burn your hair off, after all!

MRS. ELVSTED: Let me go! Let me go! I'm afraid of you, Hedda!

BERTE *(At the center opening)*: Supper's ready, ma'am.

HEDDA: Very well, we're coming.

MRS. ELVSTED: No, no! I'd rather go home alone. Now—at once!

HEDDA: Nonsense! You'll do nothing of the sort, you silly little thing. You'll have some supper and a nice cup of tea and then at ten o'clock Ejlert Lövborg will be here with vine leaves in his hair—*(She almost drags* MRS. ELVSTED *toward the center opening.)*

CURTAIN

Act Three

SCENE: *The room at the* TESMANS'. *The portières of the center opening are closed as well as the curtains of the glass door. The shaded lamp on the table is turned low. In the stove, of which the door stands open, there has been a fire which is now nearly burnt out.*

MRS. ELVSTED, *wrapped in a large shawl, reclines in the armchair close to the stove with her feet on a footstool.* HEDDA *lies asleep on the sofa, covered with a rug.*

MRS. ELVSTED (*After a pause, suddenly straightens up in her chair and listens eagerly. Then she sinks back wearily and says softly and plaintively*): Not yet—Oh, God!—Oh, God!—Not yet— (BERTE *slips cautiously in by the hall door. She has a letter in her hand.*)

MRS. ELVSTED (*Turns and whispers eagerly*): Did someone come?

BERTE (*Softly*): A girl just brought this letter, ma'am.

MRS. ELVSTED (*Quickly, stretching out her hand*): A letter! Give it to me!

BERTE: It's for Dr. Tesman, ma'am.

MRS. ELVSTED: Oh.

BERTE: Miss Tesman's maid brought it. I'll just put it on the table.

MRS. ELVSTED: Yes, do.

BERTE (*Puts down the letter*): I think I'd better put out the lamp, ma'am.

MRS. ELVSTED: You might as well—it must be nearly daylight.

BERTE (*Puts out the lamp*): It *is* daylight, ma'am.

MRS. ELVSTED: So it is! Broad daylight—and no one's come home yet!

BERTE: Lord bless you, ma'am—I thought something like this would happen.

MRS. ELVSTED: You did?

BERTE: Yes—when I saw them go off with a—certain gentleman, last night—we used to hear plenty about him in the
old days.

MRS. ELVSTED: Sh! Not so loud! You'll wake Mrs. Tesman—

BERTE *(Looks toward the sofa and sighs)*: Yes, you're right—let her
sleep, poor thing. Shall I make up the fire, ma'am?

MRS. ELVSTED: Thank you—you needn't trouble—

BERTE: Very well, ma'am. *(She goes out softly by the hall door.)*

HEDDA *(Wakes at the closing of the door and looks up)*: What—what
was that?

MRS. ELVSTED: It was just the maid—

HEDDA *(Looks around her)*: What are we doing in here? Oh yes!
Now I remember! *(She sits up on the sofa, stretches herself,
and rubs her eyes)* What's the time, Thea?

MRS. ELVSTED *(Looks at her watch)*: It's past seven.

HEDDA: When did Jörgen get home?

MRS. ELVSTED: He hasn't come.

HEDDA: Not home yet?

MRS. ELVSTED *(Rising)*: No one has come.

HEDDA: And we were fools enough to sit up half the night—
watching and waiting!

MRS. ELVSTED *(Wringing her hands)*: And waiting in such terrible
anxiety!

HEDDA *(Yawns, and says with her hand in front of her mouth)*:
Well—we might have spared ourselves the trouble.

MRS. ELVSTED: Did you manage to get a little sleep?

HEDDA: Yes, I believe I slept quite well—didn't you?

MRS. ELVSTED: I couldn't, Hedda—I couldn't possibly!

HEDDA *(Rises and goes toward her)*: There, there! There's nothing
to worry about! It's easy to see what's happened.

MRS. ELVSTED: What—tell me!

HEDDA: Brack's party probably dragged on for hours—

MRS. ELVSTED: I expect that's true, but still—

HEDDA: —and probably Tesman didn't want to come home and wake me up in the middle of the night—perhaps he was in no condition to show himself, after the famous party.

MRS. ELVSTED: But where could he have gone?

HEDDA: To his aunts', of course!—I expect he went there to sleep it off. They always keep his old room ready for him.

MRS. ELVSTED: No, he can't be there. That letter just came for him, from Miss Tesman.

HEDDA: Letter? *(Looks at the address)* Oh, yes! It's from Aunt Juliane. Well—then I suppose he stayed at Judge Brack's. As for Ejlert Lövborg—he is sitting with vine leaves in his hair, reading his manuscript.

MRS. ELVSTED: You're talking nonsense, Hedda! You know you don't believe a word of it—

HEDDA: What a little ninny you are, Thea!

MRS. ELVSTED: Yes, I'm afraid I am—

HEDDA: And how dreadfully tired you look!

MRS. ELVSTED: I am—dreadfully tired.

HEDDA: Now you do exactly as I tell you! You go into my room—lie down on the bed—and get a little rest.

MRS. ELVSTED: No, no!—I'd never be able to sleep.

HEDDA: Of course you would.

MRS. ELVSTED: Besides, your husband should be back soon; I must find out at once—

HEDDA: I'll tell you the moment he arrives—

MRS. ELVSTED: You promise, Hedda?

HEDDA: Yes—you can count on me—Go on in now, and have a good sleep.

MRS. ELVSTED: Thanks—I will try. *(She goes out through the inner room.)*
*(*HEDDA *goes to the glass door and opens the curtains. Bright daylight streams into the room. She takes a small mirror from the writing table, looks at herself in it, and tidies her hair. Then she goes to the hall door and rings the bell. A few moments later* BERTE *appears at the hall door.)*
BERTE: Did you ring, ma'am?
HEDDA: Yes—do something to the fire—I'm absolutely frozen.
BERTE: Certainly, ma'am—I'll make it up at once. *(She rakes the embers together and puts on a piece of wood. She stops and listens)* That was the front door, ma'am.
HEDDA: See who it is—I'll look after the fire.
BERTE: It'll soon burn up, ma'am.
(She goes out by the hall door. HEDDA *kneels on the footstool and puts several pieces of wood in the stove. After a short pause* JÖRGEN TESMAN *comes in from the hall. He looks tired and rather serious. He tiptoes up toward the center opening and is about to slip through the curtains.)*
HEDDA *(At the stove, without looking up)*: Good morning, Jörgen!
TESMAN *(Turns)*: Hedda! *(Approaches her)* Good heavens—are you up so early, eh?
HEDDA: Yes, I'm up very early today, Jörgen.
TESMAN: And I was sure you'd still be sound asleep—think of that, Hedda!
HEDDA: Sh! Don't talk so loud. You'll wake Mrs. Elvsted.
TESMAN: Did Mrs. Elvsted stay here all night?
HEDDA: Naturally—since no one came to call for her.
TESMAN: No—I suppose not—
HEDDA *(Closes the stove door and rises)*: Well—did you enjoy yourselves?
TESMAN: Were you worried about me, Hedda, eh?

HEDDA: That would never occur to me—I asked if you'd enjoyed yourselves?

TESMAN: Yes, we really did, Hedda. Especially at first—you see, Ejlert read me part of his book. We got there quite early, think of that—and Brack had all sorts of arrangements to make, so Ejlert read to me.

HEDDA *(Sits to the right of table)*: Yes? Well?

TESMAN *(Sits on a stool near the stove)*: Hedda, you can't conceive what a book it will be! I believe it's one of the most remarkable things that has ever been written. Think of that!

HEDDA: I'm really not very interested, Jörgen.

TESMAN: I've something to confess, Hedda—after he'd finished reading, I had such a horrid feeling—

HEDDA: A horrid feeling, Jörgen?

TESMAN: Yes. I felt quite jealous of Ejlert, because he'd been able to write such a book. Just think, Hedda.

HEDDA: Yes, yes! I *am* thinking!

TESMAN: It's really appalling, that he, with all his great gifts, should be so utterly incorrigible!

HEDDA: Because he has more daring than any of the rest of you?

TESMAN: It's not that, Hedda—he's utterly incapable of moderation.

HEDDA: Well—tell me what happened.

TESMAN: There's only one word to describe it, Hedda—it was an orgy!

HEDDA: Did he have vine leaves in his hair?

TESMAN: Vine leaves? No, I didn't see any vine leaves—but he made a long incoherent speech in honor of the woman who had inspired him in his work—that was the phrase he used.

HEDDA: Did he mention her name?

TESMAN: No, he didn't. But I can't help thinking he meant Mrs. Elvsted—just you see!

HEDDA: Where did you part?

TESMAN: When the party finally broke up, there were only a few of us left—so we came away together. Brack came with us too—he wanted a breath of fresh air; and then we decided we had better take Ejlert home—he was in pretty bad shape, you see.

HEDDA: Yes, I dare say.

TESMAN: And then, the strangest thing happened, Hedda—the most tragic thing! I'm really almost ashamed to tell you about it—for Ejlert's sake—

HEDDA: Oh, do go on, Jörgen!

TESMAN: Well—as we were nearing town, you see—I happened to drop a little behind the others—only for a minute or two—think of that!

HEDDA: Yes, yes!—Well?

TESMAN: And then, as I hurried after them, what do you think I found on the sidewalk, eh?

HEDDA: How should I know?

TESMAN: You mustn't say a word about it to anyone, Hedda— do you hear? Promise me—for Ejlert's sake.

HEDDA: Yes, Jörgen!

TESMAN (*Takes a parcel wrapped in paper from his pocket*): Just think, dear—I found this.

HEDDA: Isn't that the parcel he had with him yesterday?

TESMAN: Yes. It's his precious, irreplaceable manuscript. He had lost it, and hadn't even noticed it. Isn't it tragic, Hedda, that—?

HEDDA: Why didn't you give it back to him at once?

TESMAN: I didn't dare trust him with it, in the condition he was in.

HEDDA: Did you tell any of the others you'd found it?

TESMAN: Certainly not! I didn't want them to know—for Ejlert's sake, you see.

HEDDA: Then no one knows that Ejlert Lövborg's manuscript is in your possession?

TESMAN: No—and no one must know it.

HEDDA: What did you say to him afterward?

TESMAN: I didn't get a chance to talk to him again; he and two or three of the others gave us the slip and disappeared—think of that!

HEDDA: I suppose they took him home then.

TESMAN: Yes, I suppose they did—and Brack went home too.

HEDDA: And where have you been gallivanting ever since?

TESMAN: Someone suggested we should go back to his house and have an early breakfast there—or perhaps it should be called a late supper—eh? And now—as soon as I have had a little rest and poor Ejlert has had a chance to recover himself a bit—I must take this back to him.

HEDDA *(Stretching out her hand for the parcel)*: No, Jörgen—don't give it back to him—not right away, I mean. Let me read it first.

TESMAN: No, dearest Hedda, I daren't do that. I really dare not.

HEDDA: You dare not, Jörgen?

TESMAN: Think of the state he'll be in when he wakes up and can't find his manuscript! There's no copy of it, Hedda—think of that! He told me so himself.

HEDDA *(Looks at him searchingly)*: Tell me, Jörgen—would it be quite impossible to write such a thing over again?

TESMAN: Oh, I should think so, Hedda. You see, it's the inspiration—

HEDDA: Yes, of course—the inspiration. . . . I suppose it depends on that. *(Lightly)* By the way, Jörgen, here's a letter for you.

TESMAN: Just think—

HEDDA *(Hands it to him)*: It came just a little while ago.

TESMAN: It's from Aunt Juliane, Hedda! What can it be? *(He puts the parcel down on the other stool, opens the letter, glances through it, and jumps up)* Oh, Hedda—she says Aunt Rina is dying, poor thing.

HEDDA: Well—we were expecting that.

TESMAN: And that I must hurry, if I want to see her again—I'll just run over and see them at once.

HEDDA *(Suppressing a smile)*: Will you run, Jörgen?

TESMAN: Oh, my dearest Hedda—if you could only bring yourself to come with me! Just think!

HEDDA *(Rising. Rejects the idea wearily)*: No, no! Don't ask me to do that! I'll have nothing to do with sickness or death. I loathe anything ugly.

TESMAN: Well then, in that case—*(Rushing about)* My hat?—My overcoat?—Oh, in the hall. I do hope I won't be too late, Hedda—eh?

HEDDA: Well, after all—if you run, Jörgen—!

(BERTE enters by the hall door.)

BERTE: Judge Brack is here, sir—and wishes to know if you'll see him?

TESMAN: At this hour? No, no! I can't possibly—

HEDDA: But I'll see him. *(To BERTE)* Ask him to come in, Berte. *(BERTE goes. Rapidly, in a whisper)* Jörgen!—The manuscript! *(She snatches it up from the stool.)*

TESMAN: Yes, give it to me!

HEDDA: No, no. I'll keep it here till you come back. *(She goes over to the writing table and puts it in the bookcase. TESMAN in a frenzy of haste can't get his gloves on. BRACK enters from the hall.)*

HEDDA *(Nodding to him)*: You're certainly an early bird, Judge.

BRACK: I am, aren't I? *(To TESMAN)* Where are you off to in such a hurry?

TESMAN: I must rush off to my aunts'. Just think, Aunt Rina is dying, poor thing.

BRACK: Dear me, is she? Then don't let me detain you; every moment may be precious.

TESMAN: Yes, I really must run—good-bye, good-bye, Hedda—*(He rushes out by the hall door.)*

HEDDA *(Approaching* BRACK*)*: I hear the party was more than usually jolly last night, Judge.

BRACK: Yes, I've been up all night—haven't even changed my clothes.

HEDDA: So I see—

BRACK: What has Tesman told you of last night's adventures?

HEDDA: Oh, nothing much; some dreary tale about going to someone's house and having breakfast.

BRACK: Yes, I've heard about that breakfast party—but Ejlert Lövborg wasn't with them, was he?

HEDDA: No—he'd been escorted home.

BRACK: By Tesman, you mean?

HEDDA: No—by some of the others.

BRACK *(Smiling)*: Jörgen Tesman is certainly a naïve creature, Mrs. Hedda.

HEDDA: Yes, God knows he is! But you're very mysterious— what else happened last night?

BRACK: Oh, a number of things—

HEDDA: Do sit down, Judge, and tell me all about it! *(She sits to the left of the table.* BRACK *sits near her, at the long side of the table)*—Well?

BRACK: I had special reasons for keeping an eye on my guests—or rather some of my guests—last night.

HEDDA: One of them being Ejlert Lövborg, I suppose.

BRACK: Frankly—yes.

HEDDA: This sounds quite thrilling, Judge!

BRACK: Do you know where he and some of the others spent the rest of the night?

HEDDA: No. Do tell me—if it's not quite unmentionable!

BRACK: No. It's by no means unmentionable. Well—they turned up at an extremely gay party.

HEDDA: A *very* jolly party, Judge?

BRACK: An excessively jolly one!

HEDDA: Do go on!

BRACK: Lövborg, as well as the others, had been invited some time ago. I knew all about it. But he had refused the invitation, for he had become a reformed character, as you know—

HEDDA: At the Elvsteds', yes. But he went all the same?

BRACK: Well, you see, Mrs. Hedda, he became somewhat inspired at my place last night—

HEDDA: Yes. I heard he was . . . inspired.

BRACK: Rather violently inspired, in fact—and so, he changed his mind. We men are not always as high-principled as perhaps we should be.

HEDDA: I'm sure you are an exception, Judge. But to get back to Ejlert Lövborg—

BRACK: So—to make a long story short—he did finally turn up at Mlle. Diana's residence.

HEDDA: Mlle. Diana?

BRACK: Yes, it was she who was giving the party—to a very select circle of her friends and admirers.

HEDDA: Is she that red-haired woman?

BRACK: Precisely.

HEDDA: A sort of . . . singer?

BRACK: Yes—in her leisure moments. She is also a mighty huntress—of men. You must have heard of her, Mrs. Hedda. In the days of his glory Ejlert Lövborg was one of her most enthusiastic protectors.

HEDDA: But how did all this end, Judge?

BRACK: In a none-too-friendly fashion, it seems. After greeting him most tenderly, Mlle. Diana finally proceeded to tear his hair out!

HEDDA: What?—Lövborg's?

BRACK: Yes. It seems he accused her, or her friends, of having robbed him. He kept insisting some valuable notebook had disappeared—as well as various other things. In short, he raised quite a terrific row.

HEDDA: What did all this lead to?

BRACK: It led to a general free-for-all, in which the women as well as the men took part. Fortunately the police at last appeared on the scene.

HEDDA: The police?

BRACK: Yes. I'm afraid it may prove an expensive amusement for Ejlert Lövborg—crazy lunatic that he is!

HEDDA: How?

BRACK: They say he made a violent resistance—half killed one policeman, and tore another one's coat off his back. So they marched him off to the police station.

HEDDA: Where did you hear all this?

BRACK: From the police themselves.

HEDDA (*Gazing straight before her*): So that's what happened! Then, after all, he had no vine leaves in his hair!

BRACK: Vine leaves, Mrs. Hedda?

HEDDA (*With a change of tone*): Tell me, Judge—why should you be so interested in spying on Lövborg in this way?

BRACK: In the first place—I am not entirely indifferent to the fact that during the investigation it will be known that he came directly from my house.

HEDDA: You mean, the case will go to court?

BRACK: Naturally. However—be that as it may. But I felt it my

378

duty, as a friend of the family, to give you and Tesman a full account of his nocturnal exploits.

HEDDA: For what reason, Judge?

BRACK: Because I have a shrewd suspicion that he means to use you as a sort of . . . screen.

HEDDA: Whatever makes you think that?

BRACK: After all—we're not completely blind, Mrs. Hedda. You watch! This Mrs. Elvsted—she'll be in no great hurry to leave town.

HEDDA: Well—supposing there were something between them—there must be plenty of other places where they could meet.

BRACK: Not a single *home.* From now on, every respectable house will be closed to Ejlert Lövborg.

HEDDA: And mine ought to be too, you mean?

BRACK: Yes. I admit it would be more than painful to me if he should be welcome here. If this undesirable and superfluous person should be allowed to force his way into the—

HEDDA: —the Triangle?

BRACK: Precisely. It would simply mean that I should find myself homeless.

HEDDA *(Looks at him with a smile):* I see. So you want to be cock-of-the-walk, Judge. That is your aim.

BRACK *(Nods slowly and speaks in a low voice):* Yes—that is my aim; and for that I will fight with every weapon I can command.

HEDDA *(Her smile vanishing):* I wonder, Judge, now one comes to think of it, if you're not rather a dangerous person.

BRACK: Do you think so?

HEDDA: I'm beginning to think so. And I'm exceedingly glad that you have no sort of hold over me.

BRACK *(Laughs ambiguously)*: Well, well, Mrs. Hedda—perhaps you're right. If I had, who knows what I might be capable of.

HEDDA: Come now! Come, Judge! That sounds almost like a threat.

BRACK *(Rising)*: Not at all! For the Triangle, it seems to me, ought, if possible, to be based on mutual understanding.

HEDDA: There I entirely agree with you.

BRACK: Well—now I've said all I had to say—I'd better be off. Good-bye, Mrs. Hedda. *(Crossing toward the glass door.)*

HEDDA *(Rising)*: Are you going through the garden, Judge?

BRACK: Yes, it's a short cut for me.

HEDDA: Yes—and then it's the back way, isn't it?

BRACK: Very true; I've no objection to back ways. They are rather intriguing at times.

HEDDA: When there's shooting going on, you mean?

BRACK *(At the glass door, laughingly)*: People don't shoot their tame poultry, I fancy.

HEDDA *(Also laughing)*: And certainly not the cock-of-the-walk, Judge! Good-bye!

(They exchange laughing nods of farewell. He goes. She closes the glass door after him. HEDDA, *now serious, stands looking out. She goes up and peeps through the portières into the inner room. Then goes to the writing table, takes* LÖVBORG's *parcel from the bookcase, and is about to examine it.* BERTE *is heard speaking loudly in the hall.* HEDDA *turns and listens. She hurriedly locks the parcel in the drawer and puts the key on the inkstand.* EJLERT LÖVBORG, *wearing his overcoat and carrying his hat in his hand, tears open the hall door. He looks somewhat confused and excited.)*

LÖVBORG *(Turns toward the hall)*: I will go in, I tell you! *(He closes the door, turns, sees* HEDDA, *at once controls himself and bows.)*

HEDDA *(At the writing table)*: Well, Mr. Lövborg! Isn't it rather late to call for Thea?

LÖVBORG: And rather early to call on you—forgive me.

HEDDA: How do you know Thea's still here?

LÖVBORG: They told me at her lodgings she'd been out all night.

HEDDA *(Goes to the table)*: Did you notice anything odd in their manner when they told you that?

LÖVBORG *(Looks at her inquiringly)*: Anything odd?

HEDDA: Didn't they seem to think it—a little—queer?

LÖVBORG *(Suddenly understanding)*: Oh, of course! I see what you mean. I suppose I'm dragging her down with me—However, I didn't notice anything. I suppose Tesman isn't up yet?

HEDDA: No—I don't think so—

LÖVBORG: When did he get home?

HEDDA: Oh, very late.

LÖVBORG: Did he tell you anything?

HEDDA: He just said it had all been very jolly at Judge Brack's.

LÖVBORG: Nothing else?

HEDDA: No, I don't believe so. In any case, I was so dreadfully sleepy—

(MRS. ELVSTED comes in through the portières from the inner room. She goes to him.)

MRS. ELVSTED: Ejlert! At last!

LÖVBORG: Yes—at last—and too late!

MRS. ELVSTED *(Looks at him anxiously)*: What is too late?

LÖVBORG: Everything's too late now—it's all up with me.

MRS. ELVSTED: No, no! You mustn't say that!

LÖVBORG: You'll say the same when you hear—

MRS. ELVSTED: I don't want to hear anything!

HEDDA: Perhaps you'd rather talk to her alone? I'll leave you.

LÖVBORG: No! Stay, please—I beg of you!

MRS. ELVSTED: But I don't want to hear anything, I tell you.

LÖVBORG: I don't intend to talk about last night, Thea—

MRS. ELVSTED: No?

LÖVBORG: No. I just want to tell you that now we must part.

MRS. ELVSTED: Part?

HEDDA *(Involuntarily)*: I knew it!

LÖVBORG: I no longer have any use for you, Thea.

MRS. ELVSTED: How can you say that! No more use for me? You'll let me go on helping you—we'll go on working together, Ejlert?

LÖVBORG: I shall do no more work, from now on.

MRS. ELVSTED *(Despairingly)*: Then what shall I have to live for?

LÖVBORG: You must try and live as though you'd never known me.

MRS. ELVSTED: But you know I can't do that!

LÖVBORG: You must try, Thea. You must go home again.

MRS. ELVSTED *(Protesting vehemently)*: Never! I won't leave you! I won't allow you to drive me away. We must be together when the book appears.

HEDDA *(Whispers, in suspense)*: Ah, yes—the book!

LÖVBORG *(Looks at her)*: My book and Thea's—for that's what it is.

MRS. ELVSTED: Yes—that's true; I feel that. That's why we must be together when it's published. I want to see you showered with praise and honors—and the joy! I want to share that with you too!

LÖVBORG: Our book will not be published, Thea.

MRS. ELVSTED: Not published?

LÖVBORG: No. It never can be.

MRS. ELVSTED *(Anxiously, with foreboding)*: Lövborg—what have you done with the manuscript?

HEDDA *(Watches him intently)*: Yes—the manuscript?

MRS. ELVSTED: Where is it?

LÖVBORG: Thea! Don't ask me about it!

MRS. ELVSTED: Yes—I must know—I have a right to know.

LÖVBORG: Very well, then!—I've torn it into a thousand pieces!

MRS. ELVSTED (*Cries out*): No—no!

HEDDA (*Involuntarily*): But that's not—

LÖVBORG (*Looks at her*): Not true, you think?

HEDDA (*Controlling herself*): Of course it must be—if you say so! But it sounds so utterly incredible!

LÖVBORG: It's true all the same.

MRS. ELVSTED (*Wringing her hands*): Torn his own work to pieces!—Oh, God, Hedda!

LÖVBORG: I've torn my life to pieces—why shouldn't I tear up my work as well!

MRS. ELVSTED: And you did this last night?

LÖVBORG: Yes. I tore it into a thousand pieces. I scattered them far out on the fjord. I watched them drift on the cool sea water—drift with the current and the wind. In a little while they'll sink, deeper and deeper—just as I shall, Thea.

MRS. ELVSTED: Lövborg—this thing you've done to the book— it's as though you'd killed a little child.

LÖVBORG: You're right—it was child-murder.

MRS. ELVSTED: Then—how could you?—it was my child too.

HEDDA (*Almost inaudibly*): The child—

MRS. ELVSTED (*Breathes heavily*): It's all over then—I'll go now, Hedda.

HEDDA: But you won't be leaving town?

MRS. ELVSTED: I don't know what I'll do—there's nothing but darkness before me. (*She goes out by the hall door.*)

HEDDA (*Stands waiting a moment*): Then—you're not going to see her home, Mr. Lövborg?

LÖVBORG: I?—Do you want people to see her with *me*?

HEDDA: Of course, I don't know what else may have happened last night—but is it so utterly irreparable?

LÖVBORG: It won't end with last night—I know that only too well; and the trouble is, that kind of life no longer appeals to me. I have no heart to start it again—she's somehow broken my courage—my defiant spirit!

HEDDA *(Gazes before her)*: To think that that pretty little fool should have influenced a man's destiny! *(Looks at him)* Still, I don't see how you could be so heartless.

LÖVBORG: Don't say that!

HEDDA: What do you expect me to say! You've destroyed her whole purpose in life—isn't that being heartless?

LÖVBORG: Hedda—to you I can tell the truth.

HEDDA: The truth?

LÖVBORG: First, promise me—give me your word—that Thea will never know.

HEDDA: I give you my word.

LÖVBORG: Good. There was no truth in what I said just now—

HEDDA: You mean—about the manuscript?

LÖVBORG: Yes. I didn't tear it to pieces or scatter it on the fjord—

HEDDA: Where is it then?

LÖVBORG: But I have destroyed it, Hedda—utterly destroyed it!

HEDDA: I don't understand.

LÖVBORG: Just now, Thea said I had killed our child—

HEDDA: Yes—so she did—

LÖVBORG: One can do worse things to a child than kill it—I wanted to spare Thea the truth—

HEDDA: What do you mean?

LÖVBORG: I couldn't bring myself to tell her; I couldn't say to her: Thea, I spent last night in a frenzy of drinking—I took our child with me, dragged it round with me to all sorts of obscene and loathsome places—and I lost our child—lost it! God only knows what's become of it—or who's got hold of it!

HEDDA: But, when you come right down to it, this was only a book—

LÖVBORG: Thea's pure soul was in that book.

HEDDA: Yes—so I understand.

LÖVBORG: Then you must also understand why no future is possible for us.

HEDDA: What will you do now?

LÖVBORG: Nothing. I want to make an end of it. The sooner the better.

HEDDA *(Takes a step toward him)*: If you do make an end of it, Ejlert Lövborg—let it be beautiful!

LÖVBORG *(Smiles)*: Beautiful! Shall I put vine leaves in my hair, as you wanted me to in the old days?

HEDDA: No—I don't believe in vine leaves anymore. But—for once—let it be beautiful! Good-bye—you must go now—you mustn't come here anymore.

LÖVBORG: Good-bye, Mrs. Tesman. Remember me to Jörgen Tesman. *(He's on the point of going.)*

HEDDA: No, wait!—I want you to take something of mine with you—as a token—*(She goes to the writing table, opens the drawer, and the pistol case. Goes back to* LÖVBORG, *carrying one of the pistols.)*

LÖVBORG *(Looks at her)*: This? Is this the token?

HEDDA *(Nods slowly)*: Do you remember it? It was aimed at you once.

LÖVBORG: You should have used it then.

HEDDA: Take it!—Use it now!

LÖVBORG *(Puts the pistol in his inner pocket)*: Thanks.

HEDDA: But let it be—beautiful, Ejlert Lövborg! Promise me that!

LÖVBORG: Good-bye, Hedda Gabler.

(He goes out by the hall door. HEDDA *listens at the door a moment. Then she goes to the writing table and takes out the parcel with the manuscript, peeps inside the cover, half takes out a few sheets of paper and looks at them. Then she takes the parcel over to the armchair by the stove and sits down. She has the parcel in her lap. In a moment she opens the stove door, then opens the parcel.)*

HEDDA *(She throws part of the manuscript in the fire and whispers to herself)*: Your child, Thea—your child and Ejlert Lövborg's. Darling little Thea, with the curly golden hair. *(Throws more of the manuscript into the stove)* I'm burning your child, Thea. *(Throws in the rest of the manuscript)* I'm burning it—burning it—

CURTAIN

Act Four

SCENE: *The same room at the* TESMANS'. *It is evening. The drawing room is dark. In the inner room the hanging lamp over the table is lighted. The curtains are drawn over the glass doors.* HEDDA, *dressed in black, paces back and forth in the dark room. Then she goes up into the inner room and off left. A few chords are heard on the piano. She appears again and returns to the drawing room.* BERTE *enters from the right, through the inner room, carrying a lighted lamp which she puts down on the table by the corner sofa in the drawing room. Her eyes are red with weeping and she has black ribbons on her cap. She goes out right, quietly and circumspectly.* HEDDA *goes to the glass door, pulls the curtains aside a little, and peers out into the darkness. After a moment* MISS TESMAN *comes in from the hall. She is in mourning and wears a hat and veil.* HEDDA *goes toward her and holds out her hand.*

MISS TESMAN: Well, Hedda, here I am, all dressed in black! My poor sister has found rest at last!

HEDDA: As you see, I have heard already. Tesman sent me a note.

MISS TESMAN: He promised he would. I wish Rina hadn't left us just now—this is not the time for Hedda's house to be a house of mourning.

HEDDA *(Changing the subject)*: It is good to know she died peacefully, Miss Tesman.

MISS TESMAN: Yes, her end was so calm, so beautiful. And thank heaven, she had the joy of seeing Jörgen once more—and bidding him good-bye—He is not home yet?

HEDDA: No. He wrote me he might be detained. But do sit down, Miss Tesman.

MISS TESMAN: No, thank you, my dearest Hedda. I should like nothing better, but I have so much to do. I must prepare my darling sister for her burial. She must look her very sweetest when they carry her to her grave.

HEDDA: Can I do anything to help?

MISS TESMAN: Oh, no, you mustn't think of that! This is no time for Hedda Tesman to take part in such sad work. Nor let her thoughts dwell on it either—

HEDDA: H'm—one's thoughts—!

MISS TESMAN (*Continuing the theme*): How strange life is! At home we shall be sewing a shroud; and soon I expect there will be sewing here, too—but of a different kind, thank God!

(JÖRGEN TESMAN *enters by the hall door.*)

HEDDA: Well! Here you are at last!

TESMAN: You here, Aunt Juliane? With Hedda? Think of that!

MISS TESMAN: I am just going, my dear boy. Did you get everything done?

TESMAN: I'm afraid I forgot half of it. I'll have to run over and see you in the morning. Today my brain's in a whirl! I can't keep my thoughts together.

MISS TESMAN: But, my dear Jörgen, you mustn't take it so much to heart.

TESMAN: How do you mean?

MISS TESMAN: We must be glad for her sake—glad that she has found rest at last.

TESMAN: Oh, yes, of course—you are thinking of Aunt Rina.

HEDDA: I'm afraid it will be very lonely for you now, Miss Tesman.

MISS TESMAN: It will be at first—but I won't let poor Rina's room stay empty for long.

TESMAN: Really? Who will you put in it—eh?

MISS TESMAN: One can always find some poor invalid who needs to be taken care of.

HEDDA: Would you really take such a burden on yourself again?

MISS TESMAN: A burden? Heaven forgive you, child, it has been no burden to me.

HEDDA: But it's different with a stranger!

MISS TESMAN: I simply must have someone to live for—and one soon makes friends with sick folks; and perhaps some day there may be something in this house to keep an old aunt busy.

HEDDA: Oh, please don't trouble about us!

TESMAN: Just think! What a wonderful time we three might have together if—

HEDDA: If—?

TESMAN *(Uneasy)*: Nothing. Let's hope things will work out for the best—eh?

MISS TESMAN: Well, well, I daresay you two want to have a little talk. *(Smiling)* And perhaps Hedda may have something to tell you, Jörgen. Good-bye! I must go home to poor Rina. *(Turning at the door)* How strange it is to think that now Rina is with my poor brother, as well as with me.

TESMAN: Yes, think of that, Aunt Juliane! Eh?

(MISS TESMAN goes out by the hall door.)

HEDDA *(Gives TESMAN a cold, searching look)*: Aunt Rina's death seems to affect you more than it does Aunt Juliane.

TESMAN: Oh, it's not that alone. It's Ejlert I am so terribly upset about.

HEDDA *(Quickly)*: Have you heard anything new?

TESMAN: I called on him this afternoon. I wanted to tell him the manuscript was safe.

HEDDA: Did you see him?

TESMAN: No, he wasn't home. But later, I met Mrs. Elvsted and she said he had been here, early this morning.

HEDDA: Yes, directly after you had left.

TESMAN: And he said that he had torn his manuscript to pieces, eh?

HEDDA: That is what he said.

TESMAN: Good heavens, he must have gone completely mad! I

389

suppose in that case you didn't dare give it back to him,
Hedda.

HEDDA: No, he didn't get it.

TESMAN: But of course you told him that we had it?

HEDDA: No. Did you tell Mrs. Elvsted?

TESMAN: No, I thought I had better not. But you ought to have
told him. Just think—he might do himself some injury.
Give me the manuscript. I'll run over with it at once.
Where is it, Hedda? Eh?

HEDDA *(Cold and motionless, leaning against the armchair)*: I
haven't got it any longer.

TESMAN: Haven't got it? What in the world do you mean?

HEDDA: I've burned it—every word of it.

TESMAN *(Starts up in terror)*: Burned! Burned Ejlert's manuscript!

HEDDA: Don't shout so loud. The servant might hear you.

TESMAN: Burned! Why, good God—! No, no, no! It's utterly
impossible!

HEDDA: It's true, all the same.

TESMAN: Do you realize what you have done, Hedda? It is
unlawful appropriation of lost property. Think of that!
Just ask Judge Brack, he will tell you what that means.

HEDDA: It would be wiser not to speak of it—either to Judge
Brack or to anyone else.

TESMAN: But how could you do anything so unheard of? What
put it into your head? What possessed you? Do answer
me—

HEDDA *(Suppressing a scarcely perceptible smile)*: I did it for your
sake, Jörgen!

TESMAN: For my sake!

HEDDA: This morning when you told me that he had read it to
you—

TESMAN: Yes, yes—what then?

HEDDA: You admitted that you were jealous of his work.

TESMAN: Of course, I didn't mean that literally.

HEDDA: All the same—I couldn't bear the thought of anyone putting you in the shade.

TESMAN (*In an outburst of mingled doubt and joy*): Hedda? Is this true? But—but—I have never known you to show your love like that before. Think of that!

HEDDA: Then—perhaps I'd better tell you that—just now—at this time—(*Violently breaking off*) No, no; ask Aunt Juliane. She'll tell you all about it.

TESMAN: Oh, I almost think I understand, Hedda. (*Clasping his hands together*) Great heavens! Do you really mean it, eh?

HEDDA: Don't shout so loud. The servants will hear—

TESMAN (*Laughing with irrepressible joy*): The servants—? Why, how absurd you are, Hedda! It's only my dear old Berte! Why, I'll run out and tell her myself!

HEDDA (*Clenching her hands in despair*): Oh, God, I shall die—I shall die of all this—!

TESMAN: Oh what, Hedda? What is it? Eh?

HEDDA (*Coldly, controlling herself*): It's all so ludicrous—Jörgen!

TESMAN: Ludicrous! That I should be overjoyed at the news? Still, after all, perhaps I had better not tell Berte.

HEDDA: Why not that—with all the rest?

TESMAN: No, no, I won't tell her yet. But I must certainly tell Aunt Juliane. Oh, she will be so happy—so happy!

HEDDA: When she hears that I've burnt Ejlert Lövborg's manuscript—for your sake?

TESMAN: No, of course not—nobody must know about the manuscript. But I will certainly tell her how dearly you love me, Hedda. She must share that joy with me. I wonder, now, whether this sort of thing is usual in young wives? Eh?

HEDDA: Why not ask Aunt Juliane that, too?

TESMAN: I will, indeed, some time or other. *(Again agitated and concerned)* But the manuscript. Good God—the manuscript! I can't bear to think what poor Ejlert will do now! (MRS. ELVSTED, *dressed as on her first visit, wearing a hat and coat, comes in from the hall door.)*

MRS. ELVSTED *(Greets them hurriedly, and says in evident agitation)*: Hedda dear—please forgive my coming back so soon.

HEDDA: What is it, Thea? What has happened?

TESMAN: Is it something to do with Ejlert Lövborg, eh?

MRS. ELVSTED: Yes, I am terribly afraid he has met with some accident.

HEDDA *(Seizes her arm)*: Ah!—You think so?

TESMAN: Why should you think that, Mrs. Elvsted?

MRS. ELVSTED: When I got back to my lodgings—I heard them talking about him. There are all sorts of strange rumors—

TESMAN: Yes, I've heard them too! And yet I can bear witness that he went straight home last night. Think of that!

HEDDA: What sort of things did they say?

MRS. ELVSTED: Oh, I couldn't quite make it out. Either they knew nothing definite or—in any case, they stopped talking the moment I came in, and I didn't dare question them.

TESMAN *(Moving about the room uneasily)*: We must only hope you misunderstood them, Mrs. Elvsted.

MRS. ELVSTED: No, I am sure they were talking about him—they said something about a hospital or—

TESMAN: Hospital?

HEDDA: No, no! That's impossible!

MRS. ELVSTED: Oh, I am so terribly afraid for him. I finally went to his house to ask after him!

HEDDA: You went there yourself, Thea?

MRS. ELVSTED: What else could I do? I couldn't bear the suspense any longer.

TESMAN: But you didn't find him—eh?

MRS. ELVSTED: No. And the people there knew nothing about him. They said he hadn't been home since yesterday afternoon.

TESMAN: Yesterday! Just think—how could they say that?

MRS. ELVSTED: I am sure something terrible must have happened to him!

TESMAN: Hedda dear—supposing I run over and make some inquiries—?

HEDDA: No, no! Please don't mix yourself up in this affair.
(JUDGE BRACK, *hat in hand, enters by the hall door which* BERTE *opens and closes behind him. He looks grave and bows silently.*)

TESMAN: Oh, it's you, my dear Judge—eh?

BRACK: Yes, it's imperative that I see you at once.

TESMAN: I can see you have heard the news about Aunt Rina.

BRACK: Yes, that among other things.

TESMAN: Isn't it sad? Eh?

BRACK: Well, my dear Tesman, that depends on how you look at it.

TESMAN (*Looks at him doubtfully*): Has anything else happened?

BRACK: Yes.

HEDDA (*Intensely*): Anything sad, Judge?

BRACK: That, too, depends on how you look at it, Mrs. Tesman.

MRS. ELVSTED (*In an involuntary outburst*): Oh! It's something about Ejlert Lövborg!

BRACK (*Glancing at her*): What makes you think that, Mrs. Elvsted? Perhaps you have already heard something—?

MRS. ELVSTED (*Confused*): No, no, nothing at all—but—

TESMAN: Well, for heaven's sake, tell us. What is it?

BRACK (*Shrugging his shoulders*): Well, I am sorry to say, Ejlert Lövborg has been taken to the hospital—they say he is dying.

MRS. ELVSTED *(Cries out)*: Oh, God! God!

TESMAN: To the hospital! And dying—

HEDDA *(Involuntarily)*: So soon then—

MRS. ELVSTED *(Tearfully)*: And we parted in anger, Hedda!

HEDDA *(In a whisper)*: Thea—Thea—be careful!

MRS. ELVSTED *(Not heeding her)*: I must go to him! I must see him alive!

BRACK: I'm afraid it is useless, Mrs. Elvsted. No one is allowed to see him.

MRS. ELVSTED: But at least tell me what happened to him? What is it?

TESMAN: He didn't try to kill himself—eh?

HEDDA: Yes—I am sure he did!

TESMAN: Hedda, how can you—?

BRACK *(Not taking his eyes off her)*: Unfortunately, you have guessed quite correctly, Mrs. Tesman.

MRS. ELVSTED: Oh, how horrible!

TESMAN: Killed himself!—Think of that!

HEDDA: Shot himself!

BRACK: You are right again, Mrs. Tesman.

MRS. ELVSTED *(Trying to control herself)*: When did it happen, Judge Brack?

BRACK: This afternoon—between three and four.

TESMAN: But where did it happen? Eh?

BRACK *(With a slight hesitation)*: Where? Well—I suppose at his lodgings.

MRS. ELVSTED: No, it couldn't have been there—for I was there myself between six and seven.

BRACK: Well, then, somewhere else—I don't know exactly. I only know that he was found—he had shot himself . . . through the heart.

MRS. ELVSTED: How horrible! That he should die like that!

HEDDA *(To* BRACK*)*: Through the heart?

BRACK: Yes—as I told you.

HEDDA: Through the heart—

TESMAN: It's absolutely fatal, you say?

BRACK: Absolutely! Most likely it is already over.

MRS. ELVSTED: Over—all over—oh, Hedda!

TESMAN: You're quite positive of this? Who told you—eh?

BRACK *(Curtly)*: One of the police.

HEDDA *(Loudly)*: At last, a deed worth doing!

TESMAN *(Terrified)*: Good heavens, what are you saying, Hedda?

HEDDA: I say, there is beauty in this.

BRACK: H'm, Mrs. Tesman—

TESMAN: Beauty! Think of that!

MRS. ELVSTED: Oh, Hedda, how can you talk of beauty in such a case?

HEDDA: Ejlert Lövborg has made up his own account with life. He had the courage to do—the one right thing.

MRS. ELVSTED: No; no! You mustn't believe that! He did it in delirium!

TESMAN: In despair.

HEDDA: No! No! He didn't—I'm sure of that!

MRS. ELVSTED: I tell you he must have been delirious—as he was when he tore up our manuscript!

BRACK *(With a start)*: The manuscript? He tore up the manuscript?

MRS. ELVSTED: Yes. Last night.

TESMAN *(In a low whisper)*: Oh, Hedda, we'll never get over this!

BRACK: H'm—how very extraordinary.

TESMAN *(Pacing the room)*: To think of Ejlert dead! And his book destroyed too—his book that would have made him famous!

MRS. ELVSTED: If only there were some way of saving it—

TESMAN: Yes, if only there were!—There's nothing I wouldn't give—

MRS. ELVSTED: Perhaps there is a way, Mr. Tesman.

TESMAN: What do you mean?

MRS. ELVSTED *(Searches in the pocket of her dress)*: Look! I have kept all the notes he used to dictate from—

HEDDA *(Takes a step toward her)*: Ah—!

TESMAN: You have, Mrs. Elvsted?—Eh?

MRS. ELVSTED: Yes. I took them with me when I left home— they're here in my pocket—

TESMAN: Do let me see them!

MRS. ELVSTED *(Hands him a bundle of scraps of paper)*: I'm afraid they are dreadfully mixed up—

TESMAN: Perhaps, together, we might be able to sort them out—just think!

MRS. ELVSTED: We could try at any rate—

TESMAN: We'll do it—we *must* do it—I'll devote my life to it!

HEDDA: You, Jörgen? Your life?

TESMAN: Or at least, all the time I can spare. My own work will simply have to wait—I owe this to Ejlert's memory . . . you understand, Hedda, eh?

HEDDA: You may be right.

TESMAN: Now, my dear Mrs. Elvsted, we must pull ourselves together—it is no good brooding over what has happened. Eh? We must try and control our grief as much as possible—

MRS. ELVSTED: Yes, you're right, Mr. Tesman, I *will* try—

TESMAN: That's splendid! Now then, let's see—we must go through the notes at once—Where shall we sit? Here? No, no, we'd better go in there—Excuse me, Judge— Come along, Mrs. Elvsted!

MRS. ELVSTED: Oh! If only it were possible—

(TESMAN *and* MRS. ELVSTED *go into the inner room. She takes off her hat and coat. They sit at the table under the hanging lamp and become absorbed in examining the papers.* HEDDA *goes toward the stove and sits down in the armchair. After a moment* BRACK *joins her.*)

HEDDA *(In a low voice)*: Oh, what a sense of freedom there is in this act of Ejlert Lövborg's.

BRACK: Freedom, Mrs. Hedda? Of course, it is freedom for him.

HEDDA: I mean for me. It gives me a sense of freedom to know that an act of deliberate courage is still possible in this world—an act of spontaneous beauty.

BRACK *(Smiles)*: H'm—my dear Mrs. Hedda—

HEDDA: Oh, I know what you are going to say. For you're a specialist, too, in a way—just like—well, you know.

BRACK *(Looks at her intently)*: Ejlert Lövborg meant more to you than you are willing to admit—even to yourself. Or am I mistaken?

HEDDA: I don't answer such questions. I know that Ejlert Lövborg had the courage to live his life as he saw it—and to end it in beauty. He had the strength and the will to break with life—while still so young.

BRACK: It pains me to do so, Mrs. Hedda—but I fear I must rob you of this beautiful illusion.

HEDDA: Illusion?

BRACK: It would soon be destroyed, in any case.

HEDDA: What do you mean?

BRACK: He did not shoot himself—of his own accord.

HEDDA: Not of his own—?

BRACK: No, the thing did not happen exactly as I told it.

HEDDA *(In suspense)*: You've concealed something? What is it?

BRACK: For poor Mrs. Elvsted's sake, I slightly changed the facts.

HEDDA: What are the facts, then?

BRACK: First, that he is already dead.

HEDDA: At the hospital.

BRACK: Yes—without regaining consciousness.

HEDDA: What else have you concealed?

BRACK: That—the tragedy did not happen at his lodgings—

HEDDA: That makes no difference—

BRACK: Doesn't it? Not even if I tell you that Ejlert Lövborg was found shot in—in Mlle. Diana's boudoir?

HEDDA *(Attempts to jump up but sinks back again)*: That is impossible, Judge. He couldn't have gone there again today.

BRACK: He was there this afternoon. He went there to claim something he said they had taken from him—talked wildly about a lost child—

HEDDA: Ah—that was why—

BRACK: I thought he must have meant the manuscript. But now I hear he destroyed that himself. So I suppose it must have been his pocketbook.

HEDDA: Yes—probably. So, he was found—there.

BRACK: Yes. With a discharged pistol in his breast pocket. He had wounded himself mortally.

HEDDA: Through the heart!—Yes!

BRACK: No—in the bowels.

HEDDA *(Looks at him with an expression of loathing)*: How horrible! Everything I touch becomes ludicrous and despicable!—It's like a curse!

BRACK: There is something else, Mrs. Hedda—something rather ugly—

HEDDA: What is that?

BRACK: The pistol he carried—

HEDDA *(Breathless)*: What of it?

BRACK: He must have stolen it.

HEDDA *(Leaps up)*: That is not true! He didn't steal it!

BRACK: No other explanation is possible. He *must* have stolen it—hush!

(TESMAN *and* MRS. ELVSTED *have risen from the table in the inner room and come into the drawing room.*)

TESMAN (*His hands full of papers*): Hedda dear, it is almost impossible to see under that lamp. Just think!

HEDDA: Yes, I am thinking.

TESMAN: Do you think you'd let us use your desk, eh?

HEDDA: Of course—no, wait! Just let me clear it first.

TESMAN: Oh, you needn't trouble, Hedda. There's plenty of room.

HEDDA: No, no! Let me do as I say. I'll put all these things in on the piano.

(*She has taken something covered with sheet music from under the bookcase. She puts some added pieces of music on it and carries it all into the inner room and off left.* TESMAN *arranges the scraps of paper on the writing table and moves the lamp from the corner table over to it. He and* MRS. ELVSTED *sit down and resume their work.* HEDDA *returns.*)

HEDDA (*Stands behind* MRS. ELVSTED'S *chair, gently ruffling her hair*): Well, darling little Thea—how are you getting on with Ejlert Lövborg's memorial?

MRS. ELVSTED (*Looks up at her with a disheartened expression*): I'm afraid it's all very difficult—

TESMAN: We *must* manage it. We've simply got to do it! And you know sorting out and arranging other people's papers—that's something I'm particularly good at—

(HEDDA *crosses to the stove and sits down on one of the stools.* BRACK *stands over her, leaning on the armchair.*)

HEDDA (*In a whisper*): What was that you said about the pistol?

BRACK (*Softly*): That he must have stolen it.

HEDDA: Why stolen?

BRACK: Because any other explanation ought to be out of the question, Mrs. Hedda.

HEDDA: Indeed?

BRACK *(Glancing at her)*: Of course, Ejlert Lövborg was here this morning. Was he not?

HEDDA: Yes.

BRACK: Were you alone with him?

HEDDA: Yes—for a little while.

BRACK: Did you leave the room while he was here?

HEDDA: No.

BRACK: Try to remember. Are you *sure* you didn't leave the room—even for a moment?

HEDDA: I might have gone into the hall—just for a moment—

BRACK: And where was your pistol case?

HEDDA: It was put away in—

BRACK: Well, Mrs. Hedda?

HEDDA: It was over there on the desk.

BRACK: Have you looked since to see if both pistols are there?

HEDDA: No.

BRACK: Well, you needn't. I saw the pistol Lövborg had with him, and I recognized it at once as the one I had seen yesterday—and before that too.

HEDDA: Have you got it by any chance?

BRACK: No, the police have it.

HEDDA: What will the police do with it?

BRACK: Search until they find the owner.

HEDDA: Do you think they will succeed?

BRACK *(Bends over her and whispers)*: No, Hedda Gabler, not so long as I keep silent.

HEDDA *(Gives him a frightened look)*: And if you do *not* keep silent—what then?

BRACK *(Shrugs his shoulders)*: One could always declare that the pistol was stolen.

HEDDA *(Firmly)*: It would be better to die!

BRACK *(Smiling)*: One *says* such things—but one doesn't *do* them.

HEDDA *(Without answering)*: And if the pistol were not stolen and the police find the owner? What then?

BRACK: Well, Hedda—then—think of the scandal!

HEDDA: The scandal!

BRACK: The scandal, yes—of which you are so terrified. You'd naturally have to appear in court—both you and Mlle. Diana. She would have to explain how the thing happened—whether it was an accident or murder. Did he threaten to shoot her, and did the pistol go off then—or did she grab the pistol, shoot him, afterward putting it back into his pocket. She might have done that, for she is a hefty woman, this—Mlle. Diana.

HEDDA: What have I to do with all this repulsive business?

BRACK: Nothing. But you will have to answer the question: Why did you give Ejlert Lövborg the pistol? And what conclusion will people draw from the fact that you did give it to him?

HEDDA *(Bowing her head)*: That is true. I didn't think of that.

BRACK: Well, fortunately, there is no danger as long as I keep silent.

HEDDA *(Looks up at him)*: That means you have me in your power, Judge! You have me at your beck and call from now on.

BRACK *(Whispers softly)*: Dearest Hedda—believe me—I shall not abuse my advantage.

HEDDA: I am in your power, all the same. Subject to your commands and wishes. No longer free—not free! . . . *(Rises impetuously)* No, I won't endure that thought. Never!

BRACK *(Looks at her half mockingly)*: People manage to get used to the inevitable.

HEDDA *(Returns his look)*: Yes, perhaps. *(She crosses to the writing table. Suppressing an involuntary smile and imitating* TESMAN's *intonations)* Well? How's it going, Jörgen, eh?

TESMAN: Heaven knows, dear. In any case, it will take months to do.

HEDDA *(As before)*: Think of that! *(She runs her fingers softly through* MRS. ELVSTED's *hair)* Doesn't it seem strange to you, Thea? Here you are working with Tesman—as you used to work with Ejlert Lövborg?

MRS. ELVSTED: If I could only inspire your husband in the same way!

HEDDA: Oh, no doubt that will come—in time.

TESMAN: You know, Hedda—I'm really beginning to feel something of the sort! Why don't you go and talk to Judge Brack again?

HEDDA: Is there nothing at all—I can do to help?

TESMAN: No, thank you. Not a thing. *(Turning his head)* You'll have to keep Hedda company from now on, my dear Judge.

BRACK *(With a glance at Hedda)*: It will give me the greatest of pleasure!

HEDDA: Thanks. But this evening I feel a little tired. I'll go and lie down on the sofa for a little while.

TESMAN: Yes, do that dear—eh?
*(*HEDDA *goes into the inner room and closes the portières after her. A short pause. Suddenly she is heard playing a wild dance tune on the piano.)*

MRS. ELVSTED *(Starts up from her chair)*: Oh—what's that?

TESMAN *(Runs to the center opening)*: Dearest Hedda, don't play dance music tonight! Think of Aunt Rina! And of poor Ejlert!

HEDDA *(Sticks her head out between the curtains)*: And of Aunt Juliane. And of all the rest of them—Never mind—From now on, I promise to be quiet. *(She closes the curtains again.)*

TESMAN *(At the writing table)*: I don't think it is good for her to see us at this distressing work; I have an idea, Mrs.

Elvsted. You can move over to Aunt Juliane's and then I'll come over in the evenings and we'll work there. Eh?

MRS. ELVSTED: Perhaps that would be the best thing to do.

HEDDA *(From the inner room)*: I can hear what you are saying, Tesman. What am I to do with all those long evenings—here—by myself?

TESMAN *(Turning over the papers)*: Oh, I am sure Judge Brack will be kind enough to drop in and see you.

BRACK *(In the armchair, calls out gaily)*: Every single evening, with the very greatest of pleasure, Mrs. Tesman! I'm sure we'll have a very jolly time together, we two.

HEDDA *(In a loud, clear voice)*: Yes, that's what you hope, Judge, isn't it?—Now that you are cock-of-the-walk—
(A shot is heard within. TESMAN, MRS. ELVSTED, *and* BRACK *leap to their feet.)*

TESMAN: Now she is playing with those pistols again.
(He throws back the portières and runs in, followed by MRS. ELVSTED. HEDDA *lies stretched out on the sofa, dead. Confusion and cries.* BERTE, *alarmed, comes in from the right.)*

TESMAN *(Cries out, to* BRACK*)*: Shot herself! Shot herself in the temple! Think of that!

BRACK *(Sinks into the armchair, half fainting)*: Good God—but—people don't *do* such things!

CURTAIN